DOM AUGUSTINE BAKER

DOM AUGUSTINE BAKER

1575–1641

edited by

GEOFFREY SCOTT

GRACEWING

First published in 2012
by
Gracewing
2 Southern Avenue
Leominster
Herefordshire HR6 0QF
United Kingdom
www.gracewing.co.uk

All rights reserved. No part of this publication may be reproduced, stored in a retrieval system, or transmitted in any form or by any means, electronic, mechanical, photocopying, recording or otherwise, without the written permission of the publisher.

Compilation, editorial material and introduction © Geoffrey Scott 2012
Copyright for individual chapters resides with the authors

The right of the editor and the contributors to be identified as the authors of this work has been asserted in accordance with the Copyright, Designs and Patents Act 1988

ISBN 978 085244 774 1

Cover image of Dom Augustine Baker, courtesy of Dame Andrea Savage OSB, Abbess of Stanbrook. The picture is a replica of a painting by Ferenc Szoldatits (1820–1916).

Typeset by Gracewing

Contents

Contents v

Introduction vii

Contributors ix

1: EDMUND POWER, The Spirituality of *Sancta Sophia* 1

2: BARNABY HUGHES, Augustine Baker and the History of the English Benedictine Congregation 19

3: MARGARET TRURAN, Did Father Baker compile the Cambrai nuns' first Constitutions? 31

4: +TERESA RODRIGUES, Mortification in the teaching of Dom Augustine Baker 43

5: PETER TYLER, Mystical Writing as *Theologia Mystica* .. 51

6: GORDON MURSELL, 'On Being Loved': the Assurance of Divine Love in the works of Augustine Baker 65

7: ELISABETH DUTTON & VICTORIA VAN HYNING, Augustine Baker and the Mystical Canon 85

8: JOHN CLARK, Towards a chronology of Father Baker's writings 111

9: JAN RHODES, Abbot Blosius and Father Baker 133

10: JOHN COTTINGHAM, The Spiritual and the Philosophical Quest: Augustine Baker and René Descartes 153

11: GEOFFREY SCOTT, Baker's critics 179

12: ALBAN HOOD, Baker in the nineteenth-century English Benedictine Congregation 193

Index 203

Introduction

The annual English Benedictine Symposium, held at Douai Abbey, Reading, on 3 September, 2009, was devoted to the teaching of Dom Augustine Baker (1573–1641), the English Benedictine mystical writer. The Symposium was held to mark the retirement of Dr James Hogg, the distinguished general editor of the *Analecta Cartusiana* series, which now numbers over 300 volumes. This series deals largely with the history of the Carthusian Order, and was begun in Berlin in 1970 and transferred to Salzburg the following year. Thanks to Dr Hogg's encouragement, the series also includes nearly forty volumes of Baker's works and volumes related to Baker which have been painstakingly edited by the Reverend Dr John Clark. Until the appearance of these new editions scholars had been largely dependent on Dom Serenus Cressy's digest of Baker's teachings, known as *Sancta Sophia* or *Holy Wisdom* (first edition, Douai, 1657, New York 1857, London 1871, and later editions), for knowledge of Baker's thought. Dr Clark's work is crucial for revealing much more to us about Baker and his teachings, and an index to Cressy's sources in *Sancta Sophia* remains his ultimate objective. The 2009 Symposium brought together Benedictine monks and nuns, and friends, colleagues, and past pupils of Dr Hogg and Dr Clark, as well as a number of scholars interested in mystical literature. This volume is the first to recognise the importance of Dr Clark's recent editions of Baker, and this is illustrated by so many references to these editions found throughout the various chapters. While congratulating Dr Hogg for his enthusiasm and persistent dedication over so many years, we recognise that Dr Clark enjoys many of the same gifts and hope this celebratory volume will encourage him, *Deo volente*, to go forward and complete editions of the entire extant corpus of Baker's writings.

Geoffrey Scott
Douai Abbey
July 2011

List of Contributors

Edmund Power is Abbot of the Benedictine abbey of Saint Paul's-outside-the-Walls and was professed at Douai Abbey. His doctoral dissertation (King's College, London, 1991) is entitled *The Christian Anthropology of Augustine Baker's* Holy Wisdom.

Barnaby Hughes completed an MA dissertation at Bristol in 2003 on *Monasticism and the Marian Church. The Restoration of Westminster Abbey, 1556-59*, and since then has been interested in aspects of continuity between medieval and early modern English Benedictinism.

Margaret Truran is an English Benedictine nun who, as archivist of Stanbrook Abbey, has written extensively on the English Benedictine life for women in the seventeenth century. She is presently organising a school of Gregorian chant and liturgical spirituality at the Abbey of Santa Cecilia in Rome.

Teresa Rodrigues† was, until her sudden death in February 2010, a Benedictine nun of the Monastery of the Holy Trinity, East Hendred, Oxfordshire. For many years she was occupied with a study of Augustine Baker's spiritual teachings. Her years of work on a modernised version of *Holy Wisdom* bore fruit in an edition, *The Essence of 'Holy Wisdom', Treatises on the Spiritual Life by Augustine Baker OSB*, privately printed in 2001.

Peter Tyler is Senior Lecturer and Programme Director in Pastoral Theology at St Mary's University College, Twickenham. He has a particular interest in mystical theology and his most recent work is *The Return to the Mystical: Ludwig Wittgenstein, Teresa of Avila and the Christian Mystical Tradition* (Continuum: 2011).

Gordon Mursell has recently retired as Bishop of Stafford. His doctoral thesis on early Carthusian spirituality was published by Dr James Hogg, and he is well known for his major study, *English Spirituality from Earliest Time to 1700* (2001) and *English Spirituality from 1700 to the Present Day* (2001).

Elisabeth Dutton is Professor of Medieval English at the University of Fribourg, Switzerland. She is the author of Julian of Norwich; the Influence of Late-Medieval Devotional Compilations (Cambridge: D. S. Brewer, 2008) and an edition of Julian for Yale University Press (2008), as well as articles about devotional compilation and the transmission of medieval texts. She also publishes on and directs productions of early English theatre. **Victoria Van Hyning** is a PhD candidate who works predominantly on Augustinian convent literature as well as the writings of Augustine Baker. She holds the 'Letters and Lives' British Library studentship from the University of Sheffield.

John Clark is a retired Anglican priest who is presently engaged in compiling edited volumes of Carthusian history and spirituality for the *Analecta Cartusiana*. In addition to this, he has committed himself to providing the first published editions of Baker manuscripts, a project supported by Dr James Hogg and by the English Benedictine Congregation.

Jan Rhodes has been responsible for special collections in a number of English libraries and has written extensively on English recusant bibliography and spirituality. She is currently cataloguing the early collections in Colwich Abbey Library, which holds many Baker manuscripts.

John Cottingham is Professor Emeritus of Philosophy at the University of Reading, Professorial Research Fellow at Heythrop College, University of London, and an Honorary Fellow of St John's College, Oxford. He has published widely on Descartes, and on Moral Philosophy and the Philosophy of Religion.

Geoffrey Scott is Abbot of Douai and Chairman of the English Benedictine History Commission. He has a particular interest in eighteenth-century English Catholic and English Benedictine history.

Alban Hood is novice master at Douai Abbey and is preparing his doctoral dissertation, *From Repatriation to Revival: Continuity and Change in The English Benedictine Congregation, 1795-1850* (Liverpool, 2006), for publication.

1

The Spirituality of Sancta Sophia

EDMUND POWER

The unexpected appeal of Sancta Sophia

On a rainy morning in February 1998, while a junior monk of Oceanside in California was driving me from his Abbey to San Diego airport, the subject of Augustine Baker came up. I told him that I had done some research on *Sancta Sophia* (hereafter, *Holy Wisdom*)[1] and he responded enthusiastically, saying how much he liked the book. The incident reminded me of the experience of Dom John Main, when, in the 1970s a young man in Washington DC came to him for advice:

> I gave him Baker's Holy Wisdom as his book of study, thinking this would keep him quietly occupied for several weeks, unravelling its loping Drydenesque sentences. To my amazement, however, he reacted with real and immediate enthusiasm, to such a degree that I felt I had to read it again

---

1. The modern version of the name (*Holy Wisdom*) first appeared in the 1911 reprint of the edition of Norbert Sweeney (London: 1876.)

myself .... in Baker there is an intuitive understanding of the mantra.'²

There may, in fact, be some truth in this last claim:

> Some few souls there are to whom one only exercise, without any change or variety, may suffice for their whole life, till they arrive to perfect contemplation... after a little practice they will have it in their hearts & memories.³

But *Holy Wisdom* is not merely a 'cult book' among young Americans. The last seventy years reveal a range of positive responses: Eugene Boylan wrote in 1943 that it 'is a work to which these pages owe much, and which is in the same tradition (as the Cloud of Unknowing)';⁴ E.I.Watkin in 1953 noted that the principles of Bakerism 'can and should be the foundation of the spiritual education of Catholic children ... I know of no wiser or safer school of prayer';⁵ David Knowles in 1961 believed *Holy Wisdom* was 'indeed a book of power ... which will guide all for a part of their way, and may suffice for some for a very great part of their lives';⁶ David Lunn in 1980 argued that Baker is 'a free spirit, a universal figure, who belongs to all ages and all creeds.'⁷

Such enthusiastic responses to Baker, or rather, to Baker as known through *Holy Wisdom*, suggest that we are dealing with a work of spiritual potential, even for people of today, and not a mere period piece.

---

2. N. McKenty, *In the Stillness Dancing: the Journey of John Main* (London: 1986), pp. 79f.
3. Augustine Baker, *Holy Wisdom*, ed. G. Sitwell (London: 1964 and Wheathampstead, 1972), pp. 396-97. I use this edition for all references.
4. E. Boylan, *Difficulties in Mental Prayer* (Dublin: 1943), p. 57.
5. E. I. Watkin, *Poets and Mystics* (London: 1953), p. 235f.
6. D. Knowles, *The English Mystical Tradition* (London: 1961), p. 187.
7. D. Lunn, *The English Benedictines 1540-1688* (London: 1980), p. 217

Disclaimers

An Italian academic historian assured me recently that for the historian, the tears of Oscar Romero are no different from those of Marcel Lefebvre. I am not an historian, but clearly we need to understand the context of a book before describing or recommending its 'spirituality'. My position is that of the theologian, interested in the ascetical and monastic dimensions of the discipline, and with a particular fascination for how language is used and for the 'between-the-lines' aspects of communication.

I am not bothered by those who say that *Holy Wisdom* is not truly Augustine Baker, but merely 'Baker/Cressy'. Be that as it may, the work stands on its own merits. In the past it was certainly considered a fair presentation of Baker's ascetical theology. His faithful supporter, Abbess Catherine Gascoigne acknowledged the working and reworking that Cressy had done ...

> to give the more full satisfaction in rendering your abridgement most entirely conformable to his writings in the very expression, as much as might be... since not any that hath read your booke, and is versed in the authours works; have found any objections to make, either of anything wanting or differing from him: but all acknowledge that you have most faithfully, clearely and substantially delivered his doctrine.[8]

Nor am I concerned with the fascinating and eccentric Baker himself, who well merits a critical biography. He himself describes his spiritual development, and it is retold by his immediate followers and biographers. Despite the fact that we know a lot about him, he remains strangely remote. There are tantalising ambiguities: for instance, the fervour of the prayers and acts printed at the end of the

---

8. Augustine Baker, *Sancta Sophia*, ed. S. Cressy (Douai: 1657), vol. 1, p. 12. Catherine Gascoigne OSB was Abbess of the English Benedictine nuns of the community of Our Lady of Comfort, Cambrai, (1629–41, 1645–73).

first edition of *Sancta Sophia* that contrast strikingly with the general 'cool detachment' of the book. He was certainly a polarising figure, as evidenced by the contemporary and disparaging label, 'Bakerists'.[9] Nowadays, I would probably have more sympathy with Father Rudesind Barlow OSB, 'our old grandsir ... who ... is crafty and crewel, God forgive him. He it is that is secretly the motor and promoter of all these turbulent affayres to effect his owene designs'.[10] A supporter of Baker until the relationship turned sour, the efficient Barlow must have found Baker infuriating. The chapter in *Holy Wisdom* entitled 'How prayer is to be exercised in distractive offices' was, without doubt, written by someone who had little or no idea of the reality of distractive offices!

Finally, this paper will spend no time on the admittedly interesting question of the genesis and subsequent history of *Holy Wisdom* but will deal with the text as it stands because this is how Baker has been known and appreciated down the centuries. Nothing will be said on the relationship between the Baker manuscripts and *Holy Wisdom*. My research on *Holy Wisdom* was finished in the early 1990s, and the rush of events since then has left no time for further work. I will stick exclusively to *Holy Wisdom*, aware, however, that some of what I say may well have been superseded by subsequent publication and study.

The language of Holy Wisdom

The book is daunting: there are none of the glib and slick attractions necessary in so much modern publication. The ponderous march of the text, the systematic layout of titles and subtitles, of divisions and subdivisions, the long, long sentences, sometimes running to half a page, do not reflect

---

9. J. McCann (ed.), *The Life of Father. Augustine Baker (1575–1641) by Fr Peter Salvin & Fr Serenus Cressy* (London: 1933), p. 28.
10. J. McCann, 'Some Benedictine Letters in the Bodleian', *Downside Review*, 141, October 1931, p. 478. from a letter of Father William Walgrave, chaplain at Cambrai, dated 3 March 1655.

The Spirituality of Sancta Sophia

the style of the twenty-first century. But we have always to remember that *Holy Wisdom* is a digest, a handbook, derivative rather than original. The language itself is not always accessible: words sound quaint because they have sometimes shifted meaning over the centuries.

To illustrate the point, let us consider a passage in the first chapter of the third treatise, 'Of Prayer', where the author offers a definition of prayer:

> Prayer is an affectuous actuation of an intellective soul towards God, expressing, or at least implying, an entire dependence on Him as the Author and Fountain of all good, a will and a readiness to give Him His due, which is no less than all love, obedience, adoration, glory, and worship, by humbling and annihilating of herself and all creatures in His presence; and lastly, a desire and intention to aspire to an union of spirit with Him.[11]

The first thing to note here is the cautious style: this is not a writer in search of sound-bites. There is a tentativeness, a hesitation that seeks an absolute precision ('expressing, *or at least implying, ...*'). The array of subordinate clauses in the book as a whole, the careful qualifications, could readily make a modern reader impatient. We just haven't got that doggedness that is required not only in reading *Holy Wisdom*, but also in the spiritual life itself. The passage under consideration is one sentence, but not a particularly long one by *Holy Wisdom's* standards—it is in fact broken by a semi-colon. Without concentration, however, we lose the thread of the thought.

Then there is the vocabulary: at least three words might cause us to pause. My computer tells me that 'affectuous' doesn't exist. It does, in fact, exist, but *The Oxford English Dictionary* (*OED*) describes it as obsolete. It had a rather short career, deriving from fourteenth-century French with a 'secular' meaning and dying well before our time. We can guess its meaning, but we cannot be certain that

---
11. *Holy Wisdom*, p. 299.

Holy Wisdom is not using it in a technical sense. Interestingly, the *OED* offers a theological use of the word with precisely the same date as *Holy Wisdom* (1656, *Holy Wisdom* was published in 1657).[12] The second word, 'actuation', is not normal for us, but again, with effort, we can imagine its meaning. The *OED*, in its restrictive insularity so different from Baker's own international breadth, fails to acknowledge recusant English literature published on the Continent. It offers three theological citations for the word, dating from c. 1630, 1656 and 1699, all from Anglican authors writing in England.[13] The third word is 'annihilating' which, well before the Daleks of the 1960s, was a word already in use in 1611 with a theological sense.[14]

These three technical or semi-technical words from a short passage of *Holy Wisdom* do not prove that the Anglican sources are derivative from Baker (or from other recusant contexts). They do, however, strongly suggest a common ascetical-theological language that can be explained only by direct reciprocal influence. This is not new, of course. There are other examples in *Holy Wisdom* of technical ascetical words, the earliest known Anglican/Protestant occurrences of which come later.[15] Even if *Holy Wisdom* dates only from 1657, its sources go back considerably earlier. The happy publication of the Baker manuscripts will enable a systematic study of this interesting question.

Returning to the short text under consideration, we may note the linguistic veneration: the (masculine) pronominal and adjectival words used six times for God, always

---

12. *c.* 1656, Bishop Joseph Hall (1574-1656), 'The great mystery of godliness laid forth by way of affectuous and feeling meditation.'

13. *c.*1630 Thomas Jackson, 1656 H. Jeanes, 1699 Gilbert Burnet.

14. *Oxford English Dictionary*, vol. I (Oxford: 1933), p. 340; R. Cotgrave, A *Dictionarie of the French and English Tongues* (London: 1611).

15. e.g. *Holy Wisdom* talks of the 'mentality' of prayer (p. 315): *OED* finds the earliest written example of that use only in 1691. The phenomenon has been mentioned by others, for example, Philip Jebb, 'A hitherto unnoticed autograph manuscript of the venerable Augustine Baker', *Downside Review*, January 1986, pp. 28, 38–39.

The Spirituality of Sancta Sophia 7

with the capital "H." Even Papal documents (in English translation at least) no longer do that today. There is an instance of loose repetition ("Author and Fountain") that offers two different metaphors for the same idea, and there is a moment of warmth or fervour, that reveals itself in the slightly breathless list of devotional substantives ('no less than all love, obedience, adoration, glory, and worship ...')

Finally, there is the significant word 'herself'. 'Soul' is the prevalent word used throughout *Holy Wisdom* for referring to the human person in relation to God. Normally the author is speaking in a general way, and not, therefore, thinking of women in particular, but 'soul' invariably carries the feminine pronoun. I would like to offer a brief comment on this fact, moving beyond the specific passage we have been studying. Consider three other quotations (italics my insertion):

> Many *souls* there are that cannot content themselves ... and, therefore, my desire was to comply with all tempers, to the end that every one might find an exercise proper and profitable for *him* ... a *soul* that .. is maturely called ... to the exercise ... ought ... to take for the subject of *her* recollections...[16]

> *She* must remember that the doctrine of abstraction ... has place also even in distractive offices ... that the person is not to meddle in things that belong not to *his* present employment ... *he* must be careful ... A devout soul thus constantly discharging *her* office will come to that liberty ...[17]

> Person ... himself ... his ... him, he ... his ... him ... him ... he ... he ... a soul ... herself ... she ... she ... she ... her ... she ...[18]

It is clear that whenever *Holy Wisdom* uses any other "person" word (e.g. "Christian," "internal liver," etc) it always uses the masculine pronoun, unless speaking explicitly

---

16. *Holy Wisdom*, p. 391.
17. *Holy Wisdom* p. 412.
18. *Holy Wisdom*, p. 413.

of a woman. The use of "she" for a male is clear from the following quotation: "a soul ... quitting the world ... the questions proposed to her, and her answers, her habit, tonsure ..."[19] Imagine a soul with her tonsure!

The resolution of this ambiguity is not to be found in the fact that while English is a grammatically genderless language, "soul" in Romance (and Germanic) languages is feminine.[20] The word "person", for example, is also feminine in those languages, but for *Holy Wisdom* 'person' is always 'he'. My contention is that this 'false' gendering of the human person, considered in the context of his or her relation to God, has the effect of rarefying 'spirituality' and of separating it from the context of concrete personhood. There is no time to develop the subject here, but I believe that it would bear a detailed study. Naturally, *Holy Wisdom* is not unique in this. Maybe all spiritual books written in English from the sixteenth century until the first half of twentieth use, as a primary anthropological term, the combination of 'soul-she'. By contrast, 'The Cloud of Unknowing' (late fourteenth century) never applies the feminine pronoun to 'soul', but, as we would do today, uses 'it'.[21]

As a final comment on the 'soul-she' question, I should mention those who, influenced by a tradition of allegorical interpretation of biblical texts such as the Song of Songs, would propose a psychological explanation, suggesting, for instance, that 'female' passivity is more appropriate in the life of prayer, 'male' activity less appropriate. Historically, St Paul's communitarian concept of the Church as Bride of Christ was gradually extended to include the individual Christian as (female) beloved of a male Christ. This

---

19. *Holy Wisdom,* p. 131.
20. In classical Latin, in fact, there are two words: *animus* and *anima*. The former has the sense of the rational soul, the latter of soul as the breath of life. In the Vulgate, the latter is far more frequently used than the former. It is closer to the Hebrew *nephesh*. The Greek equivalents would be *psyche* (fem.) and *nous* (masc.).
21. e.g P. Hodgson (ed.), *The Cloud of Unknowing and The Book of Privy Counselling* (London: 1973), p. 19. 'o louyng soule only in *it-self,* by vertewe of loue...'

tendency reached an erotic apogee in Baker's older contemporary, John of the Cross (1542–91), to whom, by the way, *Holy Wisdom* makes ten references: 'upon my flowering breast / which I kept wholly for Him alone, / there He lay sleeping, / and I caressing Him / there in a breeze from the fanning cedars. // When the breeze blew from the turret / parting His hair, / He wounded [impassioned] my neck / with his gentle hand, / suspending all my senses'.[22] Even if we were convinced by the psychological stereotyping, it wouldn't really resolve the tension between 'soul-she' language and concrete personhood. There are, in addition, other ascetical-anthropological terms that would merit consideration, for example 'spirit', but there is no time to deal with them here.

To conclude the reflection on the language and style of *Holy Wisdom*, we might ask whether it is possible to take the book seriously, despite the enthusiasts mentioned at the beginning of this chapter. I believe it does repay careful reading. It is systematic and thorough; in general, it is wise and speaks with experience as well as with learned preparation; there *is* figurative language, illustrations, even humour. Sometimes, despite Cressy's editing hand, the hang-ups emerge and the bees buzz in the bonnet. Sometimes, more movingly, a fervour, even a tenderness, breaks through the straitjacket of scholastic discipline.

Spirituality

The 'spirituality' of *Holy Wisdom* is conveyed by its style and form as well as by its content. Having looked at the style, I wish now to consider some of the content. But before that let us take issue with the vexed word 'spirituality'. It has, firstly, a legal meaning (spirituality as opposed to temporality, lords spiritual as opposed to lords temporal); secondly, it has a practical religious meaning (a body

---

22. John of the Cross, *Collected Works of St. John of the Cross*, trans. K. Kavanaugh & O. Rodriguez (Washington DC: 1991), pp. 711–12.

of practices, ways of praying, fasting etc.); thirdly, it has a theoretical religious meaning (a theology of the ways in which the human being relates to God by way of practices of various kinds). Just as there are theology and theologies, so there are spirituality and spiritualities. *Holy Wisdom* has a lot to say in terms of practical religious meaning, but it also tries, albeit often indirectly, to articulate theoretical religious meanings. The theory (or theories), however, frequently need to be coaxed out of hiding. How *Holy Wisdom* understands incarnation, redemption, the make-up of the human person as an individual and as a social being etc., needs to be drawn from the coils of the text. Interestingly, *Holy Wisdom* uses the word 'spirituality' on at least one occasion when it discusses 'ways of spirituality'.[23]

Holy Wisdom is rarely explicit about its linguistic methodology. Consider, however, this passage:

> it is generally the custom of those that write treatises of spiritual doctrine to begin with a division of the several stations or ascents ... in the spiritual progress.[24]

Here, at least, it reveals an awareness of the subject of metaphor or model. This aspect of *Holy Wisdom* stands in contrast with, for example, the fascination of the author of 'The Cloud' with regard to linguistic and methodological questions, perhaps surprising in a writer of such evocative prose, but then the Cloud is by a prose-poet; *Holy Wisdom* is not.[25]

---

23. *Holy Wisdom*, p. 352.
24. *Holy Wisdom*, p. 350.
25. Cf. J. Walsh (ed.), *The Cloud of Unknowing* (New York: 1981), p. 218 and p. 241, for two examples of The Cloud's linguistic awareness: '... we need to be greatly on our guard in the interpretation of words which are spoken with spiritual intent ... it is particularly important to be careful about this word "in" and this word "up" ...", and 'take care not to interpret bodily what is meant spiritually, though it be spoken in bodily metaphor, as these words "up" or "down," "in" or "out," "behind" or "before," "on one side" or "on the other." ... For no matter how spiritual a thing may be in itself, yet when we come to speak of it, since speech is a bodily exercise

When I studied *Holy Wisdom* in the 1980s, I was on the attack against a spirituality, present in *Holy Wisdom* but characteristic of most of what I would call the 'soul-she' period. 'Soul-she' is a glib sound-bite. The spirituality was characterised by an evaluative dualism that saw the human person as divided, not merely in the simplistic and obvious sense of having sinful tendencies at the same time as tendencies towards the good, but radically, in his or her very constitution. I would be more patient with Baker today; or maybe age has made me more pessimistic about human capacity.

Holy Wisdom and Prayer

Instead of continuing in this rather theoretical way, I will now consider a fundamental and concrete aspect of *Holy Wisdom's* spirituality, namely its teaching on prayer. This will be done in three sections entitled the Divine Office, *Lectio Divina*, and The Higher Stages. The Divine Office and *Lectio Divina* are not perhaps of major interest to *Holy Wisdom*, but they are to monastics of today, therefore it is valuable to reflect on what *Holy Wisdom* says or at least implies, ('expressing, or at least implying') on the subject.

1. The Divine Office

For *Holy Wisdom* vocal prayer represents a preliminary level that barely enters in its scheme of degrees of prayer, the first of which is discursive prayer or meditation. Consider the following three quotations:

> (Vocal prayer is) suitable for simple and unlearned persons (especially women) as are not at all fit for discursive prayer.[26]

---

performed with the tongue ... it is necessary that bodily metaphors be used'.

26. *Holy Wisdom*, p. 304.

> In vocal prayer there is a continuous variety and succession of images ... the which do distract ...[27]

> God only desires our hearts or affections, without which our tongues or brains are of no esteem at all.[28]

The basic principle of *Holy Wisdom's* theory of prayer is already implied here: that prayer is rooted in the will ('our hearts or affections'), that the function of the intellect or the faculty of understanding (*Holy Wisdom* frequently uses 'understanding' as a substantive, but rarely uses 'intellect') is not of great importance ('without which ... are of no esteem at all'), and that prayer requires an absence of 'images', whether visual or expressed by words. Images 'do distract'. From what do they distract? From an abstracted attention to God. *Holy Wisdom's* theory is essentially the same as that of 'The Cloud' and its 'naked intent unto God'.

Monks and nuns, however, must spend several hours a day praying the Divine Office, which is essentially words. We know that Baker's monastic observance was at best idiorhythmic, at worst, plain disobedient. He never learnt to live in community. But he couldn't just jettison the Divine Office. What *Holy Wisdom* offers, in fact, is an interesting and, indeed, nuanced, way of inserting the Divine Office into its own scheme of degrees of prayer. The author proposes three levels of increasing profundity in the praying of the Office:

> 1. Attention or express reflection on the words ... Now this attention being, in vocal prayer, necessarily to vary and change according as sentences in the Psalms etc, do succeed one another, cannot so powerfully and efficaciously fix the mind or affections on God, because they are presently to be recalled to new considerations or succeeding affections'.[29]

> 2. By occasion of such reciting raising in themselves an efficacious affection to God, do desire without

---
27. *Holy Wisdom*, p. 310.
28. *Holy Wisdom*, p. 312.
29. *Holy Wisdom*, p. 305.

The Spirituality of Sancta Sophia 13

variation to continue it ... not at all heeding whether it be suitable to the sense of the present passage which they pronounce ... attention to God though not to the words.[30]

3. Whereby vocal prayers do become mental; that is, whereby souls most profoundly and with a perfect simplicity united to God can yet ... attend also to the sense and spirit of each passage that they pronounce.[31]

These three stages, as a description of a process of deepening or maturing in prayer, are convincing. In the first stage, the rapid movement of words (and therefore of ideas or images), if followed with attention and concentration, would leave the person metaphorically breathless. The restless succession prevents the stable resting necessary if the will is to fix itself on its true object. So there is the second level: this is characterised by stability ('without variation to continue it'). The will fixes itself on God, but the price to be paid is the abandonment of attention to the flow of words which thus become a mere background sound, more or less helpful. We might have expected *Holy Wisdom* to conclude here, seeing the Office merely as an environment potentially conducive to prayer of the will. But the author goes a step further: a still more perfect stage is where the words themselves (presumably not *all* of them but occasional phrases), become the 'acts' which merge into 'aspirations'.[32] They become the darts of the will. This is possible because the person is already 'with a perfect simplicity united to God'.

Those who have prayed the Divine Office for many years will probably respond positively to *Holy Wisdom's* advice. Intuitively, the two extremes represented by the first and second stages do not really satisfy. The first proves to be exhausting or, in fact, impossible in practice. The second

---

30. *Holy Wisdom*, p .305.
31. *Holy Wisdom*, p. 306.
32. See below for discussion on 'acts' and 'aspirations'.

seems, ultimately, to deny any real value to the Office. The third, however, 'sacramentalises' the words.

2. Lectio Divina

Before considering how the teaching of *Holy Wisdom* might relate to *lectio divina*, let us note the book's way of describing 'degrees of prayer'. The author tells us how various spiritual writers propose various schemes.[33] He himself, however, will follow a variation of that of Barbanson.[34] Where the latter offers six stages, *Holy Wisdom* will offer only three, telescoping Barbanson's final four into one. The three proposed are:

> 1. Discoursive prayer or meditation.
>
> 2. The prayer of forced immediate acts or affections of the will, without discourse preparatory thereto.
>
> 3. The prayer of pure active contemplation or aspirations ...[35]

Holy Wisdom will be particularly interested in the second and third stages, but it is at the first stage that we might see a connection with *lectio divina*. *Holy Wisdom* never talks directly about *lectio divina* in our (re-discovered) sense. In Baker's day, it did not have the distinctive monastic status that it enjoys today. But if *Holy Wisdom* is to be a help to modern Christians who consider *lectio divina* an essential part of their spirituality, we must seek to establish some kind of relationship between the two. At first sight, there seems little ground for a rapprochement:

> and meditation, in which discourse is employed, is, so far, little more than a philosophical contempla-

---

33. *Holy Wisdom*, p. 350f.
34. Constantine Barbanson, Capuchin (1582–1631) and a slightly younger contemporary of Baker.
35. *Holy Wisdom*, p. 351f.

tion of God, delaying this fixing of the heart and affections on God ...³⁶

Even if the author does not have a high opinion of meditation, he offers some interesting comments on it. Let us first recall the traditional four phases of *lectio divina*: reading, meditating, praying and contemplating (in Latin: *lectio, meditatio, oratio, contemplatio*),³⁷ remembering also that they are not to be taken in an inflexible, linear way. Now consider *Holy Wisdom's* comments on meditation:

> Let her not trust her memory for the points that she is to meditate on, but have the book ready that she may look on it as she shall have need ... *[LECTIO]* ... (1) with her memory and understanding let her think on the matter of that point *[MEDITATIO]*; (2) out of which let her draw a reason or motive, by which the will may be inclined some way or other toward God *[MEDITATIO to ORATIO]*; (3) and thereupon let her produce an act of the will (as of humiliation, adoration ...), abiding in such application of the soul to God as long as the will hath life and activity for it, or as long as she shall be able to do it *[ORATIO to CONTEMPLATIO]*; (4) the which failing and growing to be disgustful, let her proceed to the next point, therein behaving herself likewise after the same manner, so proceeding in order to the others following till she have spent a competent time in her recollection' *[back to LECTIO]*.³⁸

Clearly, we need to make some adjustments. The 'points' for meditation are replaced by a biblical text ('have the book ready ...'). The meditation entails the use of the lower faculties of memory and understanding, but this pondering provokes a movement of the higher faculty of the will that expresses itself through an 'act'. If the orientation of

---

36. *Holy Wisdom*, p. 310.
37. The *locus classicus* of this description of *lectio divina* is found in the Carthusian, Guigo II (1140–1193), *Epistola de Vita Contemplativa (Scala Claustralium)*.
38. *Holy Wisdom*, p. 369, italics mine.

the will to God expressed in the act continues, the prayer may become 'aspirative', which prayer *Holy Wisdom* would describe as 'pure, active contemplation'. When this fails, the person returns to the text ('the next point') to read again. Note, by the way, the dominance of the feminine particles, because the person-word is, of course, 'soul'.

3. *The Higher Stages*

The practice of 'discursive prayer or meditation', even though it includes elements of the two higher stages, is only a preliminary for *Holy Wisdom*. The moment arrives when

> a contemplative soul, hath for some reasonable time practised meditation ... she ought to forbear meditation, and to betake herself to the exercise of immediate acts ... the end of all meditation etc. is the producing acts of the will.[39]

It is interesting to note that there was uneasiness about jettisoning the Bible entirely. *Holy Wisdom* is generally positive about the teaching of the Capuchin, Fr Benet Canfield,[40] but on this subject he distinguishes his position. Canfield, with other authors, holds that exercises of the understanding must be left behind in favour of those of the will (here *Holy Wisdom* is entirely in agreement), except for the case of the Passion of Our Lord (here *Holy Wisdom* differs). The ground for differing is not unconvincing: the Passion is indeed important, but, in the higher reaches of prayer, it is to be experienced and lived rather than meditated upon by means of the understanding.[41]

I have already mentioned the technical words 'acts' and 'aspirations' that represent the core elements of *Holy Wis-*

---

39. *Holy Wisdom,* p. 375f.
40. Father Benet Canfield or Fitch (1562–1610), a slightly older contemporary of Baker.
41. *Holy Wisdom*, p. 377, *cf.* p. 465.

The Spirituality of Sancta Sophia

dom's second and third stages. A quotation will clarify the difference between them:

> 1. The exercise of forced acts or of affections of the will, produced either immediately according to the person's present disposition, without a distinct or express motive represented by the understanding ... : these are called forced acts, because after that a soul has become indisposed to prosecute the exercise of meditation, it will be long before that good affections do ... naturally flow from her, so that she will need to use some force upon herself for producing the said acts of the will, which are imperfect contemplation.
>
> 2. The exercise of aspirations, which, though they be in substance little differing from the former, yet by reason of the facility wherewith they are produced without force, foresight, or election ... we therefore give them another name, and call them not acts, but aspirations, the constant exercise of which is proper and perfect contemplation'.[42]

In (1) a conscious effort is required to produce the act. In (2) the act seems to 'say itself', or to emerge spontaneously, and is then called an 'aspiration'. *Holy Wisdom* explicitly chooses this word in preference to others that mean the same: 'Elevations, inward stirrings of the spirit, Aspirations etc ... we will ... use ... Aspirations'.[43]

Conclusion

In this selective consideration of *Holy Wisdom's* spirituality, I have dealt primarily with its teaching on prayer. The book does attempt to deal with other aspects of prayer: for example, silence, passive unions and the great desolation, but with more detachment and maybe less success. David Knowles rightly points out that the note of personal authority in *Holy Wisdom* diminishes as the author describes the

---
42. *Holy Wisdom*, pp. 384–85.
43. *Holy Wisdom*, p. 456.

higher reaches of prayer.[44] Certainly, beyond the description of the three major stages, there is a quality of increased tentativeness and greater reliance on other authorities. Was the Baker manifested in *Holy Wisdom* a mystic? Knowles, from his narrow framework of definitions, thought not.[45] It all depends, of course, on how one chooses to define a mystic. The person who was present in Baker's last hours confirmed that 'perfect resignation and a total subjection to the will and good pleasure of Almighty God was plainly seen to be performed by him to his last breath'.[46] One could hardly ask for more.

---

44. D. Knowles, *The English Mystical Tradition* (London: 1961), p. 187.
45. Knowles, *Mystical Tradition*, p. 160f.
46. J. McCann (ed.), *The Life of Father. Augustine Baker (1575–1641) by Fr Peter Salvin & Fr Serenus Cressy* (London: 1933), p. 138, words of Baker's landlady in London in 1641.

2

Augustine Baker and the History of the English Benedictine Congregation

BARNABY HUGHES

The most substantial history of English Benedictine monasticism is still that published at Douai in 1626 and entitled *Apostolatus Benedictinorum in Anglia*, a massive volume that has neither been translated nor reprinted. Augustine Baker, although known to be one of the principal authors of that work, is largely unknown and unrecognised as an historian. Perhaps rightly, attention has been focussed on Baker's spiritual writings. In order to broaden our perspective on Augustine Baker I here aim to shed light on his historical work. As far as I am aware, the only person to have specifically written at any length on Baker's historical work is T. P. Ellis in his *Welsh Benedictines of the Terror* (Newtown, 1936). While Ellis' account is still substantially accurate, its main weakness is the lack of references, though it is not difficult to discover what his sources are. I want only to look more closely at the primary sources and supplement them with more recent scholarship, and in doing so, to say something about Augustine Baker's role in the composition of the *Apostolatus Benedictinorum in Anglia*. What I do not aim to speak about is Baker's place in the history of the English Benedictine Congregation, although something must inevitably be said about this, since Baker was one of the most important figures in its early history. To begin with, it is worth asking where Baker's interest in history came from. Baker himself gives no indication of having done any historical reading in his 'Autobiography', no doubt because it is unfinished. This lack notwithstanding, I venture to presume that Baker read little, if any, history before becoming a monk. My guess is that his interest in history, and specifically the history of the English Benedictines, was ignited by meeting Dom Sigebert Buckley and the events surrounding the latter's aggregation of the monks Edward Mayhew and Vincent Sadler to himself on 21 November 1607.[1] Undoubtedly, Baker was largely responsible for the legal aspects of this affair, due to his education in law at the Inns of Court, but I must disagree with the judgement of Ellis that 'it was to him (Baker), to his legal and historic instinct, that the importance of preserving the continuity of the Congregation occurred.'[2] Moreover, Ellis argues that while Anselm Beech and Thomas Preston were looking after the aged Baker upon his release from prison, 'they probably never considered, or even knew of, the pre-Reformation Congregation; its very existence had been almost forgotten, and Dom Buckley himself, when he was questioned, was more than hazy on the subject.'[3] Ellis is here almost certainly basing himself upon the account of Dom Leander Prichard, who writes of Buckley in *The Second Treatise concerning the Life and Writings of the Venerable Father, F. Augustin Baker*:

---

1. J. McCann & H. Connolly (eds.), 'Memorials of Father Augustine Baker and other documents relating to the English Benedictines', *Catholic Record Society*, vol. 33 (London: 1933), pp. 279, 291, for Baker's unfinished 'Autobiography'; B. Hughes, 'Dies Memorabilis: Continuity in English Benedictine Monasticism' in *The American Benedictine Review* 61:1 (March 2010), pp. 3–18.
2. T. P. Ellis, *Welsh Benedictines of the Terror* (Newtown: 1936), p. 110.
3. Ellis, *Benedictines*, p. 110.

> This old man did the Italian monks [i.e. Beech and Preston] respect and honour as a venerable piece of antiquity, and as a relique of our Order in former days in England. But Mr Baker shewed them many speciall and perticuler points, in which this old man might be useful to them. And namely how far the modern laws, and much more how far the ancient laws, both of the Kingdom and Church of England, did approve or favour the surviving and continuation of rights in few or one only person of a body politick or religious.[4]

But this account differs from that of Baker himself, who related in his *Treatise of the English Benedictine Mission* that Anselm Beech knew of Buckley's importance as early as 1600.[5] In describing Beech's petition to the pope in favour of sending English monks on the mission, Baker noted that one of the principal reasons for this was that the said monks might be united and aggregated to Sigebert Buckley, and

> thereby the old English Benedictine congregation would be kept ever alive and continued... whereas otherwise it would cleane perish by the death of the said remaininge monke who was now extreamely aged, and so could not live longe but would die before these fathers could come in as missioners, if they came not in with the more speed.[6]

But how did Anselm Beech know of Buckley's existence in 1600, that is, while Buckley was still in prison and before Beech and Preston had even gone to England and met him? David Lunn says that it was through a certain Henry Constable, a layman and courtier politically active on behalf of English Catholics. Beech met Constable while acting as

---

4. McCann & Connolly (eds.), 'Memorials', p. 95.
5. McCann & Connolly (eds.), 'Memorials', p. 171.
6. McCann & Connolly (eds.), 'Memorials', p. 171; D. Lunn, *The English Benedictines 1540–1688: From Reformation to Revolution* (London: 1980), pp. 24–26, for fuller and clearer details of the petition's history than those provided Baker.

apostolic penitentiary to English pilgrims in Rome.⁷ Constable, however, is unlikely to have actually met Buckley, since the latter had been imprisoned throughout Constable's early life, for in 1591 Constable had gone into exile and resided mostly in France.⁸ Yet Constable was well-connected and well-informed of English Catholic affairs, both at home and abroad, so it is certainly possible that he knew of Buckley's existence. Beech and Preston, therefore, did not need Baker to tell them about the special importance of Buckley in continuing the English Benedictine Congregation, since they had already learned this from Constable, but Baker probably did aid them in showing exactly how any aggregation might be legally effected.

Around this time, that is, at the time when Baker, Buckley, Beech, and Preston were arranging the all-important aggregation, Baker related another chance occurrence that would influence events at least as much as had the meeting of Beech and Constable in Rome. This was the discovery of

> an abstract or summary of all the decrees held by a certeine generall chapter of the order in England, held in the time of Henry the sixt kinge of England...and there was expressed there the title of the session, place, day, and yeare, and the names of the two Presidents, specifieinge that it was for the whole order in England, that was not subiect to transmarin howses.⁹

This 'abstract or summary', Baker wrote, was written in the back of 'an old printed Turrecremata upon our Rule, which one whom I know [which is probably Baker himself] happened to buy amonge the booke-sellers of Duck-lane.'¹⁰ This glimpse into the medieval history of the English Benedic-

---

7. Lunn, *English Benedictines*, p. 25.
8. G. Wickes, 'Henry Constable, Poet and Courtier (1562–1613)' in *Biographical Studies* 2, 4 (1953–54), pp. 272–300.
9. McCann & Connolly (eds.), 'Memorials', p. 181.
10. McCann & Connolly (eds.), 'Memorials', p. 180. The book in question must have been the *Expositio Super Regulam Beatissimi Patris Benedicti* by Cardinal Ioannes de Turrecremata or Juan de Torque-

tines, at a time when Baker was trying to find out as much as he could from Buckley, would certainly have ignited his interest into the history of the English Benedictine Congregation, the existence of which Baker was only beginning to be conscious. Yet, it seems that he had little opportunity to engage in serious historical study until the 1620s.

I must make a short digression now in order to put Baker's historical researches into context. In 1619, Edward Mayhew, one of the first two monks aggregated to Buckley in 1607, began to publish his *Congregationis Anglicanae Ordinis Sancti Benedicti Trophaea* (Rheims, 1619–20 and 1625).[11] This book appeared in three instalments: the first in 1619 concerning the history of the English Benedictines, the second in 1620 concerning its saints, and the third in 1625 concerning its writers. The year 1619 is, of course, the year when the union of the Spanish and English monks was effected to form the present English Benedictine Congregation. Not every monk of the Spanish Congregation, however, wished to join the English Congregation. Two such monks were John Barnes (died 1661) and Francis Walgrave (1581–1668) who had become chaplains attached to the nuns at Chelles. For their maintenance, the abbess of that house managed to acquire for them French benefices, which meant that they had to become French citizens and, furthermore, because the benefices belonged to a Cluniac priory, they had to transfer themselves to the Order of Cluny. Having left the Spanish Congregation without permission, Barnes and Walgrave found themselves in some trouble with their former superiors. They began to promote the Cluniac Order at the expense of the English

---

mada. The Bodleian Library, Oxford, has an edition published at Paris in 1491.

11. R. H. Connolly, 'A Rare Benedictine Book: Father Edward Maihew's *Trophaea*' in *Downside Review* 50 (1932), pp. 108–25, and his, 'Father Maihew on the Restoration of the English Congregation' in *Downside Review* 50 (1932), pp. 490–497; A. F. Allison and D. M. Rogers, *The Contemporary Printed Literature of the English Counter-Reformation between 1558 and 1640*, vol. 1 (Aldershot: 1994), nos.757–59; Allison and Rogers, *Literature*, 1, no. 70.

Congregation, Barnes publishing in 1622 a book with the polemical title of *Examen Trophaeorum congregationis pretensae Anglicanae*, in which he argued that there never had been an English Benedictine Congregation, but that all of the medieval English Benedictine houses had been subject to Cluny.[12]

The English Benedictines in France and the Low Countries, therefore, found it necessary to refute Barnes's book, enlisting the aid of Augustine Baker, then in London and well placed to undertake the necessary historical research. Baker compiled six volumes of transcriptions from medieval manuscripts relating to English monasteries at this time. Four of these survive as Jesus College MSS 75–78 in the Bodleian Library, Oxford. A note at the end of the first volume, which Baker wrote at Cambrai in 1627, reads as follows:

> This tome together with five other tomes manuscripte do conteyn certein collections which I made out of some olde MS. books that I founde in divers mens hands in Englande, concerning some principall houses of our order. My purpose was to have collected farre more and better things, but was hindred by ye persecution arising in Englande, which thereuppon I lefte and came over to this side the seas. And this that I have donne I did in the peaceable tyme that was in Eglande, which was in the tyme of ye treatie of ye match betweene ye Prince of Englande and ye Infanta of Spaine; what I meant further to have donne was chieflie out of ye MS. librarie of sir Robert Cotton, whence though I have taken many things, yet is there yet there to be hand an infinit store of matter more than I have taken out, yea better matter, for indeed I spent my tyme most, in other mens libraries heere and there, esteming

---

12. Y. Chaussy, *Les Bénédictins Anglais Refugiés en France au XVIIe Siècle, 1611–1669* (Paris: 1967), pp. 95–128, and his, 'New Evidence on the English Benedictines' in *Downside Review* 88 (1970), pp. 36–56.

myself sure of sir Roberts librarie, as I had ben, if ye tyme had helde for it.[13]

Prichard's *Life of Augustine Baker* further supplies the details that Baker himself omits, namely that he employed a scribe who travelled with him and copied out most of the contents of the Jesus College manuscripts, and that this laborious work was accomplished at Baker's own expense to the sum of nearly two hundred pounds.[14] It is evident from this note, however, that Baker had to leave his researches unfinished and flee to the continent, where he stopped at Douai briefly before being sent to the nuns at Cambrai in 1624.

I now want to dwell on these manuscripts for a moment before turning to the *Apostolatus Benedictinorum in Anglia*, which was written using these manuscripts and published four years after the publication of Barnes's *Examen*. The first and longest of these manuscript volumes (616 fols.) contains material relating to the Benedictine houses in Canterbury—St. Augustine's and Christchurch—and the abbeys of Reading, Bury St Edmunds, and Westminster. The second volume (262 fols.) concerns Ely, the third volume (322 fols.) St Albans, and the fourth volume (215 fols.) Ramsey, Lindisfarne, and Durham. Naturally, one might wish to speculate about the contents of the missing fifth and sixth volumes. In this connection, David Knowles published in 1954 a very intriguing review of the third volume of Walther Holtzmann's *Papsturkunden in England*, a collection of papal documents relating to medieval England. Knowles noted that the most interesting documents in Holtzmann's collection, hitherto unpublished, were a series of more than eighty privileges and bulls from the abbey of St Albans. 'These', he wrote, 'together with other monastic records, seem to have formed part of the transcripts made by Dom Augustine Baker and his associates for Reyner's

---

13. H. O. Coxe, *Catalogus Codicum MSS qui in Collegiis Aulisque Oxoniensis Hodie Adservantur*, 2 vols. (Oxford: 1852), Collegii Jesu, 27–28.
14. McCann & Connolly (eds.), 'Memorials', p. 110.

Apostolatus and other works; they found their way into the library of the Bollandists and thence into the Bibliothèque Royale (Brussels), but have never been printed or used by modern monastic historians.'[15] Knowles then went on to describe some of these particular privileges of St Albans and their significance for historians. What I would like to know is whether it is Knowles's or Holtzmann's opinion that these transcripts were part of the original Baker collection, and if so, whether or not anyone has followed up such a suggestion? It might certainly end speculation as to the contents of one, if not both, of the missing volumes.

Yet it is possible that the original volumes have been subsequently divided, seeing as the first Jesus College manuscript contains more than twice as many pages as the other three. I do not know if Baker's working methods were entirely consistent, but on the evidence of the Jesus College manuscripts, he grouped his material together by monastery, not interspersing material relating to different houses. For there to be another manuscript volume in existence, therefore, containing material relating to St Albans, in addition to Jesus College MS 77 devoted exclusively to St Albans, presents an anomaly unless that manuscript has been subsequently divided. But these are just speculations. Perhaps a more reliable method of discovering the contents of the missing volumes would be to conduct a careful analysis of the *Apostolatus* to see how its authors have made use of the extant material in the Jesus College manuscripts, and then to work out which similar parts of the *Apostolatus* do not rely on that material. Thus, by a process of elimination, it might be possible to work out the contents of the missing volumes.

Having discussed Baker's preparatory researches, it is now time to turn to the *Apostolatus* itself, which is composed of three parts of roughly equal length: two treatises and appendices of primary sources. The first treatise,

---

15. D. Knowles, review of W. Holtzmann (ed.), *Papsturkunden in England*, vol. 3 (Gottingen: 1952) in *English Historical Review* 69 (1954), pp. 433–36.

divided into three parts, argues that the conversion of England was effected by Benedictine monks; it is in this connection that the transcriptions in the Jesus College manuscripts were chiefly used. The second treatise, in six parts, certainly the most important of the three, as it refutes Barnes's book, argues that the English monasteries were a Congregation, distinct from all other Congregations, and subject to no foreign Congregation. The final part of the *Apostolatus*, the appendices, includes official documents relating to the re-establishment of the English Benedictine Congregation in 1619 as well as much older documents, such as the tenth-century *Regularis Concordia*. According to his first biographer, Leander Prichard, Augustine Baker was responsible for drafting both of the *Apostolatus's* treatises, and presumably he was also responsible for collecting the documents that make up the appendices. Leander Jones, says Prichard, 'who penned it in Latin' and 'had the trimming and pollishing of it', deserves to have the second place in the composition of the *Apostolatus* after Baker.[16] The only other person mentioned in connection with the composition of the *Apostolatus* is Clement Reyner, whose name appears on the title page; he is said to have been the 'Secretary and subscribed the dedicatory epistle.'[17]

Although Augustine Baker undoubtedly used his medieval manuscript sources to great advantage in the composition of the *Apostolatus*, he did not neglect more contemporary published histories. In scrutinising his account of Abbot John Feckenham at the end of the first treatise, which could not have been written from medieval manuscripts, one can see that Baker's sources are divided between Catholic exiles and Anglican antiquarians.[18] Baker makes extensive use of Thomas Stapleton's *A Counterblast to M. Hornes Vayne Blast against M. Fekenham* (Louvain,

---

16. McCann & Connolly (eds.), 'Memorials', p. 111.
17. McCann & Connolly (eds.), 'Memorials', p. 112.
18. Initially I was under the impression that Baker had based his account of Feckenham solely on Henry Holland (1550–1625), a kinsman of the abbot.

1567) and Nicholas Sander's *De Origine ac Progressu Schismatis Anglicani* (Cologne: 1585), both of which must have been available to him in Douai. Of the Anglican antiquarians, Baker met some of them at Sir Robert Cotton's house, one being William Camden, whose work he also used extensively.[19] It is possible, though unacknowledged, that Baker also consulted Father Henry Holland (1550–1625), who was a kinsman of Abbot Feckenham and taught theology to French monks in Flanders at the time Baker was writing.[20] Holland wrote a substantial biographical poem 'In Laudem Ioannis Fecknami', which survives among his other Latin poems in Harley MS 3258 in the British Library.[21]

The *Apostolatus Benedictinorum in Anglia* was, and still is, a monumental work of scholarship. While I think it would be perhaps unfair to criticise it, say, for describing St Augustine of Canterbury as a Benedictine, which we now know to be false, we can certainly commend Augustine Baker's generous use of manuscript sources, something his modern successor David Knowles never accomplished. As David Farmer noted in a previous English Benedictine Symposium paper, the *Apostolatus* printed for the first time the *Regularis Concordia* and Lanfranc's *Monastic Constitutions*.[22] Much more work remains to be done on the *Apostolatus*, chiefly an examination of its relationship to the Jesus College MSS. Additionally, if we are to better appreciate Baker's role as an historian, a new edition of his *Treatise of the English Benedictine Mission*, one that reproduces the entire text and not just the portion edited by

---

19. McCann & Connolly (eds.), 'Memorials', pp. 112–13.
20. P. Millward, 'Henry Holland', *Oxford Dictionary of National Biography* (Oxford: 2004),
21. E. Bishop (ed.), 'In Laudem Joannis Feckenham, O.S.B.' in *Downside Review* 1 (1882), pp. 430–33.
22. D. Farmer, 'Historical Influences on the Early Development of the EBC' in *EBC History Symposium Papers* (1981), p. 6.

Hugh Connolly for the Catholic Records Society,[23] is also needed. While Augustine Baker is remembered fondly for the spiritual foundations that he laid for the English Benedictine Congregation, he deserves to be better remembered for similarly laying its historical foundations.

---

23. McCann & Connolly (eds.), 'Memorials', pp. 155–189. Subsequent to this paper, John Clark has edited Baker's *An Introduction or Preparative to a Treatise of the English Benedictine Mission* in *Analecta Cartusiana*, 119:35 (Salzburg: 2011), and, in the near future, hopes to edit more material from Baker's treatises relating to the English Mission.

3

Did Father Baker compile the first Constitutions of the English Benedictine nuns at Cambrai?

MARGARET TRURAN

In 1987 members of the English Benedictine Congregation's History Commission travelled to Lille in the north of France.[1] Their work on listing the archives there for the community of Our Lady of Consolation, formerly at Cambrai and subsequently at Stanbrook, gave Dame Eanswythe Edwards, Stanbrook's archivist, the incentive to obtain a photocopy of the first item in the calendar, the constitutions of 1631.[2] During the course of Dr John Clark's careful editing of Father Baker's writings, this text has proved invaluable in answering his enquiries. That raises the question of whether the constitutions in turn shed light on Father Baker's role at Cambrai. Did he have a hand in their compilation?

Certainly his legal training and expertise, laid at the service of the Congregation, qualified him to do so. Throughout his nine years as confessor and spiritual guide at Cambrai, however, his position was anomalous. The President of the Congregation, Dom Rudesind Barlow, sent him in 1624 as a 'tabler' or lodger to help the nine foundresses during their

---

1. R. Jones, OSB (ed.), 'Calendar of Lille, Archives du Nord 20 H' in *EBC History Symposium Papers 1987*, pp. 49–89.
2. Lille, Archives du Nord, 20 H 1.

noviciate. 'For near three years within the first six years of his being there', according to Father Serenus Cressy, he supplied as 'Vicarius Monialium' or vicar of the nuns, an office that included powers of government shared with the abbess and her council.[3] He never, however, held the post officially and his presence was increasingly resented by the Vicarius appointed by the General Chapter of 1629, Father Francis Hull, 'a verie vertuous good man', remarked Dame Christina Brent, 'but he was not well versed in the words of St Jhon Baptist: I am not.'[4] The conflict between the two men was brought before the next General Chapter in 1633 and, though Father Baker's teaching was vindicated, he was removed from Cambrai.

What clues to the history of their compilation do the constitutions offer? The title page, set out by hand with care, as if printed, does not give much away: 'CONSTITUTIONS compiled for the better obseruation of the holie Rule of our most glorious Father and Patriarch S. Bennet: confirmed by the Regiment[5] of the English Benedictine Congregation, and by it deliuered to the English Religious Dames of the same Order and Congregation, liuing in Cambray; and to all their successors.'[6] On page 111, above the word FINIS, appear in confirmation the signatures of 'B. Leander' and 'B. Rosendo'. Dom Leander Jones, as Prior of St Gregory's, Douai, was Ordinary of the monastery of Our Lady of Comfort at Cambrai. He and Dom Rudesind ('Rosendo') Barlow, who had erected the house at Cambrai, were former Presidents and two of the most learned

---

3. J. McCann (ed.), *The Life of Father Augustine Baker, O.S.B. (1575–1641)* (London: 1933), p. 108. Father Edward Maihew died two months after his appointment as 'Vicarius' in July 1625.
4. F. Gascoigne, *An Apologie for myselfe about Fr. Baker's doctrine*: Abbess Christina Brent, *Discourse concerning Father Baker's doctrine* in J. Clark (ed.), *Analecta Cartusiana*, 119:34 (Salzburg: 2011), p. 100.
5. Now called the 'Regimen'; in Baker's time, the council of the President-General.
6. I am grateful to Dame M. Peter Smith of Oulton Abbey for checking my transcriptions from the constitutions.

men in the English Benedictine Congregation. Father Baker had turned to them in 1629 for approbation of his spiritual writings. At the bottom of the same page, a paragraph in a cursive secretary hand reads:

> This copy of the constitutions hath beene by us underwrytten examined & compared with the copy sygned by the Very RRd fathers of the Regiment accordinge to the power giuen us by them, & beinge found in all to agree[,] wee by theyre authority ordayne & command that these constitutions bee read, published & practised in our Conuent at Cambray. Giuen at St Gregories in Dowaye 3° Octob. 1631. Br. Sebert Bagshaw President.[7]

A passage in Father Baker's *Exposition of the Rule*, 'And as for the Constitutions lately ordained for this house by the Regimen, by order of the General Chapter ...', confirms that the 1629 General Chapter determined that constitutions should be drawn up.[8] That this coincided with Dame Catherine Gascoigne's appointment as the first elected abbess of the community was surely no accident. Work began swiftly, to judge from the date of the specimen form of council minutes on page 52: 'Anno Domini. 1630: 20. of Januarie'. The text of the constitutions, 112 pages in all, falls into three parts: 'Pietie' (page 3); second, 'Certain perticular persons, offices, and businesses' (page 50); and third, 'Of things external and temporal. Of the Visit[ation], both ordinarie and extraordinarie' (page 97). On the last page, after the approbation and notice of promulgation, an amendment reveals that in November 1631 President Bagshaw was at Cambrai to implement the constitutions, not without some discussion about the fifth paragraph in the chapter on bedding:

---

7. In the seventeenth century 'conuent' (Latin *conventus*) did not imply female religious, but was used indiscriminately for communities of either monks or nuns.
8. Augustine Baker, *St Benedict's Rule* in J. Clark (ed.), *Analecta Cartusiana*, 119:24 (Salzburg: 2005–06), vol. 2, p. 322.

> I doe heerby declare that the meaninge of this constitution was principally to forbid the use of featherbeds, & by pillowes wee vnderstand as well great ones in manner of boulsters as little ones, & therfore every one maye haue as many feather boulsters or pillowes vnder her head as the Lady Abbesse shall thincke necessary.[9]

Who drew up the constitutions? Close attention to their text and that of Baker's other writings suggests that General Chapter asked Father Baker, on the basis of his considerable experience at Cambrai as well as his legal knowledge, to compile the document. What follows is not a comprehensive, let alone exhaustive, survey of what evidence there is, but may claim to be indicative.

Two explicit references by Baker to the constitutions are significant. One occurs in *Vox Clamantis in Deserto Animae*, written in the second half of 1632. Originally intended as an introduction to an edition of Hilton's *Scale of Perfection*, this work became a lengthy defence of Baker's teaching on divine calls, disputed in the summer of 1632 by Father Hull. Baker had already taught in *Doubts and Calls*, completed in 1629, that interior prayer is a response to the divine call or initiative, that is the promptings of grace, and had summarized his teaching in three pithy words, 'Observe your call'.[10] These two treatises, *Doubts and Calls* and *Vox Clamantis*, are central to Baker's exposition of the interior life.[11]

---

9. *Constitutions*, p. 112; *cf.* Part I, chapter 7, p. 41. His clarification was countersigned by the same two members of the Regimen, Father Leander and Father Rudesind, and in 1639 approved by General Chapter.
10. Augustine Baker, *Doubts and Calls* in J. Clark (ed.), *Analecta Cartusiana*, 119:10, (Salzburg: 1999), p. 48.
11. Augustine Baker, *Vox Clamantis in Deserto Animae* in J. Clark (ed), *Analecta Cartusiana*, 119:22 (Salzburg: 2004) and *Doubts and Calls*, in J. Clark (ed.), *Analecta Cartusiana*, 119:10 (Salzburg: 1999). These books provide the matter for section two of the first treatise in *Sancta Sophia* (Douai: 1657), Father Serenus Cressy's digest of Baker's teaching.

Did Father Baker compile the first Constitutions? 35

The passage in *Vox Clamantis* runs:

> And the Constitutions latelie made for this house doe accordinglie and worthilie prouide that the Nouices shall be taught mentall praier according to their calling, which the instructer or instructrix are to obserue, and accordinglie to direct the scholer ...[12]

One might expect to find this stipulation, 'that the Nouices shall be taught mentall praier according to their calling', in the directives on the office of the novice mistress. Not so; it is enshrined in the very opening of the constitutions, the second sentence of Part I:

> And because this is the chiefest end of a monastical life; to wit, to become spiritual and contemplatiue spirits, we ordaine that the Father Vicarius, Lady Abbesse, and Maistresse of Nouices haue a special care of them, that during the yeare of their Nouiship they be well exercised and instructed in mental prayer, according to their capacitie, and diuine calling: and therefore let them be often examined touching this point; and with this we charge the consciences of the three aforesaid.[13]

Vocabulary, teaching, emphasis on the primacy of mental or interior prayer, all proclaim Father Baker's pen. The approach is unmistakable. In *The Substance of the Rule* (1631), a work contemporary with the constitutions, he underlines the same doctrine in a parallel context, the passage in the

---

12. *Vox Clamantis*, p. 33. 'Scholer' was used of someone who had entered 'the school of the Lord's service' (Prologue to the Rule of St Benedict), either as a schoolgirl or as a postulant in the noviciate. See Part II, last section of chapter 4, 'Of the Mistresse of the Nouices, and of their reception, education, or dismission of them', §7: 'Being entred they must liue six months as scollers vnder the Mistresse of Nouices to be taught and tried before they beginne their Nouitiat ...'

13. Lille, Archives du Nord, 20 H 1, p. 3.

Rule of St Benedict that exhorts the novice master to watch the novice carefully to see if he truly seeks God:[14]

> In what maner to praie Interiorlie, or how otherwise to proceed towards Perfection of Praier, our Holie Father doth not teach, nor shew. For that office of Teaching he knew well belonged to God, and to the parties owne observation of the Divin Interior Calls, guidances, and Enablements. He knew that his Disciples were therein to have the same Maister, which himself had had for his Internall Praier, when he lived in the Wildernes and Solitude.[15]

The second explicit reference to the constitutions, already partly quoted, is from Baker's *Exposition of the Rule*. At Abbess Catherine's request, Father Baker spent five months in early 1631 on this work, which nicely provides a *terminus ante quem* for the completion of the text of the constitutions. Baker writes,

> And as for the Constitutions lately ordained for this house by the Regimen, by order of the General Chapter, there is (in the later end of the Constitutions) a Declaration to free you from scruples about them, expressly determining & declaring that they do not bind under any sin, as you may see more fully by the said Declaration itself in the said place. And whereas in the ordinances made upon every visit[16] there is usually in the beginning of them one in these words or to this effect, That first & above all things the President doth ordain & strictly command, as well the Abbess as the Dames & Sisters, that they diligently observe & keep the commande-

---

14. Augustine Baker, *The Substance of the Rule of St Bennet*, ed. Benedictines of Stanbrook, from Dom Leander Prichard's manuscript of c. 1650, Downside 26595, (Worcester: 1981), Chapter 58.
15. Augustine Baker, *Substance of the Rule of St Bennet*, p. 27. This appears on pp. 498–99 of Augustine Baker, *St Benedict's Rule* in J. Clark (ed), *Analecta Cartusiana*, 119:24 (Salzburg: 2006), vol. 3. Clark's base text is the later transcript by Dom Dunstan Hutchinson (d. 1730), which offers the only complete version of the whole *Exposition of the Rule*.
16. Namely Visitation.

ments of God & his Holy Church, our Holy *Rule*, the *Constitutions* & ceremonies of our Congregation; Now you are not to take or understand this to be a precept binding under any manner of sin, but only to be a general fatherly exhortation & admonition to look to & fulfill your duties & obligations; nor doth, nor ever did our Very Rd F. President intend thereby to put any further bond on you for the observances of those things, then allready was otherwise on you; & that is plainly to be gathered both out of the matter & manner of this ordination or Declaration made as you have heard. The meaning thereof was only in a generall manner to revive & represent unto your memories your duties & obligations in all respects, admonishing you not to be careless, but vigilant in the performance, leaving such penalties on everything as allready was otherwise on it, without diminishing or adding of any penalty of sin or other penalty.[17]

This time the passage in question occurs at the very end of the constitutions of 1631, under the heading 'Of the obligation of the Constitutions':

1. These are the Constitutions of this our Congrega-[tion *word left unfinished*] for the Religious woemen of all the Monasteries of the same; compiled for the more perfect observance of their holy Rule, and better liuing in Religious vnitie and comformitie: which although they ought to be of high esteeme and authoritie with the children of obedience; yet to avoid scruples...

2. We declare, that no Constitution, law, statute, ceremonie, or definition of the aforesaid, imposeth any further obligation of sinne vpon their consciences, then the verie nature of the things, and reason it selfe shall require, or enforce...[18]

---

17. Augustine Baker, *St Benedict's Rule* in J. Clark (ed.), *Analecta Cartusiana*, 119:24 (Salzburg: 2005), vol. 2, p. 322.
18. Lille, Archives du Nord, 20 H 1, pp. 108–9.

As confessor, Baker had discovered that scrupulosity, particularly about making confession, was one of the besetting temptations at Cambrai. He had given detailed guidance in the *Treatise on Confession* (approved in 1629) and also dealt with the subject in *A Secure Stay in all Temptations* (1629).[19]

We cannot expect to find many direct allusions to the constitutions in Baker's writings at Cambrai, given that most of these were penned at an earlier date. Further evidence, however, can be gleaned from comparisons of content, thought and vocabulary. *The Substance of the Rule* opens with the words:

> In the Rule two things are to be considered. The one, what is the Ende whereat the Rule aimeth. The other what be the Meanes prescribed by the Rule for attaining to the said Ende.
>
> The Ende of the Rule is to bring a Soule by the Practise of it, to a Perfect Union with God.[20]

Compare the opening of the preface to the constitutions:

> Religious persons are to know, and ayme at two things: the first is the end of their profession; the second is the meanes to attaine to this end. Their end is to serue their Creatour, and saue their owne soules with all religious perfection possible: that is, to come to a perfect vnion of their spirit with God.[21]

The context is different, but this serves to highlight the identical theological approach through the two objectives of end and means, and the identical language; in both cases 'the end is ... perfect union with God'. The preface goes on to identify four 'meanes to attaine to this end':

> 1. abstraction of life, silence and solitude. Secondly prayer, which includeth both mental and vocal, the

---

19. Augustine Baker, *Five Treatises; The Life and Death of Dame Margaret Gascoigne; Treatise of Confession* in J. Clark (ed.), *Analecta Cartusiana*, 119:23 (Salzburg, 2006), and *A secure stay in all temptations* in J. Clark (ed.), *Analecta Cartusiana*, 119:8 (Salzburg: 1998).
20. Augustine Baker, *Substance*, p. 1, and *St Benedict's Rule*, vol. 3, p. 476.
21. Lille, Archives du Nord, 20 H 1, p. 2.

diuine office, together with the due, discreet and deuout frequentation of the Sacraments. Thirdly mortification of their vnruly passions, sensual appetites, peruerse inclinations, and disordinate affections, a total abnegation of their selfe-will, selfe-loue, and selfe-iudgement; and a perfect and pure resignation of themselues to the diuine will, in all things, times, and places; in life and death, for time and eternitie. Fowerthly the last is a discreet and courageous perseuerance in the three aforesaid exercises, vntill death.[22]

Abstraction of life, prayer and mortification, 'long exercise wherein': these are the classic pillars of Father Baker's spirituality.[23]

The prescriptive text of the constitutions matches less easily the content of Baker's spiritual writings, but the regulations about the councillors, the making and hearing of confessions, and above all the principle that two half-hours should be spent in mental prayer each day offer some scope for comparison. In his *Directions for Contemplation, Book D* (*c.* 1627) Father Baker had recommended:

> The mentall prayer to be twise a day (if it may be), scz. at seauen in the morning ... The second mentall prayer is to be at fowre in the afternoone.[24]

By 1630 the timetable had been adjusted a little, but the principle remained. The opening sentence of the first part of the constitutions decrees:

> There must be an hower everie day allowed and employed by all in mental prayer conuentually ... according to the distribution of time, heerafter to be set downe.[25]

---

22. *Ibid.*
23. Augustine Baker, *Substance*, p. 1, and *St Benedict's Rule*, vol. 3, p. 476.
24. Augustine Baker, *Directions for Contemplation: Book D* in J. Clark (ed.), *Analecta Cartusiana* 119:11 (Salzburg: 1999), pp. 47–48.
25. Lille, Archives du Nord, 20 H 1, p. 3.

Chapter nine, 'Of the distribution of time', establishes the daily timetable in detail, first for the morning,

> 2. ... At the halfe hower [after six] punctuallie beginne prime, then their full halfe hower of mentall prayer in the quire conuentuallie...[26]

then for the afternoon,

> 9. At fower, halfe an hower of recollection in their cells: and then halfe an hower of mentall prayer in the quire conuentuallie, to which they shall be called by a little bell, and end it at the peale to supper.[27]

Once again *The Substance of the Rule* echoes the prescription in the constitutions:

> And by Order [presumably the timetable laid down in the constitutions] of this House there is but one howre of the day limited for Mentall Praier; and that howre divided into two partes, which makes the Ordinance farre the more tolerable and the easier to be performed; one halfe being to be donne after Prime, and the other half howre next before Supper. And therefore she is verie sluggish, and hath the divell (though invisible to our darke and unworthie eyes) sitting on her skirts, that will not bestirre herself at least for those two short Seasons.[28]

Seven and a half pages about the council and councillors rather surprisingly begin the second part of the constitutions and precede slightly shorter chapters on the vicarius and abbess. Once again Baker's hand can surely be detected. In the second of his *Five Treatises*, 'About the Electing of Worthy and Fit Counsellers within this House', probably drawn up in preparation for the first election in 1629 of an abbess, and subsequent election of her councillors, he had emphasized,

---

26. Lille, Archives du Nord, 20 H 1, p. 46
27. Lille, Archives du Nord, 20 H 1, p. 47.
28. Augustine Baker, *Substance*, p. 44, and St Benedict's *Rule*, vol. 3, p. 513.

> There is not any one point of such moment in this house (as, more concerning the honour of God, and the good, both spirituall & temporall, of this house) as is the election of fit & worthy councillors ...[29]

since they were responsible for the appointment of the chief officials in the house, as also for the admission of suitable candidates to the novitiate:

> And in the natures & qualityes of those that shall be admitted to the habit, will all the happinesse & misery of the house consist. For such will the convent be, as are the spirits of those who make the convent.[30]

Finally the regulations on confession in the first chapter of the constitutions deal with a difficulty experienced by Father Baker, given his unofficial standing:

> 5. That the Religious may be the more free in their confessions, we require the Abbesse and Vicair not to be difficult in graunting them leaue to confesse, or conferre their conscience with the other Priests of our Congregation which liue in the lodging of the Confessarius of the Nunnerie; so they be persons able to performe that dutie with edification, and haue authorite from the Ordinarie.[31]

There are similar representations in the section in Part II on the vicarius:

> 2. He shall haue with him one or two Monkes of our congregation, of mature age, and exemplarie life, sufficient learning and spirituallitie, that shall assist the-saied vicarious in saying or singing of Masse, in taking the confessions of the Dames, and directing them in theire deuotions and exercises. Which notwithstanding they shall not undertake of their

---

29. Augustine Baker, *Five Treatises; The Life and Death of Dame Margaret Gascoigne; Treatise of Confession* in J. Clark (ed.), *Analecta Cartusiana*, 119:23 (Salzburg: 2006), p. 5.
30. Augustine Baker, *Five Treatises*, p. 5.
31. Lille, Archives du Nord, 20 H 1, p. 4.

owne choyse, but onlie at the appointment of the vicarious, and ouer such persons as he shall commend unto them, and in that order and measure as he shall prescribe, and noe otherwise; unlesse he chance to be a definitour of the congregation, or some person so quallified for antiquitie, learning, age, and offices borne in the congregation (and haue authoritie of the ordinarie) that he maie be intyrelie trusted to deale with such matters without anie further leaue or instruction, then [i.e. 'than'] the verie placing of him in that imployment ...[32]

'Unless he chance to be a definitour of the congregation ...' Father Baker had been appointed as definitor at the General Chapter of 1625.[33] Presumably he attended the 1629 General Chapter in this capacity. Given his labours during the previous five years to place the young community at Cambrai on firm spiritual foundations, it would have been natural to ask him to draw up the constitutions for the nuns.

The foregoing comparison with Father Baker's other writings reveals that his voice is clearly heard in the preface and the most significant sections of all three parts of the constitutions. The regulations laid down reflect existing practice at Cambrai, which he himself had done so much to establish. The corpus of Father Baker's writings should surely be expanded to indicate that he had a major hand in compiling the Cambrai constitutions of 1631.

---

32. Lille, Archives du Nord, 20 H 1, p. 58.
33. J. McCann & H. Connolly (eds.), 'Memorials of Father Augustine Baker' in *Catholic Record Society* vol. 33 (London: 1933), p. 118.

4

Mortification in the teaching of Dom Augustine Baker

Teresa Rodrigues ✠

Augustine Baker had only two major guidelines to set before those of us whom he hoped to direct towards union with God: prayer and mortification. He is rather repetitive, as we know, but he has packed into his treatment of both an amplitude of experience and acuity of observation of the human psyche that covers the entire spectrum of thought and action, emotion and volition, self-indulgence and self-discipline. His treatment of mortification covers a whole range of human conduct that would not seem amiss in a modern manual of behavioural science. The point to take is that the vast repertoire of human emotions, quirks of character, evasive strategies, self-serving devices, manipulative scheming, power struggles and so on, serve to blind the would-be contemplative to the real issues inherent in the call to holiness. Baker's concern is to unmask the devil within and teach us to handle and eventually master the interior tendencies that inhibit the search for God.

Mortification, then, is not concerned with fasting, hair-shirts, disciplines or the like. In fact Baker is deeply suspicious of penitential practices; he sees them as superficial, generally a manifestation of self-will or self-conceit, and harmful to those undertaking them. He offers his own definitions of what he means by mortification:

> If you ask me what a spiritual or interne life is, I shall expresse it in no other maner then in this generall one that it is a life consisting of the serious prosecution of mentall prayer and mortification; and by mortification I meane nothing else but the exercise of all vertues pertaining to us to exercise, under what title soever, among which is competent abstraction as one of the most necessary.[1]

> By [mortification] I intend a breaking or contradicting of the will, be it the will of sensuality or the will of the superior soul...by the word mortification I do intend mortifications of necessity and not voluntary mortifications...Those are abstraction of life, mortification of the tongue, the mortification of prayer, patience, mildness, resignation, and all those other mortifications which I have told you to be of necessity, being such as God or the state and condition of your life hath laid on you, and being such as that you have no election in them nor can without sin or imperfection forbear to undergoe them...[2]

The end of the Rule (of St Benedict) is to ensure a recollected life but this cannot be done unless the monk is actually living in the monastery and desirous of having an abbot over him:

> If [a monk] have not an abbot to breake his will, his will will never become broken and mortified; and most frequently doth our holy father signify soe much in severall places in the Rule, the which way of obedience together with that of recollectedness, he tearmeth to be the arcta via quae sola ducit ad caelum, especially in his third and fourth degrees of humilitie, in the which fourth degree he sheweth the great patience necessarie in the monke, with

---

1. Augustine Baker, *Conversio Morum*, vol. 1 in J. Clark (ed.), *Analecta Cartusiana*, 119:25 (Salzburg: 2007), p. 37.
2. Augustine Baker, *Discretion* in J. Clark (ed.), *Analecta Cartusiana*, 119:9 (Salzburg: 1999), pp. 78–79.

perseverance therein to his lives ende, under (especially) the heavy or bitter yoake of obedience... and the persecution must be from the superiour himselfe, or from others with his concurrence, connivency or bidding; for if the superiour doe favour him and stand on his side, others will not be able to hurte him nor will goe about to persecute him; and such cross proceedings by the Abbot, or his instruments, are those dura et aspera quae itur ad Deum.[3]

To some this may be intolerable stuff. Are we really expected to deny our humanity in this way in the search for God? Are superiors really to act as little Hitlers for the good of our souls? Baker has some striking passages in which he describes a monastery where all is done as St Benedict prescribes as a veritable paradise, the Superior being the first to honour and respect every monk in his charge. Love, not persecution, is what is required of the abbot. But Baker is well aware that the best of us is a flawed product of original sin and only too prone to set ourselves up as the Alpha and Omega of our little world. It is not self that is the enemy, but self-will in all its manifestations. Augustine Baker's programme is to set us free from the chains of self in order to enter into the freedom of the sons of God. For him there are only two ways to achieve this freedom: through the unremitting discipline of interior prayer and, with the light obtained in prayer, to deny ourselves the satisfaction of doing what self-centredness, whim or fancy dictate. The Superior may be a paragon of virtue but inevitably there will be friction between abbot and monk, between brother and brother. Baker confessed that one of the things he had lacked in his own life was a hard superior. To the nuns at Cambrai he extolled the advantages of community life under a superior:

> You may hope to have a good, crosse superior if you pray hard for having such an One; or that God will

---

3. Baker, *Conversio Morum*, vol. 1, p. 13.

see it necessary to send you such an one, who shall break and contradict your wills.[4]

Those who lead distracted lives wholly committed to the pursuit of natural desires live according to the flesh. The opposite is to lead a recollected life. What does Baker mean by a recollected life, or competent abstraction?

> It is a state or condition in soule transcendent to the senses and sensualitie and swaying over them, or being in the very way of towards such transcendance and sway... [5]

More comprehensively:

> There is a poverty of possession, and there is a poverty of affection, and in this later doth Christian perfection consist. And this poverty of spirit extendeth to all things that are inferior to God, as are all created things, be they externall or internall, corporall or spirituall, naturall or supernaturall, consist they in knowledge or in love or affection, in the will or in the vnderstandinge, be they things of this life or things of the future life. All these things, if they be but created things are not to be sought, loved or affected for their owne sakes; but as to our affection to them, we must be poore and naked in spirit, lovinge them but only for God and in God, and for the service of God, who is above them all, in whom our love is to end.[6]

If we would follow Baker into the lower regions of our own frailty in order to identify the impediments to prayer, we need carefully to assess those actions and reactions that we probably regard as normal, even imperative indications of normality. Baker's approach to the subject is uncompromising: suffering is necessary and it will hurt:

---

4. Augustine Baker, *Secretum* in J. Clark (ed.), *Analecta Cartusiana*, 119:7 (Salzburg: 1997), p. 48.
5. Baker, *Conversio Morum*, vol. 1, p. 40.
6. Augustine Baker, *Directions for Contemplation: Book D* in J. Clark (ed.), *Analecta Cartusiana*, 119:11 (Salzburg: 1999), p. 44.

It is really no mortification if that nature be not hit right, and the party touched and as it were let bloud in the right vein.⁷

Nor is suffering occasional; it is hourly, daily, life-long. A decision has to be made and constantly renewed in prayer to submit ourselves to whatever suffering or contradiction presents itself and under whatever form. It will often be an expression of the struggle between our own desires and exterior constraints:

> We are at first prowd, self-willed, and unconforme to the will of God in our interiour, desiring more to have our owne wills, the which is contrarie to humilitie...[it] is a kind of rebellion, and want of resignation and due subiection to God's will, which we see by dailie experience in our tergiversation or unwillingness to accept of the providences and permissions of God in matters contrarie to our naturall wills. Wheresoever we find our will not readily conforme in any accident or matter to the will of God therein, there so farre is proprietie and immortification of self-will in us...Out of such propriety a man covets many things against the will of God; as for example an ambitious man inordinatly seeketh after dignitie and out of the same humour will not endure to undergoe contempts or disgraces...and in like manner is for millions of other matters wherein we are not dulie conforme to the will of God.⁸

The word itself, 'Abstraction', gives a clue to Baker's conviction that this is one of the major components of mortification as agent of our freedom. It is initially the very concrete call to observe enclosure, to live quietly within the monastery in a setting designed to facilitate our religious aspirations. Living peaceably within the enclosure there is still need to mind one's own business, to avoid meddling with what does not pertain to us or chase after items of knowledge

---

7. Augustine Baker, *Discretion* in J. Clark (ed.), *Analecta Cartusiana*, 119:9 (Salzburg: 1999), p. 59.
8. Baker, *Conversio Morum*, vol. 1, p. 133.

that have no bearing on our spiritual life. Yielding to ambition in whatever form indicates a lack of honesty in our relationship with God. Our secret aim is to wrest from him the control of events for our own aggrandizement. We may covet the position of abbot; failing that, we may scheme to get our candidate elected so that we may piously exercise the position of *eminence grise*. Baker rules out even the slightest desire to exercise spiritual authority over others. Our spirits are to be held in a state of suspension, receiving from the hand of providence whatever comes, good or ill, harsh treatment or honourable, responsibility or rejection, recognition or disdain.

St Benedict cautions his monks against too much talk. Interestingly, Baker attacks the fallacy that it doesn't matter if such talk is carried on between monk and superior:

> (We must have a) care in conversation with our superiour, withdrawinge all inordinate affection to him or her, or to his or her company, or seekinge inordinately to please or satisfy his or her humours... or spendinge time unprofitably with them, intertaininge hurtfull or distractive talks, and to take heed of that same foolish and desperate opinion that we cannot do amisse in our treaties and conversations with our superiours; for there are greater perils in it then in conversations with others in regard of the fairnes of the pretence of superiority, as if nothing could come amisse in such a case; but I say...it is otherwise and therefore do you use abstraction in this poynt, at least as much as you would and should from the companies and conversations of others...No superior can commaund or dispense with the things that God hath forbidden, be they little or great matters, amonge which are idle words and time idly spent, inordinate affections one to the other, feedinge themselves with needless talkes about other folkes imperfections.[9]

---

9. Augustine Baker, *Directions for Contemplation: Book F in* J. Clark (ed.), *Analecta Cartusiana* 119:12 (Salzburg: 1999), p. 16.

Baker calls for a sober exterior, common sense, no clowning for the sake of an imagined self-humiliation, no outbursts, expostulations, back-biting, gossip—a quiet domination of our emotions and a demeanour that enables us to live and let live since we have our centre in God and are riveted to that centre with single-minded purposiveness.

What holds the act together is *custodia cordis*, a careful watchfulness of our own actions and reactions and the persevering will always to act as grace dictates. Nothing, however, is possible to the contemplative in the immense task of mortification of self without the primary mortifying agent, interior prayer, pursued daily and unremittingly in a boundless act of love.

5

Mystical Writing as *Theologia Mystica*

PETER TYLER

The argument in this chapter is that if we examine the form of writing associated with certain medieval writers usually referred to as 'mystics' we often find a distinctive 'Language Game'[1] which I will refer to here as the *theologia mystica*. This Language Game depends, I will argue, upon the enactment of certain manoeuvres or strategies of what I term 'performative discourse'. I shall refer to two of these strategies here: that of 'unknowing' and that of 'embodiment'. As someone familiar with this tradition Augustine Baker would, I suggest, have been familiar with this technique in his writings.

The Theologia Mystica

From the twelfth and thirteenth centuries onwards we see in Europe the rise of a type of discourse that has been referred to as Affective Dionysianism. Central to this movement was the group of theologians that arose around the Abbey of Saint-Denis near the schools of Paris. This group

---

1. *Sprachspiel*. The notion is taken from the later writings of Ludwig Wittgenstein. For more on this concept see my *The Return to the Mystical: Ludwig Wittgenstein, Teresa of Avila and the Western Mystical Tradition* (Continuum: 2011).

of writers and commentators associated with the Abbey of St Victor in Paris[2] took particular interest in the Dionysian corpus which was in the process of being retranslated by theologians such as Sarracenus and Robert Grosseteste in a manner which replaced the deficiencies of the older translations by Hilduin and Eriugena. Sarracenus produced his version of the *corpus* in 1166–7, the first full translation since Eriugena, some three hundred years earlier. Sarracenus used the glosses of Anastasius and Hugh of St Victor to perfect and advance his own translation. Generally in his translation he smoothes out some of the inconsistencies and hard edges in Eriugena to present a more flowing Latin text. In particular, he avoided the strange Greek-Latin hybrid words that Eriugena often produced from his straightforward transliterations of Greek terms. Thus Sarrecenus renders θεοσοφίας in Dionysius' *De Mistica Theologia* as *divina sapientia* (literally *divine wisdom*) rather than Eriugena's *theosophia* (literally, *theosophy*). However, he does retain the *super*—terms introduced by Hilduin and Eriugena (ὑπέρθεε changes gender from *superdeus* to *superdea* in *De Mistica Theologia* presumably in reference to the holy *Sapientia*. However the text remains ambiguous with the reference to *trinitas*).[3]

The Abbey of St. Victor was founded by William of Champeaux, a master of the schools of Paris and described by Abelard as 'the first dialectician of his age', who established the abbey after retiring from the schools in 1108. He set up a small community at the site of an old hermitage on the left bank of the Seine just beyond the walls of Paris. Almost, it seems, by accident a community grew up around William who departed in 1113 to be made Bishop of Chalons. His disciple, Gilduin, was elected first Abbot

---

2. C. H. Haskins, *The Renaissance of the 12th Century* (New York, 1957), pp. 377–79; C. Morris, *The Discovery of the Individual 1050 –1200* (London: 1972), pp. 48–49; D. Knowles, *The Evolution of Medieval Thought*, (London: 1962), chapter xii.

3. H. Dondaine, *Le Corpus dionysien de l'université de Paris au XIIIe siècle* (Rome: 1953), p. 64.

of the community in the same year and under his leadership the abbey grew and flourished. Following the *Rule of St Augustine*, the community was at the forefront of clerical renewal through prayer, study and liturgy. The abbey grew with the schools of Paris and was open to the new theological developments of the university and from its inception it was concerned with questions on the relationship between the *intellectus* and *affectus*. The distinctive Victorine tradition established in the abbey combined 'a vigorous program of Bible study, serious and creative theological investigation and disciplined pursuit of contemplation all set in the context of a community orientated towards liturgical regularity and shared experience'.[4] Within the texts of Dionysius the 'Victorines', as they became known, discovered a form of writing that allowed scholars to combine the 'intellect' with the 'affect'. This, it will be argued, formed the basis of much of the later medieval tradition of what has been termed 'Affective Dionysianism'. Here, as has been pointed out, the affective interpretation of Dionysius begins to surface. Influenced by Augustine (as passed down from Richard and Hugh of St Victor), Thomas Gallus, for example, also incorporated the influences of the newly inspired Cistercian movement, especially in Bernard's inspiration found in the Song of Songs. The translation and commentary of Thomas Gallus added a new dimension to the Dionysian corpus by its emphasis on the affective and on the 'ray of darkness' and 'cloud of unknowing'.[5] Dionysius' mystical union with God is now made through love (*affectus*) rather than intelligence. It is this thread of interpretation of the Dionysian corpus made by subsequent writers that creates what we term the *theologia mystica*. In subsequent printings of the Dionysian corpus into the

---

4. Richard of St Victor, *The twelve patriarchs; (and) The Mystical Ark; (and) Book three of the Trinity*. Trans. G. A. Zinn (London: 1979), p. 3
5. P. Rorem, *Pseudo-Dionysius. A Commentary on the Texts and an Introduction to their Influence* (Oxford: 1993), pp. 214–219; B. McGinn, 'Thomas Gallus and Dionysian Mysticism', *Studies in Spirituality*, 8 (Kampen: 1998), p. 93.

early modern periods the work of Gallus and Grosseteste was combined with that of the other authors mentioned. Thus, the Strassbourg printing of the corpus of 1502–03 contains the Grosseteste ('Lincolniensis') and Sarracenus translations and commentary together with the 'Extractio' of Gallus. As McEvoy comments:

> It cannot be too much emphasised that the entire later interpretation of the Mystical Theology was deflected into the path it actually followed through the combined influence of Thomas Gallus and Robert Grosseteste. These earliest Latin commentators provided the context within which not only the mystical theology of monastery and university but also the actual spiritual experience of countless souls was to be formed.[6]

Thus by the time we reach the writings of Jean Gerson, Chancellor of the University of Paris, we find that he is able to instruct students of the university that there are two types of theology – the *theologia speculativa*, the theology of the *intellectus*, which is concerned with sharpening our understanding of the *logos* of Christian life (largely the type of theology taught in British universities today), and what he terms the *theologia mystica*, the theology of the 'affectus', which is concerned with the *pathos* of Christian life, and what is often now referred to as 'Christian Spirituality'. Thus, in the 'Tractatus Primus Speculativus' of Gerson's *De Mystica Theologia*, the Chancellor begins by asking: 'whether it is better to have knowledge of God through penitent affectus or investigative intellectus?' (*an cognitio Dei melius per penitentem affectum quam per intellectum investigantem habeatur*) . After much discussion Gerson makes it quite clear the 'strategies' that he will employ in his discourse, thus in Section 27 he declares:

---

6. *Opera veteris ac novae translationis cum Hugonis, Alberti, Thomae et aliorum*, (Strassbourg: 1502) copy in Salisbury Cathedral library, A 5.8. See also J. McEvoy (ed.), *Mystical Theology: The Glosses of Thomas Gallus and the Commentary of Robert Grosseteste on* De Mystica Theologia (Paris: 2003), p. 128

Thus we see that it is correct to say that as contemplatio is in the cognitive power of the intelligence, the mistica theologia dwells in the corresponding affective power. (*et cognoscamus quoniam, appropriate loquendo, sicut contemplatio est in vi cognitive intelligentie, sic in vi affective correspondente reponitur mistica theologia'*).[7]

Therefore 'knowledge of God through mystical theology is better acquired through a penitent *affectus* than an investigative *intellectus*'. In this passage Gerson contrasts a 'theologia mystica' that depends upon strategies of unknowing and affectivity to the intellectual or speculative knowledge acquired through the 'theologia speculativa'. He rests with Hugh of Balma's definition of the 'theologia mystica' as 'the extension of the animus in God through the desire of love'(*extensio animi in Deum per amoris desiderium*) supplemented by the definitions, 'a raising movement in God, through fervent and pure love' (*sursum ductiva in Deum, per amorem fervidum et purum*), and 'cognition experienced of God through the embrace of unitive love'(*cognitio experimentalis habita de Deo per amoris unitive complexum*). Here, he explicitly follows Dionysius when he states that 'mystical theology is irrational and beyond mind and foolish wisdom, exceeding all praise' (*theologia mystica est irrationalis et amens, et stulta sapientia, excedens laudantes*). He later returns to this theme when he explains 'theologia mystica is an experimental cognition of God through the union of the spiritual affectus with him' (*mistica theologia est cognitio experimentalis habita de Deo per coniunctionem affectus spiritualis cum eodum*): 'theologia mystica is an experimental

---

7. Jean Gerson, *De Mystica Theologia*, 1, Prol.1. & 1.27.7. My translations, but *cf.* 'On Mystical Theology: The first and speculative treatise', in Jean Gerson, *Early Works* in B. P. Maguire (ed.), *Classics of Western Spirituality*, (New York/Mahwah: 1998), p. 262. *Ioannis Carlerii de Gerson De Mystica Theologia* in A. Combes (ed.), Jean Gerson, *Early Works* (Lugano: Thesaurus Mundi, 1958).

cognition of God through the union of the spiritual affectus with him'.[8]

Therefore, for Gerson, the 'theologia speculativa' resides in the 'potentia intellectiva' whilst the 'theologia mystica' resides in the 'potentia affectiva'. Thus, speculative theology uses 'reasoning in conformity with philosophical disciplines'. 'Theologia mystica', on the other hand, needs no such 'school of the intellect' (*scola intellectus*). It is aquired through the 'school of the affect' (*scola affectus*) and, following the importance Gerson attached to the purfication of the 'affect', through the exercise of the 'moral virtues' that 'dispose the soul to purgation'. This is acquired through the 'school of religion' (*scola religionis*) or 'school of love' (*scola amoris*). The acquisition of the 'theologia mystica' does not therefore require great knowledge or extensive study of books. Rather, the mystical theology may be acquired by 'any of the faithful, even if she be an insignificant woman or someone who is illiterate' (*a quolibet fideli, etiam si sit muliercula vel ydiota*). Concurring with St Bernard, Gerson suggests speculative theology can never be complete without mystical theology but the contrary can be the case: we all must acquire this 'affectivity' to reach a right relationship with God. Therefore 'the language of mystical theology is to be hidden from many who are clerics or learned or who are called wise in philosophy or theology, so it can be conveyed to many who are illiterate and naïve, provided they have faith'. At this point, as with Dionysius, Gerson employs the strategy of concealment, for the 'language of mystical theology' is 'to be hidden from many who are clerics or learned or are called wise in philosophy or theology' lest they 'tear apart with the teeth of dogs what they do not understand'. As he later states, 'To explain these matters an endless succession of words could be added, but for experts these few words

---

8. Gerson, *Theologia*, 1. 28. 1, 5; 1. 43. 2. Pseudo-Dionysius, *The Complete Works, The Divine Names* in C. Luibheid, P. Rorem, R. Roques (eds.), *Classics of Western Spirituality* (New York/Mahwah: 1987), p. 105.

will suffice, for the inexpert no words will ever suffice for full comprehension'. It is an 'irrational and mindless wisdom' (*irrationalis et amens sapientia*) going beyond reason and mind and translating into the affectus.[9]

Unknowing and Embodiment in the Theologia Mystica

How then does the theologia mystica 'work'? I referred at the beginning of this paper to the 'theologia mystica' as 'a style of writing', 'performative discourse' or *Sprachspiel*. My reason for choosing these phrases is to distinguish it, as Gerson does, from the conceptual or theoretical characteristics of the 'theologia speculativa'. If, as I argue, the 'theologia mystica' is to be understood as a distinctive type of learning then, as Gerson does, we must distinguish its style of learning from that of the 'theology of the schools'. And this is where it gets interesting, for, following Dionysius, I argue here, the Victorines, Gerson (and ultimately the Spanish school of Teresa of Avila and John of the Cross which derived from Francisco de Osuna) are all using a performative discourse to work on the reader's affect as much as his or her intellect. Theology, for Dionysius, is as much 'intitiation' into a way of life as a 'discourse' on that way of life. This is the 'indirect initiation' of Hierotheus, reflecting the *myesthai* of the classical initiation into the Dionysian cult where the whole of Christianity is described as a 'mystery religion'. As von Balthasar points out, even the term *thiasōtēs*, a participant in the cult of Dionysius, is used by Dionysius in *The Celestial Hierarchy* and *The Ecclesiastical Hierarchy*. Dionysius, following Plato and his neo-Platonic interpreters, makes a contrast between the rational philosophy that persuades by dialectic and the means of *logos* and reason. and this latter kind of 'initiation' that is formulated through the pathos:

---

9. Gerson, *Theologia*, 1. 30. 2, 3, 5; 1. 31. 1; 1. 42. 9; 1. 43. 3.

> The tradition of the theologians is twofold, on the one hand ineffable and mystical, on the other manifest and more knowable; on the one hand symbolic and presupposing initiation, on the other philosophical and capable of proof—and the ineffable is interwoven with what can be uttered. The one persuades and contains within itself the truth of what it says, the other effects and establishes the soul with God by initiations that do not teach anything.[10]

Theology in these texts does not so much 'say' as 'show', and this is the purpose of the discourse. This latter method, the method of *pathein*, suffering, is the one explicity used by Dionysius' master Hierotheus:

> Whatever he learned directly from the sacred writers, whatever his own perspicacious and laborious research of the scriptures uncovered for him, or whatever was made known to him through that more mysterious inspiration, not only learning (mathōn) but also experiencing (pathōn) the divine things. For he had a 'sympathy' with such matters, if I may express it this way, and he was perfected in a mysterious union with them and in a faith in them which was independent of any teaching.

Just as for the ancients in their Dionysian initiation, so Christians contemporary with Dionysius 'cannot grasp the breadth and length, the height and depth' of the revelation of Jesus Christ, as St Paul (Ephesians 3:18) teaches.[11]

If such 'divine names' transcend all conception and words, how, then, can we speak of them? For 'the union of divinised minds with the Light beyond all deity occurs

---

10. Pseudo-Dionysius, *Letter 9*.
11. Pseudo-Dionysius, *The Divine Names*, 1. 8; 2. 9; 3. 1, 2; ' The Celestial Hierarchy' , 2. 1; 3. 2; 'The Ecclesiastical Hierarchy', 1. 1; H. U. von Balthasar, *The Glory of the Lord. A Theological Aesthetic*, vol. (Edinburgh: 1982–89), p. 110; A. Louth, *Denys the Areopagite*, (London: 1989), p. 24–25, quoting from Dionysius, Letter 9. Louth also draws the parallel with Aristotle's distinction within the Eleusian mysteries, that the initiate does not *learn (mathein)* anything but *experiences or suffers (pathein)* something.

in the cessation of all intelligent activity'. Drawing from scripture, the names are primarily praised. Thus Dionysius in the second chapter of *The Divine Names* introduces his 'hyper-terms' ('supra-essential subsistence, supra-divine divinity, supra-excellent goodness, supremely individual identity') which will be reproduced at the beginning of his 'Mystical Theology'. For Dionysius, God is 'beyond every assertion and denial', for in the following chapters of *The Divine Names*, Dionysius does not try and describe the divine reality but rather plays with various models and pictures of the divine. On the level of thought (*intellectus*) the divine is utterly unknowable. This is the point of the incomprehensibility (*aporia*), heralded by the strategy of unknowing which leads to the necessary transformation described in Dionysius' writings.[12]

Despite his neo-platonic credentials, Dionysius is primarily a Christian author and these processes take place within specifically Christian engagement, in particular the Divine Liturgy and the message of the Scriptures (referred to by Dionysius as the 'divine oracles'). The *theologia mystica* is born within this context and it would be misguided to try and divorce it from this context as some nineteenth- and twentieth-century devotees of 'mysticism' tend to. Following the process of Dionysius, if knowledge of the Divine is not possible, how do we access the 'supra-real'? Here, Dionysius relies on the other key strategy of the *theologia mystica*—the strategy of embodiment. In the fourth chapter of *The Divine Names*, Dionysius introduces his discussion of *eros* and the erotic and how *eros* connects us to the deity. In McGinn's words:

> The Dionysian program is a cosmic one in which the divine Eros refracts itself into the multiple theophanies of the universe, which in turn erotically strive to pass beyond their multiplicity back into simple unity.[13]

---

12. Pseudo-Dionysius, *The Divine Names*, 1. 5; 2. 4.
13. B. McGinn, *The Presence of God. A History of Western Mysticism. Vol. 1. The Foundations of Mysticism. Origins to the Fifth Century*, (London:

All movement in the hierarchy of creation, for Dionysius, comes from above and is 'fundamentally erotic'. Not only do all things strive erotically for the Beautiful and the Good, as he teaches in the fourth chapter of *The Divine Names*, but the Deity itself is *Eros*: 'Divine Eros is the Good of the Good for the sake of the Good'. Using the Proclean procession of *monē*, (remaining), *proodos* (proceeding) and *epistrophē* (reverting), God in God's being as *eros* is able to proceed out to all creation and remain in the Godhead at the same time:

> It must be said that the very cause of the universe in the beautiful, good superabundance of his benign eros for all is carried outside of himself in the loving care he has for everything. He is, as it were, beguiled by goodness, by agape and by eros and is enticed away from his dwelling place and comes to abide within all things, and he does so by virtue of his supernatural and ecstatic capacity to remain, nevertheless, within himself. [14]

Thus, the 'sympathetic' initiation described above is also an erotic initiation. *Eros*, is the occasion for the 'special experience of knowing' (*pathein*) in contrast to the 'knowing by mental effort' (*mathein*). It is the arena of the initiation of Hierotheus, the teacher of Dionysius:

> By some more divine inspiration, not only learning the things of God but experiencing them, and through this sympathy with them, if we may say this, having been consummated in initiation into mystical union and faith in them which cannot be taught. [15]

1992), p. 161.
14. McGinn, *Presence*, p. 167, translation of *The Divine Names*, 4.10, 13.
15. McGinn, *Presence*, p. 172. Following Rorem, McGinn points out that *sympatheia* is a key term in late Neoplatonism in making the connection between the different levels of the 'theurgy' possible: '*sympathy* for Dionysius is not so much an ontological bond by which material things are manipulated to acquire an access to the upper world as it is an affinity for 'reading' the inner meaning of the hierarchies as manifestations of the Thearchy.' Hence Dionysius' adoption of the

Mystical Writing as Theologia Mystica   61

Or to put it in our terms above, it is a knowing which involves the libidinal or *affectus* as much as the *intellectus*. Within Dionysius' mystical game the strategy of deconstruction is complemented by the strategy of embodied, erotic affectivity.

'What cannot be demonstrated' by the Church, McGinn suggests, is according to Dionysius 'made present both on the material level of symbols used by scripture and in liturgy and also by extension, on the conceptual or intellectual level, where the negation of names and eventually the removal of both affirmation and negation bring the soul to union with the divine mystery'. This union, we suggest, being the erotic union engendered by *eros* through the *affectus* and the libido. This is the ex–stasis, the ecstasy: 'Through ecstasy we pass beyond the human condition and become divinised'. Dionysius' *Letter Nine* describes God as a drunken lover 'standing outside all good things, being the suprafullness of all these things'. The model here being St Paul, Dionysius' ecstatic teacher and erotic initiator, spoken of in *Divine Names*, Book 4:

> This is why the great Paul, swept along by his yearning for God and seized of its ecstatic power, had this inspired word to say: 'It is no longer I who live, but Christ who lives in me' (Gal 2:20). Paul was truly a lover and, as he says, he was beside himself for God (2 Cor: 5.13), possessing not his own life but the life of the One for whom he yearned (in eros), as exceptionally beloved.[16]

Following René Roques, McGinn sees Dionysius' concept of union as based on the transcendentalisation of knowing into unknowing and yearning *eros* into ecstatic possession. The two processes we have identified as key to the 'mystical strategy' of the *theologia mystica* are intimately connected. Dionysius' exposition of the unknowing-embodied strat-

---

phrase 'so as to speak' to suggest he is adapting a term from the Neoplatonic school.
16. McGinn, *Presence*, p. 173, 179, 180. Pseudo-Dionysius, *The Complete Works*, 'The Letters', Letter 9, 5.

egy thus allows, I would argue, later Christian writers such as Teresa of Avila and John of the Cross to mine the erotic side, especially through the medium of the exposition of the Song of Songs. As McGinn points out, Dionysius here is standing in already established Christian tradition of equating the *agape* of the New Testament with the *eros* of the Platonic tradition, beginning, he suggests, with Origen's *Commentary on the Song of Songs*:

> The power of love is none other than that which leads the soul from earth to the lofty heights of heaven, and… the highest beatitude can only be attained under the stimulus of love's desire.[17]

Conclusion: Augustine Baker and the The Heritage of Mystical Writing as Theologia Mystica

I have argued in this paper for a particular style or form of writing that arises in the Parisian schools of the twelfth and thirteenth centuries, and subsequently plays a significant role in Christian theological development in the late Middle Ages. I have argued that this *theologia mystica* has a unique way of proceeding that distinguishes it from the theoretical abstractions of the *theologia speculativa*. Owing to its unique method of working on the *affectus* it develops, I argue, particular *strategies* to go about its business. I mentioned their importance to the sixteenth century Spanish school of mystics, in particular Saints Teresa of Avila and John of the Cross. The first English reference to the latter's writings is found in Augustine Baker's *Secretum*,

---

17. R. Rocques, 'Contemplation', in M. Viller et al, *Dictionnaire de Spiritualité* volume II (Paris: 1953), cols. 1908–10; E. A. Matter, *The Voice of My Beloved: The Song of Songs in Western Medieval Christianity* (Pennsylvania: 1990); D. Turner, 'Eros and Allegory: Medieval Exegesis of the Song of Songs', *Cistercian Studies* 156 (Kalamazoo: 1995); McGinn, *Presence*, p. 119.

his commentary on the *Cloud of Unknowing*.[18] Baker was clearly tutored in the school of *theologia mystica* and would have been familiar with its methods from various sources, including these. With a new scholarly edition of Baker's writings now available due to the sterling work of Fr Clark there is now the possibility of tracing exactly how Baker developed his own version of *theologia mystica* using, like St John of the Cross before him, the resources of the later medieval schools.

In our present time of spiritual crisis and tumult there are many devout Christians today who long for a form of theology that articulates their deepest desires in a way which they cannot find in the *theologia speculativa* of our schools, colleges and Universities. The great masters of *theologia mystica*, Baker amongst them, will perhaps enable contemporary Christians to rediscover the sources of this transformational theology to begin the urgent task of renewal in individual Christian lives and in our churches.[19]

---

18. See J. Clark, *Introduction and Notes to Fr Augustine Baker OSB Secretum* in *Analecta Cartusiana* (2003), p. 65
19. Useful for further study on Dionysius are: P. Chevalier, *Dionysiaca. Recueil donnat l'ensemble des traditions latines es ouvrages attribués au Denys de l'Aréopagite*, 2 vols. (Paris: 1937–1950); P. Dubourg, 'La Date de la Theologia Mystica', *Revue d'ascetique et de mystique*, 8 (1927), pp 156–61; L. M. Harrington, ed., *A Thirteenth-Century Textbook of Mystical Theology at the University of Paris. The Mystical Theology of Dionysius the Areopagite in Eriugena's Latin Translation with the Scholia translated by Anastasius the Librarian and Excerpts from Eriugena's Periphyseon* (Paris: 2004); E. von Ivánka, *Plato Christianus: Übernahme und Umgestaltung des Platonismus durch die Väter* (Einsiedeln: 1964); A. Louth, *Denys the Areopagite* (London: 1989). A. M. Ritter, G. Heil. B. Suchla (eds.), *Corpus Dionysiacum* (Berlin: 1990); A. Solignac, 'Jean Sarrazin, traducteur du Pseudo-Denys' in M. Viller et al (eds.), *Dictionnaire de Spiritualité* Vol. XIV (Paris: 1990), cols. 352–55. On Gerson see: Ioannis Carlerii de Gerson, *De Mystica Theologia* in Combes, Jean Gerson, *Early Works*; Steven Chase, *Contemplation and Compassion: The Victorine Tradition* (London: 2003); G. Dumeige, *Richard de Saint-Victor et l'idée chrétienne de l'amour* (Paris: 1952); R. Javelet, 'Thomas Gallus et Richard de Saint-Victor mystiques' in *Recherches de théologie ancienne et médiévale*, 29/30 (1962/1963), pp. 206–233.

6

'On being loved'—The Assurance of the Divine Love in the Writings of Father Augustine Baker

GORDON MURSELL

The Herculean labours of Fr John Clark have made critical editions of many of Augustine Baker's works available to a far wider public. Fr Clark has himself pointed out that all Baker's works were produced in response to particular needs and circumstances, rather than as parts of a systematic theology.[1] But there are of course fundamental themes in his writings which give coherence and shape to his thought; and the purpose of this paper is to explore one of them: the Christian belief in the assurance of the divine love for human beings, and the difference that belief makes to Baker's theology of the spiritual life.

The use of the term 'assurance' at once invites comparison with the Protestant Reformers, and in particular with the theology of John Calvin, whose own doctrine of assurance (closely linked to his doctrine of double predestination) has been crudely satirized in that First World War soldiers' song:

> The Bells of Hell go ting-a-ling-a-ling
> For you but not for me:

---

1. Augustine Baker, *Secretum* in J. Clark (ed.), *Analecta Cartusiana*, 119:20 (Salzburg: 2003), p. 20. All quotations from Baker's works quoted in this chapter have been modernized.

> For me the angels sing-a-ling-a-ling,
> They've got the goods for me.
> Oh! Death, where is thy sting-a-ling-a-ling
> Oh! Grave, thy victory?

It is no part of my purpose to suggest some link between Baker and Protestant soteriology. But it is my purpose to suggest that underlying all that Baker wrote and believed about the spiritual life is a profound awareness of, and response to, the reality of God's love—and that this, rather than some absolute conviction of salvation, was the heart of any Catholic understanding of assurance. He could not, for example, have agreed with the great Puritan Richard Baxter's statement that:

> A sincere Christian may attain to an infallible knowledge of his own sincerity in grace, or his performance of the conditions of the covenant of life, and consequently of his justification, adoption, and title to glory; and this without any extraordinary revelation.[2]

A good place to begin is with the definition of love provided in *Holy Wisdom*. There Baker points out that love is the originating (and in a sense controlling) impulse in our lives, defining love as 'an internal complacence and inclination to an object from the goodness or beauty that is believed to be in it'.[3] The trouble is that we are inclined to love ourselves more than anything or anyone else. And (he goes on):

> the only possible remedy for this horrible and universal deordination in us... is to have a new contrary Divine principle imprinted in our hearts, by which we should be averted from the falsely seeming happiness that self-love promises us in creatures, and converted to our first and only end, which is God;

---

2. *The Saint's Everlasting Rest* (1650) 3:11 in W. Orme (ed.), *The Practical Works of the Rev Richard Baxter* (London: James Duncan, 1830), vol. 23:2.

3. Augustine Baker, *Holy Wisdom* 2:2:2, edited by S. Cressy OSB & J. N. Sweeney (London: Burns Oates, 1950), p. 243.

and this can be no other but Divine love or charity shed abroad in our hearts by the Holy Ghost.[4]

He goes on to distinguish between sensual love and that charity which 'is seated in the superior [as distinct from the sensual] soul, being a quiet but most resolute determination of the superior will to seek God and a perfect union with Him.'[5] But this charity cannot be obtained quickly:

> at the first it is very imperfect, and much allayed by self-interest, and seeking contentment to nature even in the actions done for God; so that were it not that ordinarily during such a state of imperfection God cherishes the soul with sensible comforts and gusts which she feels in the exercise of her love to Him, she would scarce have courage enough to proceed.[6]

So Baker concludes: 'in a word, the difference between heaven and hell is, that hell is full of nothing but self-love and propriety; whereas there is not the least degree of either in heaven, nor anything but the fulfilling of God's will and seeking of His glory. This is the beatitude of all saints and angels, and no other way do they nor can they love themselves but by loving God only.'[7] This emphasis on an absolute opposition between love of self and love of God is close to the teaching of the *Cloud of Unknowing*, where the author tells us that 'it is the condition of a perfect lover, not only to love that thing that he loves more than himself, but also in a sense to hate himself for the sake of the thing that he loves'.[8]

As with St Augustine, it is for Baker the right *ordering* of our love that matters. God alone is worthy to be the true and ultimate object of our love. In *Holy Wisdom*, Baker

---

4. Baker, *Holy Wisdom*, p. 244.
5. Baker, *Holy Wisdom*, 2:2:3, p. 246.
6. Baker, *Holy Wisdom*, p. 247.
7. Baker, *Holy Wisdom*, 2:2:4, p. 249 .
8. *Cloud of Unknowing*, 43 (original text slightly modernized), in P. Hodgson (ed.), *The Cloud of Unknowing and Related Treatises* in *Analecta Cartusiana* 3 (Salzburg: 1982), p. 45.

alludes to the First Letter of John in declaring that 'God loved us first, not because we deserved it, but to the end to make us deserve His love, and because we were His creatures, capable of enjoying His perfections and happiness; and we love Him because He loved us first.'[9]

Baker presses the Augustinian emphasis on loving God purely for God's own sake, entirely disinterestedly, in his *Spiritual Alphabet for the Use of Beginners*, where he says it is important that:

> one do love God and wish well unto him merely for *his own sake*, and for his own worth and excellency, without regard of reward for loving him, or of punishment for not loving him. Insomuch that if there were neither Heaven nor Hell, nor any reward nor punishment at all, yet the soul would love God and serve him and adhere unto him, only because he is God, and is most good, and is so good that he deserveth merely for his own sake to be loved and honoured by all creatures. And this is the love which we are to seek and labour (by the means of spiritual exercises) to have within us towards God.[10]

Now Baker is fully aware that this unconditional love for God is not easy. In *A Secure Stay Against All Temptations*, he argues that temptation is not only willed by God but is precisely the means by which we can, if we wish, strengthen our love for him.[11] By 'temptations' he means also daily difficulties: 'which if we had not, we should become rusty and daily more and more impure in soul, and by little and little forget both God and ourselves; as neither to regard our duty towards him, nor seek to make any progress in our own soul.'[12] Thus, he goes on,

---

9. Baker, *Holy Wisdom*, 2:2:5, p. 260.
10. Augustine Baker, *A Spirituall Alphabet for the Use of Beginners*) in J. Clark (ed.), *Analecta Cartusiana*, 119:16 (Salzburg:, 2001), pp. 18–19.
11. Augustine Baker, *A Secure Stay in All Temptations* in J. Clark (ed.), *Analecta Cartusiana*, 119:8 (Salzburg: 1998), 1 p. 7.
12. *A Secure Stay*, 1, p. 7.

as God doth send or permit a temptation only out of love towards her, so let her out of answerable love accept of the will of God in it, and be contented to undergo all the bitterness of it, and to endure all the pain & difficulty of contending with it. This consideration of love, to a well-minded soul, cannot but make all things more tolerable, if not somewhat pleasant, that otherwise would be bitter enough and very painful to her nature.[13]

And it is in this work, *A Secure Stay Against All Temptations*, that we find Baker's Augustinian theology of love in its most fully developed form. Baker again presses this theology to its ultimate—some might say beyond its ultimate—conclusion, by arguing that there is a sense in which God cannot but love humanity. He writes:

> I say first, that the love of God towards man is so great that it exceedeth all speech and understanding of man or angel, and it is inseparable from God, (I mean, his love towards man is), and is as it were so natural and inherent to him, that so far as lieth in him and belongeth to him, he cannot choose but love man. And this proceedeth out of this, that he made man according to his own image, by which man doth in some manner participate of the divinity, and is thereupon capable (by way of participation or communication) of that felicity which is proper & natural only to God himself. And hence it is that God for his part cannot choose but wish the eternal good & happiness of man, as he enjoyeth and joyeth in his own happiness; as also to impart all means to man (if he would but dispose himself for the same) for attaining to such eternal happiness, and to remove all impediments of the same.[14]

The suggestion that God has no choice but to love humanity is not, surely, intended as a check upon the divine freedom, even though at one point in *A Secure Stay* Baker

---

13. *A Secure Stay*, 1, p. 18.
14. *A Secure Stay*, 1, p. 34.

even describes the love of God for us as 'excessive.'[15] Rather, Baker wants to *reassure* (and we will return to that word) his fellow-religious that the God whom they seek in the cloister is a God whose love for them can be deflected *only* by their free decision to reject it. It is, he says, a love even greater than that of a mother for her child, despite the infinite distance between us and him. Only a freely-willed decision on our part to cut ourselves off from God, for example by freely choosing to commit mortal sin, can in fact cut us off from him.[16] And, again and again, Baker seeks to encourage those to whom he writes, warning them against too readily assuming they have committed mortal sin when they haven't. Unless they really have, he writes,

> God winketh at matters, being as it were very loath & sorry & unwilling to find a hole in his coat; I mean, a mortal sin… Will you think that a small matter can bring a soul from such great love & favour with God to become so most odious unto him, that he will not vouchsafe to look on her or think on her, but as of one whom he hateth and detesteth with all the hatred that can be imagined?[17]

Instead, he argues, we have to will actively to be separated from him: only then will this happen.[18] It follows therefore that it must be some 'great matter,'

> that shall clean cut asunder that tie of great love which God beareth towards a soul, since that even in the friendship of the world, as imperfect as it is, and which is so infinitely inferior to the trueness and greatness of the love of God to a soul, a small matter will not destroy such friendship.[19]

---

15. *A Secure Stay*, 1, p. 47.
16. *A Secure Stay*, 1, p. 47.
17. *A Secure Stay*, 1, p. 35.
18. *A Secure Stay*, 1, p. 37.
19. *A Secure Stay*, 1, p. 43.

Instead, Baker says, the soul must be *assured* that she has committed some mortal sin for it really to have taken place.[20]

Baker is not here presenting a form of humanism in which the work of our redemption is reduced to a sideshow. Later in *A Secure Stay*, he makes it absolutely clear that the soul cannot aspire to the perfection of our humanity, which is love of and union with God, 'but that she already hath the love of God in her, at least in such measure as will suffice to save her soul.'[21] Following (indeed quoting) Walter Hilton, Baker goes on to argue that we must seek the love of God

> not because I am worthy, but because I am unworthy, therefore would I love God. For if that I had his love, it would make me worthy. And since that I was created for that end (viz. for the loving of God), though I should never come by it, yet will I covet it; and therefore will I pray and think how I may get it, and will labour for it.

And then [he goes on],

> if thy enemies see that thou beginnest to grow bold, courageous and resolute in thy said purpose, they begin to grow afraid of thee.[22]

We may note here the implicit reference to the Cross: we are made worthy to love God precisely through the self-giving love of God for us in Christ. In *Book H*, Baker explicitly says that it is 'the merits of our Saviour's Passion' which are 'the means of our salvation.' At the same time, it is worth noting too Baker's emphasis on the need for Christians to be 'bold, courageous and resolute'[23] in seeking to make that love their own. What Baker offers his nuns, and later readers, is a pastoral Augustinianism, a nuanced and deeply

---

20. *A Secure Stay*, 1, pp. 43–4.
21. *A Secure Stay*, 2, p. 128.
22. *A Secure Stay*, 2, p. 149.
23. Augustine Baker, *Book H* (*Directions for Contemplation: Book H*) in J. Clark (ed.), *Analecta Cartusiana*, 119:14 (Salzburg: 2000), p. 6.

Catholic theology of love in which the soul is invited to respond to the prevenient and unconditional love of God, avoiding both an easy self-confidence on the one hand and an unhealthy preoccupation with sin on the other.

This pastoral theology is surely also paramount in what Baker says about knowledge of God. In *A Spiritual Treatise...Called A.B.C.*, Baker cites the Jesuit Alvarez de Paz's contrast between the knowledge of God had by science and that which is to be had through contemplation. De Paz compares what we would call the academic musicologist with the musical performer: the first knows all the rules but can't sing or play. His or her knowledge is ultimately futile. And Baker continues

> Even just so we, who have learned scholastic divinity do talk and speak many things of God, eloquently and truly, but like parrots... which understand not what they speak; many documents of moral and theological virtues we teach, wonderful things of contemplation and of the inward matters of the soul we discourse and talk of; but that, being empty and void of true virtue, and of the experience of spiritual things, (when we live and work otherwise then we teach), we do but expose ourselves to be laughed at.[24]

This depreciation of a narrowly academic knowledge may well be influenced by Baker's study of the *Cloud of Unknowing*: thus he can, in speaking of contemplative prayer, say that in such prayer the soul accomplishes a unity beyond words,

> knowing [God] most perfectly by ignorance...and conversing with Him...by silence...remaining in this silent busy idleness and negative knowledge, more

---

24. Augustine Baker, *A Spiritual Treatise...Called A.B.C.*, in J. Clark (ed.), *Analecta Cartusiana*, 119:17 (Salzburg: 2001), C pp. 92–3. The analogy appears in de Paz's *De vita spirituali eiusque perfectione* 2.

full of fervour and light than all the speculations of the schools or studious meditations of cloisters,[25] like a mother directing all her love to her child. The latter is an unusual image of the soul towards God, rather than vice versa. But this is surely the point. Here too, as always, Baker is conscious of his audience: he is not writing an academic treatise, but seeking to equip women religious to grow in the spiritual life; and for that growth, it is love and experiential knowledge of God, albeit firmly grounded in solid theology, which is paramount.

Now this is not to argue that Baker is concerned to produce a kind of a theology delivered *de haut en bas*, watered down to suit the needs of humbler people. Thus, in *A Secure Stay*, Baker frequently comments on the dangers of an excessive fearfulness among his audience of women religious, effectively seeing it as their besetting sin. He argues that

> pursuit of mental prayer is the most efficacious means to refrain such a melancholy nature, and to draw the soul out of it, whereby she will in time come to a merry and lightsome heart... For indeed such practice, and no other, will come to perfect both body and soul, altering and reforming the natural humours of them both, making them joyous and confident in God, all servility being driven out.[26]

Baker is not talking down to his audience. Rather he wants to free his women religious from an inappropriate fear, whether (as we have seen) of thinking they have committed a mortal rather than a venial sin, or of not considering themselves worthy of the God they seek in the cloister. We shall return to this point in a moment, for it brings us at last to a consideration of his use of the word 'assure' or 'assur-

---

25. *Holy Wisdom*, 3:3:7, pp. 497–9; for the 'silent busy idleness'. Cf. *Doubts and Calls* in J. Clark (ed.), *Analecta Cartusiana*, 119:10 (Salzburg: 1999) 1, pp. 9–10: 'this is that which is called *otium sanctum*, a holy rest or holy idlenesse, and that best part which Mary had chosen.'
26. *A Secure Stay*, 2, p. 112.

ance', and of how he sought to reassure those to whom he wrote that they were loved, and thus capable of, if not absolutely certain of, eternal salvation.

We may briefly recall the significance of this word in Reformation debate. Here is Martin Luther, in his *Commentary on Galatians*:

> I have used many words to declare that a Christian must assure himself that he is in the favour of God, and that he hath the crying of the Holy Ghost in his heart. This have I done, that we may learn to reject and utterly to abandon that devilish opinion of the whole kingdom of the Pope, which taught that a man ought to be uncertain and to stand in doubt of the grace of God towards him. If this opinion be received, then Christ profiteth nothing...Let us therefore give thanks unto God, that we are delivered from this monstrous doctrine of doubting.[27]

We may note in passing that, for all Luther's and Calvin's emphasis on assurance as the fruit of justification by faith, not all Protestants were so certain. John Bunyan writes movingly of his own doubts as to salvation in his spiritual autobiography *Grace Abounding to the Chief of Sinners*, when he says

> About this time I took an opportunity to break my mind to an ancient Christian; and told him all my case. I told him also that I was afraid that I had sinned the sin against the Holy Ghost; and he told me, he thought so too. Here therefore I had but cold comfort, but, talking a little more with him, I found him, though a good man, a stranger to much combat with the devil. Wherefore I went to God again as well as I could, for mercy still.[28]

What does Augustine Baker have to say about assurance? He takes a theologically nuanced and pastoral view of it.

---

27. M. Luther, *Commentary on Galatians* 4:6. 1575 edition, English translation, edited by P. S. Watson (London, 1953), pp. 370–1.
28. J. Bunyan, *Grace Abounding to the Chief of Sinners*, edited by R. Sharrock (Oxford: 1962), para. 180.

'On being loved' — The Assurance of the Divine Love

This is what he writes in his *Spiritual Alphabet*: when spiritual writers

> say that the soul being then in high union with God, is certified to be then accepted of God, as if then she were assured to be in the state of grace, (which in this life one cannot be without special revelation), this certification is to be understood [as] a strong and vehement conjecture of being in the state of grace, and not to be farther understood.[29]

He then immediately goes on to cite the Carmelite theologian Thomas a Jesu (1564–1627), who found it hard to believe that a soul

> in that case of streight [sic] union with God can be doubtful of her then being in his grace; but that she is made secure of it either by special revelation, or out of the force of that divine union. But whether she be then as well certified of her future glory in Heaven he doubteth; but yet he rather thinks it more probable, and more beseeming the goodness of God, that she is sure of it, and of her perseverance in grace to the end of her life, though perhaps this decree of God is kept from her knowledge, to keep her in yet more awe and greater humility.[30]

Like Thomas a Jesu, Baker wants the soul to be assured of God's love, but not to be so assured of her salvation that she feels no need to continue to grow in response to the work of grace within her. The word 'assurance' and its cognates recur frequently in *A Secure Stay*, usually in a positive and pastoral (rather than a strictly soteriological) context: thus

> she [the woman religious] must also assure herself that God, who in his providence laid the temptation on her, will ever assist her with his grace, greater or lesser, according to the measure of the temptation; and that he continually looks on her and her demeanour in it, her industry, patience, & combat;

---

29. *A Spiritual Treatise...Called A.B.C.,* A p. 12.
30. *A Spiritual Treatise,* p. 13.

and that he is most present with her in the tribulation.'[31]

So also, he argues that well-meaning souls should not judge themselves to be guilty of mortal or even venial sin 'unless they know most certainly and assuredly that they are guilty thereof.'[32] The soul should aim daily to 'grow more and more confident in love, with decay of servile fear [fear of divine punishment according to St Thomas] and self-love'—for 'the natural fear within them' is 'as great an impediment as could be to the divine union and love wherein our only happiness doth consist.'[33] Here again, Baker is trying to exorcise fear from his readers and fellow-religious—indeed in *Holy Wisdom* he goes so far as to describe servile fear as 'the greatest enemy of love.'[34] But (and this is crucial) he does not want to replace servile fear with an easy certainty about salvation which would, in his view, remove both any need to continue to respond to divine grace and any human freedom of choice in doing so.

Thus, although we cannot in this life be certain of salvation, Baker does encourage the nuns to whom he wrote *A Secure Stay* not to become morbidly convinced that they have committed mortal sin and so excluded themselves from salvation too readily unless they are certain that they have voluntarily *willed* to commit such a sin. Thus he writes

> And therefore do you understand it well, fix it for perpetuity in your memory, and put it in practice upon all occasions; and it will ease, rid, and secure you from thousands of doubts, anxieties, scruples, fears, consultations, confessions and perplexities, which otherwise would possess your spirit and perhaps oppress it, and will hold you in a plain, clear and quiet way of the true and most pleasant and

---

31. *A Secure Stay*, 1, p. 6.
32. *A Secure Stay*, 1, p. 21.
33. *A Secure Stay*, 1, p. 24.
34. *Holy Wisdom*, 3:3:5, p. 471.

satisfactory love of God, with daily increase of confidence in him.³⁵

They are not to esteem themselves to be children of the Devil but instead to be children of God, 'as you may well hope and assure yourselves (with such assurance as God allows a soul to conceive) to be, so long as you be of such good will and affection, that wittingly and willingly you would offend him in nothing.'³⁶

Here surely is the heart of what for Baker is true Christian assurance, 'such assurance as God allows a soul to conceive'—not the absolute certainty of future salvation but the childlike conviction of being unconditionally loved which alone frees the soul from those 'thousands of doubts, anxieties, scruples, fears' and so on and holds it in that 'true and pleasant and satisfactory love of God, with daily increase of confidence in him.' In a beautiful passage later in *A Secure Stay*, Baker points out that a soul may, during temptations and desolation,

> use such industries as she is able; and if she seems able to do nothing, yet let her offer up that nothing to God. In the midst of such a case, let her seek to make a breach upwards towards God through all the said confusions, making election of God with that free will which at all times and in all cases is in her. For no case is there, nor can be, wherein she may not by the grace of God make choice of him, to be (as he is) her God, her Saviour, her protector and refuge, her last end and final felicity. This choice she may (I say) at all times and in all cases make, and this our Faith assureth us of.³⁷

And he goes on to say that the soul may equally freely choose to reject God, and that our faith assures of this too.³⁸

---

35. *A Secure Stay*, 1, p. 29.
36. *A Secure Stay*, 1, p. 54.
37. *A Secure Stay*, 2, p. 101.
38. *A Secure Stay*, 2, p. 101.

In *Holy Wisdom*, Baker uses the term 'assurance': in what he describes as the state of intellectual passive union with God,

> there is thereby [i.e. via the understanding] a divine light communicated, not revealing or discovering any new verities, but affording a most firm clear assurance and experimental perception of those verities of Catholic religion which are the objects of our faith, which assurance the soul perceives to be divinely communicated to her.[39]

And he continues by saying that 'surely the first knowledge and assurance that the primitive Christians had of the mysteries of our religion came by such contemplations communicated to the Apostles, &c (as St Paul witnesses of himself for one), who saw and even felt the truth of what they preached and delivered by tradition to others.'[40]

For Baker, then, our faith assures us that we are loved; it assures us that we have the freedom to choose for or against God; and it may, when we have progressed far in the spiritual life, assure us within our own experience of the transforming truth of Christian faith. Nothing less than such assurance would inspire and equip a soul to leave the world for God, or to risk persecution and martyrdom for the sake of truth. But anything more than that, anything that leads us to believe with absolute certainty in this life that we are assured of salvation, would for Baker rob our lives of their freedom, and divine grace of its subtle and distinctive character; and before concluding we need briefly to reflect on the importance of grace in Baker's theology of the spiritual life. In the *Conversio morum*, he says that, because of the Fall, humanity can no longer remain in 'continual amorous actuation of soul towards God', even when wishing to do so: sensuality, and what Baker calls

---

39. *Holy Wisdom*, 3:4:4, p. 533.
40. *Holy Wisdom*, 3:4:4, p. 534.

'deordinations' that draw us away prevent it.[41] Later in the same work, Baker applies some Aristotelian logic to show how the grace of God draws fallen humanity back to him:

> It is a principle in philosophy, that everything must be served by his first cause, otherwise the thing so caused corrupteth and perisheth. As for example, water that naturally is cold, if it be made hot by fire, it must also be conserved in such its heat by the same cause of fire, otherwise by little and little it will return to its own natural coldness. Accordingly (spiritually) is it in the matter of grace, that makes the soul acceptable to God. Such grace is not granted or given by God (who is the cause and sole giver of it) to an adult person, but by this means and after this manner, viz. that God inciteth and moveth the soul to convert itself by love towards him; the which the soul doing, in virtue of such incitement God powereth his foresaid grace into the soul where none was before; or if there were, then such incitement and conversion causeth an increase of such grace so already being in the soul.[42]

And, for Baker, this process by which the soul may, if it chooses, respond to the work of grace within it is what he calls mental prayer.[43] In *Holy Wisdom*, he tells us that the aim of the spiritual life is 'the conversion of the soul to God in prayer.'[44] Prayer, then, occupies an exceptionally important part in the life of the Christian—especially, of course, the cloistered religious who form Baker's primary audience. But we need to return to his theology of grace. In *Conversio morum*, Baker cites Jesus' parable of the talents: we will be condemned if we don't use the talent that has been given to us: 'and the talents which God properly

---

41. Augustine Baker, *Conversio morum*, in J. Clark (ed.), *Analecta Cartusiana*, 119:25, 2 vols. (Salzburg: 2007), 1, pp. 53–4.
42. *Conversio morum*, 3, p. 189.
43. *Ibid*.
44. *Holy Wisdom*, 2:2:9, p. 286.

bestows on souls is his aforesaid grace or the increase of it.'⁴⁵ The difficulty for us is that

> both towards the getting, conserving, and increasing of grace, violence must be used… upon nature, that is always rising up, and seeketh to stain, weaken, corrupt and clean eject grace out of the soul.⁴⁶

Growing in grace is, therefore, though first and foremost a response to God's 'incitement and enablement,'⁴⁷ a matter both of desire and of practice: Baker quotes in this regard Leviticus 6:12 *'ignis in altari semper ardebit'* (the fire on the altar will always burn).⁴⁸ He concludes:

> In sum the answer may be, that God would have us (and without obeying him in it, we cannot continue secure as to [the] soul's health), by our actuations to correspond so frequently and so intensively to his continual incitements, as corporal infirmity and necessary external occasions will permit us to do.⁴⁹

And here too this is above all a matter of prayer: the person who grows in mental prayer and nourishes such grace 'prospereth well, and grows better both in internal state of soul and in external carriage.'⁵⁰

We should note that parenthetical warning: 'without obeying [God] in it, we cannot continue secure as to [the] soul's health': only in and through our response in prayer to the action of grace in the soul do we, so to speak, enable that grace to become effective, and so acquire some sense of assurance about our salvation. Elsewhere (in *Doubts and Calls*) Baker cites Aquinas' distinction between sanctifying grace (*gratia gratum faciens*), which confers eternal life (and is thus primarily for the good of the person to whom it is

---

45. *Conversio morum*, 3, p. 190.
46. *Conversio morum*, 3, p. 191.
47. *Conversio morum*, 3, p. 194.
48. *Conversio morum*, 3, p. 192.
49. *Conversio morum*, 3, p. 193.
50. *Conversio morum*, 3, p. 195.

given), and graces freely given (*gratiae gratis datae*), which are given above all for the good of others. The first of these is fundamental: this is

> that grace which whosoever hath and dyeth having it, hath eternal life. This none can have that is in mortal sin; and when one gets out of the state of mortal sin, then one is in the state of grace, which again is lost by committing a mortal sin. And this grace, though no man (without special revelation from God) is sure and certain that he hath it, yet certain it is that he who hath it, hath (through the promise and goodness of God) a right and title to everlasting life.[51]

Baker makes it clear that

> this grace in effect is but charity or the love of God. And this grace God doth bestow on a soul for her own good and salvation... ever to be sought after and prayed for, that it may come into us, remain in us, and continually increase and grow stronger in us, which in effect is but to desire that we may more and more love God; and to have this affection is but to affect and love God himself, which is not only lawful but also necessary for us to do. And to come to this affection doth serve the right ordering of all other affections.[52]

We may conclude this exploration with a few final quotations. In *Holy Wisdom*, reflecting on the important but easily-misunderstood notion of resignation, Baker summarizes his position on assurance thus:

> the point of resignation lies in this, that a soul ought to content herself not to know how and in what manner God will dispose of her after death. Her anchor is hope, which she ought to cherish and fortify all she can, and the best way for souls to fortify that is to make as few reflections on themselves as may be, and to employ all their thoughts and affections

---

51. Augustine Baker, *Doubts and Calls*, 2 pp. 98–9.
52. *Doubts and Calls*, 2, p. 98.

directly upon God. It is divine love alone that is at least the principal virtue that brings souls to beatitude, and therefore fearful souls, though they were in as dangerous a state as they suspect, must needs rationally argue thus: that the way to procure and strengthen love is by fixing their minds upon the mercies, goodness, and perfections of God, and to contradict or forget all arguments or motives of servile fear, the greatest enemy of love...Surely, at the close of our lives we ought to practise after the best manner we can the best actions, and most acceptable to God, which is to relinquish ourselves, and to contemplate, trust, rely, and roll ourselves upon Him...Let the soul withal consider that He which hath denied unto her an assurance and forbidden her to presume, hath yet commanded her to hope.[53]

Baker does not quote the Letter to the Hebrews, but it is surely its famous insistence that faith is 'the assurance of things hoped for' which is utterly central to his theology.[54] Three short final quotations help give us a flavour of what that means in practice. First, from his *Book D*:

> Observe the grace that God gives you and do not outrinne it, nor yet be behind it but as it were accompany it. And contrast yourself with that measure of grace that he gives you, and use it the best you can, and when he gives you more, make you the more use of it.[55]

Spiritual life is the attentive and sensitive process of co-operation between fickle human wills and the subtle personal initiatives of divine grace. And that grace is utterly central to our hope of salvation. Here is Baker in Augustinian form in *Holy Wisdom*:

> It is certain, yea, and faith obliges us to believe, that in all the good actions we do, or good thoughts

---

53. *Holy Wisdom*, 3:3:5, pp. 471–3.
54. Hebrews 11:1.
55. Augustine Baker, *Book D* (*Directions for Contemplation: Book D*) in J. Clark (ed.), *Analecta Cartusiana* 119:11 (Salzburg: 1999), p. 20.

we entertain, we so do and think in virtue only of a precedent and concomitant illumination of our understanding and inclining of our will, both which are immediately caused by God.[56]

Finally, co-operating with that grace is, for Baker as for Augustine, not so much a *process* as an *adventure*, for (as he says in *Book D*):

> the ways by which God calls a soul are infinitely various and changing, strange-seeming, impertinent, above all reason; and therefore the soul must dispose herself to follow the call and tract of God, through thick and thin, sour and sweet, light and darkness, with reason and without it, as having neither understanding nor will of her own, and this both for the interior and for the exterior; and having such a guide she can never err in her way, which ever tends to the mortification of herself and renouncing her proper will, and finally in the perfect love of God.[57]

---

56. *Holy Wisdom*, 1:2:8, p. 124.
57. Augustine Baker, *Book D*, p. 20.

7

Augustine Baker and the Mystical Canon

ELISABETH DUTTON AND VICTORIA VAN HYNING

In the emerging field of Augustine Baker studies we benefit from being cross-disciplinary—attending to a multiplicity of scholarly voices and discourses from the fields of English, theology, and history, amongst others. From Barbara Constable, Serenus Cressy, Leander Prichard, Dom Justin McCann, to John Clark and Ben Wekking, many scholars, readers, and editors, often Benedictine or from other religious orders, have laid the groundwork for current Baker studies. We are enormously indebted to James Hogg for printing the *Analecta Cartusiana* Baker volumes, as well as to a whole host of scholars who have passed Baker's writings on to us: their acts of transmission are in some ways similar to Baker's own in passing on the writings of other authors which he perceived to be the fine spiritual heritage of the Cambrai nuns.

The present authors both came to study Baker through an interest in medieval mysticism, originating in studies of Julian of Norwich and the influence of the Benedictine readership of Julian's *Revelation of Divine Love* during the seventeenth century. The ideas presented here stem from our shared interest in what is commonly referred to as the 'Middle English Mystics Canon'—a concept which, in the faculties of English literature in which we work, has become contentious. Specifically we will discuss Baker's use and possible coining of the term 'mystick-author' as it relates to Baker's role as a writer.[1]

Thus far, Baker has not made a big splash in the English literary academy, in large part because his style is parenthetical, self-referential, repetitive and hard to follow. If he deserves a place in the study of English Renaissance literature, as opposed to the canon of spiritual guidance literature, it is likely to be as a reader of and commentator on medieval and early modern texts, responsible for translating, transmitting and canonizing particular authors, rather than as a literary figure in his own right. Although Baker's name is not yet well known to students of literature, he is sometimes cited for his 1629 letter to Robert Cotton, which requests the loan of medieval books, including works by Richard Rolle and Walter Hilton, for the nuns of Cambrai.[2] This letter is only one example from amongst many texts of Baker's which demonstrate his desire to maintain connections to a pre-Reformation English tradition. This letter, and the body of evidence we will detail below, suggests that Baker, in gathering texts and forming reading lists for the Cambrai nuns, was purposefully building a canon in the sense of designating *useful* works that he felt his readership needed in order to achieve mystical union with God. This canon was large, encompassing not only pre-Refor-

---

1. This is discussed in more detail in V. Van Hyning, 'Augustine Baker Mystic-Maker: Three Modes of Self-Authorization' (MA Thesis, Oxford: 2008).
2. The letter is preserved in BL Cotton MS Julius III, f. 12r-v. For critical discussions of this letter see J. Summit, *Memory's Library: Medieval Books in Early Modern England* (Chicago and London: University of Chicago Press, 2008). See also H. Wolfe, 'Reading Bells and Loose Papers' in V. E. Burke and J. Gibson (eds.), *Early Modern Women's Manuscript Writing: Selected Papers from the Trinity/Trent Colloquium* (Aldershot: Ashgate, 2004), pp. 135-56; and Fr M. Barrett, OSB, "Such a world of books': Spiritual Reading in Augustine Baker.' available at: www.benedictines.org.uk/theology/2007/Barrett.doc [Accessed 1 December 2011].

mation English writers, but contemporary and patristic works from all over Europe and Britain.

Ten years ago Nicholas Watson observed that 'the canon of "Middle English mystics" and the term "mysticism" have... largely outlived their usefulness to scholars'.[3] His question was simple: why do we have a separate group of Middle English mystics at all? Watson traces the identification of this group to the work of early twentieth-century scholars with a confessional bias—most notably Evelyn Underhill.[4] Watson writes:

> The study of Middle English mystics is the product of a modern, not a medieval reality—for, in actual fact, there was no such group as the 'Middle English mystics' until it was created after the turn of the [twentieth] century... Hilton, Rolle and the *Cloud* author did form part of a group of 'canonical' authors on the spiritual or 'contemplative' life, but the group also included a variety of ascetic, pastoral and other kinds of writers, and excluded [Margery] Kempe and Julian, who were not widely known in their own times.[5]

Watson outlines a medieval contemplative canon, as opposed to a mystical canon, which was broad and included: Richard Rolle of Hampole, the fourteenth-century hermit whose Latin and English works were some of the most widely-circulated and imitated in the medieval period, Walter Hilton, the Augustinian Canon who wrote *The Scale of Perfection*, the '*Cloud of Unknowing*-author', along with numerous anonymous as well as known spiritual writers. Evelyn Underhill's canon, on the other hand,

---

3. N. Watson, 'The Middle English Mystics' in D. Wallace (ed.), *Cambridge History of Medieval English Literature* (Cambridge: 1999) vol. I, p. 539.
4. *Ibid.*, p. 540, note 5. Watson also includes, amongst others: J. Colledge and E. Walsh (eds.), *A book of showings to the anchoress Julian of Norwich* (Toronto: 1976), and W. R. Inge, *Studies of English Mystics* (London: 1907).
5. Watson, 'Mystics', pp. 543–4.

was not broadly contemplative but specifically and narrowly 'mystical': it took Rolle, Hilton, the *Cloud*-author and added to the mix Julian of Norwich, whose *Revelation of Love* has been the most widely published and read 'Middle English mystical' text inside and outside the academy in the twentieth century.

When Nicholas Watson writes that the medieval 'canonical' authors on the contemplative life included 'Hilton, Rolle and the *Cloud*-author' as well as 'a variety of ascetic, pastoral and other kinds of writers', the presence of 'the *Cloud*-author' signals a complication to his statement. This author is himself a creation of modern scholarship, and does not look like an author in the modern sense of the word. Modern scholars have grouped together several texts—most notably *The Cloud of Unknowing* and its 'sequel', the *Epistle of Privy Counselling*—and attributed them to one writer; this writer has no name, and no identity beyond 'probably Carthusian'. Many of the so-called *Cloud*-author's works are translations, albeit loose ones— *Deonise Hid Divinity*, a translation of the *Mystical Theology* of Pseudo-Dionysius the Areopagite, *An Epistle of Discretion of Spirits*, a translation of a sermon of Bernard of Clairvaux, *A Treatise of the Study of Wisdom that Men Call Benjamin*, a translation of Richard of St Victor's *Benjamin Minor*. This writer's anonymity and focus on translation demand an examination of the *sense* of Watson's designation 'author'. His group of 'canonical authors' might be better termed a group of 'canonical works'.

Baker and Underhill, on the other hand, focus on the author's lifestyle in their grouping of English mystics. Both authors highlight that these writers were solitaries themselves or writing with a concern for those living as solitaries. This emphasis privileges the lived experience of an author as part of what makes them a mystic. In *The Mystics of the Church* Underhill outlines her criteria for choosing the English mystics as follows:

> It is a peculiarity of their writings that all are connected with the solitary or, as they called it, the 'singular life', which seems at this period to have had a deep attraction for all who sought spiritual perfection. Rolle at his conversion chose the career of a hermit; Julian of Norwich was an anchoress. *The Cloud of Unknowing* and *Scale of Perfection* were apparently addressed respectively to a male and a female recluse. All wrote in the vernacular, and were indeed among the first so to do, for Latin was still the literary tongue. They did so in order to widen their circle of appeal, for they addressed themselves... to their 'even-Christians'; that is, to the middle class, lay and religious, and especially the country population, always the home of our peculiar English earnestness.[6]

Both Baker and Underhill group together the English mystics on the grounds of their solitary life or their writing for solitaries, but their motivations are quite different. Underhill desired a group of author-mystics whose experiences, she felt, transcended history, time, and place—whose works she argued were intended for a medieval lay, English middle class, an appealing idea for a twentieth-century scholar who spent her working lifetime trying to make mystical experience accessible to the average Christian. Underhill states that she also grouped together these writers because they composed in the English vernacular (an important reason for their appearance on medieval literature courses in English faculties today).[7] By highlighting

---

6. E. Underhill, *The Mystics of the Church* (New York: 1971), pp. 110–11.
7. The 'Middle English mystics' are central to current discussion of 'vernacular theology', a term first used by A. I. Doyle, then developed by Bernard McGinn, and promoted by Nicholas Watson. See A. I. Doyle, *A Survey of the Origins and Circulation of Theological Writings in English in the 14th, 15th, and Early 16th Centuries with Special Consideration of the Part of the Clergy Therein* (Ph.D. diss., Cambridge: 1953), vol. 1, pp. 5–7; B. McGinn, 'Introduction: Meister Eckart and the Beguines in the Context of Vernacular Theology', in B. McGinn (ed.), *Meister Eckhart and the Beguine Mystics: Hadewijch of Brabant,*

features of these texts that appear to be concerned with broadening access, Underhill overlooks the fact that the *Cloud*-author addressed his writings to a limited audience, and did not want his works read by just anyone. Moreover, Julian is the only author to address explicitly her work to an 'even-Christian' audience. In the extract above, Underhill appropriates phrases and facts about the individuals in her canon, and generalizes them to the group. As Watson points out, these acts of elision promote belief in a long tradition of medieval English mystical writers with a concern not for the spiritual elite, but for the average Christian.

For Baker, who was writing for the enclosed Cambrai nuns, it was of enormous value to be able to designate texts by or for solitaries as 'mystical' or flowing from a higher degree of spiritual understanding, because this served to connect the nuns' experiences of solitude and enclosure with the potential for mystical union. In his *Apologie* for his works, Baker explains that the treatises he wrote at Cambrai about mystical works such as the *Cloud* were composed for and appropriate for the nuns because they lived in near '… eremiticall estates. & for such persons the ordinarie instructions that are vsually giuen to & exercised by such as liue not retired liues, are little or nothinge profitable or proper.'[8] Therefore it made sense for Baker to highlight links between his medieval authors' concerns and ways of life and those of his enclosed female audience. In his focus on the mystic as author then, Baker anticipates Underhill by four centuries, yet his motives for delineating a 'mystics' group is radically different from Underhill's: whereas

---

Mechthild of Magdeburg, and Marguerite Porete (New York: 1994) pp. 1–14; also Idem, *The Flowering of Mysticism: Men and Women in the New Mysticism (1200–1350)* (New York: 1998), pp. 19–24; N. Watson, 'Censorship and Cultural Change in Late-Medieval England: Vernacular Theology, the Oxford Translation Debate, and Arundel's Constitutions of 1409', *Speculum* 70 (1995), pp. 822–64; also Watson, 'Mystics', pp. 539–65.

8. Augustine Baker, *The Anchor of the Spirit; The Apologie; Summarie of Perfection* in J. Clark (ed.), *Analecta Cartusiana*, 119:30 (Salzburg: 2008), p. 61. Hereafter *Apologie*.

Underhill argues for a wider Christian audience than was intended by writers such as the *Cloud*-author, Baker argues consistently for a narrow audience, highlighting, as we will discuss later, the need for mystical texts, appropriate guidance literature, and most importantly, an expositor or teacher, who explains the meanings of mystical works to those hoping to achieve contemplative union.

Though an admirer of *Sancta Sophia*, Cressy's digest of Baker's works, Underhill was apparently unaware of Baker's broader involvement in the transmission of the *Cloud*, *Revelation* and other pre- and post-Reformation mystical texts. Given Underhill's explicit grouping together of these writers as mystics, and the fact that she does not indicate that any other scholar has influenced her rationale[9], it is unsurprising that Watson locates the genesis of the English mystical canon with writers such as Underhill, and the 'English Catholic scholars' (Watson's term) such as Colledge and Walsh—who produced the first critical edition of Julian's *Revelation*, classifying it as a medieval mystical text.[10]

Watson's interrogation of the canon leads him to claim that the concept of a separate canon of medieval English mystics, and indeed the concepts 'mystic', 'mysticism' and 'mystical theology', are all non-medieval coinings, and so we cannot speak of a medieval mystical canon as in any

9. Van Hyning has argued that Underhill was not aware of Baker's part in preserving the *Cloud*, nor was she aware of Baker's true writing style, being familiar with Serenus Cressy's meticulous digest of Baker's works, entitled *Sancta Sophia* rather than original Baker compositions. Whereas Underhill praises Cressy's heavily edited *Sancta Sophia*, she deeply criticizes the style of the first printed edition of the *Cloud*, not realizing that it was Baker's translation: see H. Collins (ed.), *The Divine Cloud* (London: 1871). Although Underhill was unaware of Baker's impact on this edition of the *Cloud*, she was aware that it was read by Baker and the Cambrai women, but it is unclear if this influenced her in classifying the *Cloud* as 'mystical'. Van Hyning discusses this in greater detail in, 'Augustine Baker Mystic-Maker', pp. 14–15.

10. For further comments on Colledge and Walsh see Watson, 'Middle English Mystics,' p. 542.

way stemming from medieval sensibilities.[11] Correct as Watson undoubtedly is to argue for the reintegration of the works of these mystical authors into the mainstream of medieval English literature—for this is the thrust of his argument—his assertion that the grouping is a creation of twentieth-century scholarship is complicated by Baker's explicit designation of Rolle, Hilton and the *Cloud*-author as 'mistick-authors' four centuries before Underhill.[12] Furthermore, like Underhill, Baker knew and admired Julian, and several of the Cambrai nuns knew and read the long text of Julian's *Revelation*. Julian's importance to the Cambrai nuns may be demonstrated by a passage in Baker's *Life* of Margaret Gascoigne: in his account of her death, he refers to her insistence that an excerpt from the *Revelation* be put beneath the crucifix upon which she, like Julian, gazes from her sickbed.[13] However, Baker does not categorise the *Revelation* as 'mystical' because, as Van Hyning has argued, 'Julian does not offer her experience as a template for contemplation' to her readers—nor does she speak about achieving mystical union in any way.[14] We will return to Baker's treatment of the *Revelation* below.

---

11. Watson. 'Middle English Mystics', p. 544.
12. Baker had access to a tract written by William Flete titled: 'The remedy ayenst the troubles of temptacyons,' which he believed to be a Rolle text, because it was mis-represented as such by Winken de Worde in his 1519 edition of this work. Rolle is explicitly mentioned several times in Baker's writings, see for instance the book list appended to Augustine Baker, *Directions for Contemplation: Book H*, in J. Clark (ed.), *Analecta Cartusiana*, 119:14 (Salzburg: 2000), pp. 79–81, the final item being '27. Richard of Hampoll'.
13. See Downside MS 42, fols 234–6. For discussion, see R. Lawes, *Accounts of Intense Religious Experience in Autobiographical Texts by English Catholics 1430–1645, and in the Writings of George Herbert* (Oxford D. Phil thesis: 2001), p. 188 n. 67.
14. Van Hyning argues this point in further detail emphasizing that Julian's *Revelation* is not an account of how to achieve mystical union, but rather an account of understanding gained from visionary experience, and thus not easily appropriated by Baker into his canon of 'mystick-authors'. 'Augustine Baker Mystic-Maker', p. 12.

It seems Baker's impetus to develop the 'mystick-author' concept stemmed from his strong belief that the nuns under his direction *could* successfully pursue mystical union by reading and practising the methods laid out by particular authors. But Baker's attitude to the authors he cites, translates, and adapts into his own works is rather complex.[15] At times he exemplifies an approach to his authors which is thoroughly medieval, and which may appear to the modern reader rather paradoxical: on the one hand, the citation of earlier *auctores* is essential to establishing a subsequent work as authoritative and canonical; on the other hand, citations from the validating *auctores* may be made in a manner which pays little heed to the original—authorial—context, intention, or even form.[16] Medieval texts are often crammed full of quotations from classical, scriptural, patristic authors which are freely mis-cited and mis-attributed, but which still serve to validate the texts in which they appear, by demonstrating to the reader the author or compiler's familiarity with a range of authorities. Similarly, Baker is sometimes rather free in his treatment of the *Cloud*, for instance, interpolating, extracting, and—whether deliberately or in a sincere but mistaken attempt to explain or modernize—directly gainsaying his *auctor*.

Baker's treatise on the *Cloud*, entitled *Secretum Sive Mysticum*, is filled with explanatory phrases in which he changes the *Cloud*-author's meaning or original text. For instance, he writes: 'Albeit ye same Author doe speak only in a generality of a *blind stirring* or *Springing of Love*, yet must we understand th^t there be, or may be, Many &

---

15. For further discussion of Baker's and the nuns' attitudes to textuality and authority, see C. Walker, 'Spiritual Property: The English Benedictine Nuns of Cambrai and the Dispute Over the Baker Manuscripts', in N. E. Wright, M. W. Ferguson and A. R. Buck (eds.), *Women, Property and the Letters of the Law in Early Modern England*, (London: University of Toronto Press, 2004), pp. 237–55.

16. This is true of both secular and religious texts: on the relevance of this treatment of *auctores* to late medieval religious texts see E. Dutton, *Julian of Norwich: the Influence of Late Medieval Devotional Compilations* (Cambridge: 2008), especially chapter 2.

various changes of Such Exercises...';[17] and 'whereas our Author Speaketh much & often of seeking to Suppresse & Keep under y^e *clowd of forgetting*... all images th^t would presse in or offer themselves whilest th^t ye Soul is in her Exercise of Love, this is more to be understood to be practice in ye Exercise of Acts of Love...'[18] Baker is specifically trying to reconcile the terminology of the *Cloud* with the other texts he is writing about in *Secretum*, including Benet of Canfield's *Of the Will of God* and Constantin de Barbanson's *Secres Sentiers*.[19] Thus, Baker's near-contemporaries de Barbanson and Canfield become commentators, to be read alongside or even over the *Cloud* author, often at the expense of one or all of these authors' meanings.

Baker's practice of discoursing beyond what was contained in a text, for the sake, as will be discussed below, of better communicating what he believed its original author felt they could not say, is exemplified in his discussion of the term 'mystic' as an adjective. Although in his writings 'mistick' functions predominantly as a noun, the word does have adjectival connotations as well. The Middle English lexicon contained the following terms with the root '*misti*': '*misterial*', meaning mysterious or symbolic; '*misticke*,' as an adjective meaning 'symbolical; figurative'; and '*mistik(e)*' as

---

17. Augustine Baker, *Secretum Sive Mysticum*, in J. Clark (ed.), *Analecta Cartusiana*, 119:7 (Salzburg: 1997), p. 141.
18. Ibid., pp. 142–3.
19. Van Hyning, 'Augustine Baker Mystic-Maker' pp. 18–19, 'By positioning the *Cloud* alongside two seventeenth-century texts, and declaring that the *Cloud* is the 'first text' to discuss 'mystical' matters, Baker is devising an origin-story for mystical writing as pre-Reformation, Catholic and English, while using contemporary texts, one English, exiled, and one generation older than Baker, the other continental and contemporary, to unpack the meaning and significance of the first. Baker explicitly claims the *Cloud*-author for a pre-Reformation English tradition when he states "I do not take it to be any Translation, but to have bin first penned in ye English tongue, as we have it." (Baker, *Secretum*, p. 3) By drawing upon this past and framing it as the generator of mystical writing, Baker is inscribing the origins of contemplative tracts within an English tradition, yet reconciling its purpose to the perceived present needs of his audience.'

a noun derived from the adjective, and meaning 'spiritual or symbolical meaning or interpretation.'[20] Baker's use of the adjective 'mistick' is infrequent, but he does occasionally use 'mistick' to mean 'hid' or 'privy.' In his discussion of the title *Secretum Sive Mysticum*, he writes:

> This Treatise of mine I call *Secretum*, both because it Containeth Mystick matters (& *Mysticum* and *Secretum* are both of one Sence and Meaning), and such as S. Denis (whose writings are as it were the Text whereon both our Author of y^e *Clowd* & other Mystick Authors (do Comment), forbiddeth to be Communicated to such as do more use their externall Senses then internall & Spirituall exercises; as also because it Conteineth / Certain Particular Passages wch the Author hereof doth not think fit to be made known to All, nor indeed to any, save such as do really Lead or pursu internall lives...[21]

Here, Baker defines 'mistick' as 'secret,' 'privi' or 'hid' in the Middle English sense, as beyond the knowing of certain people. This adjective in Middle English generally pertained to God's 'mistick' knowledge or way, as opposed to man's, and indeed describes that which is hidden from human understanding. When the *Middle English Dictionary* does refer to 'misti' or 'misticke' texts, these are Biblical or patristic. Baker's identification of the *Cloud* and his *Secretum* as 'mistick' texts thus align these with a tradition of authority in which God's meaning is pursued by humans, but remains impenetrable: this identification also practically requires Baker to serve as an expositor of the text's mystical meaning.

This tradition of divine authority as dependent on that which is secret, mystic, or 'privy' is exemplified in Julian

---

20. See S. M. Kuhn and J. Reidy (eds.), *Middle English Dictionary* (Ann Arbor: 1975), pp. 593, 596. The earliest record for 'mistick(e)' as a noun is 1333, in Shoreham, *Poems* 23, lines 630–1: 'Cryst and hijs membrys, men, O body beþe ine mystyke. Wet hys mystyke ne mey non wete... Bote wanne þer hys o þyng yked, An o þer to onderstonde þer-inne.', p. 595.

21. Baker, *Secretum*, p. 2.

of Norwich's *Revelation of Love*, but it is interesting to note a manipulation of Julian's teaching on this theme in the extracts from her work which appear in the Upholland manuscript, formerly at St Joseph's College, Upholland. Although the precise degree of Baker's involvement in the production of the Upholland Julian extracts is still open to question,[22] it is certain that Baker was a vital influence in the spiritual formation of those who copied and read both this manuscript and the two earliest surviving full long-text witnesses of the *Revelation*:[23] Baker's works of guidance, including his 'modernizations' and commentaries, contribute to the seventeenth-century reading context of the *Revelation*. It cannot be proven that Baker modernized or adapted the *Revelation* at all: Julian's teaching is in many ways in conflict with Baker's, and her *Revelation* may therefore seem an unlikely candidate for Baker's transmission to the Cambrai nuns. On the other hand, the high degree of selection and adaptation of Julian's text which may be

---

22. H. W. Owen and L. Bell, 'The Upholland Anthology: An Augustine Baker Manuscript', in *Downside Review* cxcvii (1989), pp. 274–92, and H. W. Owen, 'More extracts from the Upholland Anthology: An Augustine Baker Manuscript', *Downside Review*, ccclxx (1990), pp. 133–43. Hywel Owen identified this MS as an anthology of extracts from medieval and post-Reformation spiritual classics translated by Baker. On Baker's possible contribution to the Julian extracts in Upholland, see E. Dutton, 'Augustine Baker and Two Manuscripts of Julian of Norwich's *Revelation of Love*,' *Notes and Queries*, New Series 52, no. 3 (Sept. 2005) pp. 329–37, and E. Dutton, 'The Seventeenth-Century Manuscript Tradition and the Influence of Augustine Baker', in L. H. McAvoy (ed.), *A Companion to Julian of Norwich* (Cambridge: 2008), pp. 127–38.

23. Paris, MS Bibliothèque Nationale, Fonds Anglais No. 40 (late sixteenth or early seventeenth century), is associated with the nuns of Cambrai, and BL MS Sloane 2499, is tentatively ascribed to Anne Cary, in religion Clementia (1615–1671), founder of Cambrai's sister house in Paris, and Prioress. See the *Who were the nuns?* database project for biographical details: http://wwtn.history.qmul.ac.uk/search/nsearch.html, ID: CB027. For this ascription see: G. Ronan Crampton (ed.), *The Shewings of Julian of Norwich* (Kalamazoo, MI: Medieval Institute Publications, 1994), and online: http://www.lib.rochester.edu/camelot/julianin.htm#f26 [Accessed 1 December 2011].

observed in the Upholland manuscript could be held as evidence of the concern of an adaptor to rework the teaching of the *Revelation* radically. Baker professes concern at the lack of books 'proper' for the nuns and suggests that 'there were manie <good> English bookes in old time, wherof thoughe they have some, yet they want manie'.[24] In the light of this paucity of suitable material, he may have been reluctant to suppress even the most—to him—unappealing of old books. Furthermore, the attraction of 'Iulian the Ankress of norw*ich*'[25]—a woman who received visions, and lived as a solitary—as an inspiration for the Cambrai nuns, may have been irresistible. Although Julian does not claim her visionary experience as exemplary at all, Gascoigne's death-bed imitation of Julian and evocation of her text indicates a surprising use of the *Revelation* in religious imitatory practice.[26]

---

24. The quotation is from Baker's letter to Robert Cotton—see note 2, above. This citation from fol. 12ʳ.
25. MS Colwich Abbey 18, p. 155: on the significance of this manuscript see Dutton, 'Augustine Baker and Two Manuscripts...'
26. N. Watson and J. Jenkins, *A Vision Showed to a Devout Woman* and *A Revelation of Love* (Pennsylvania: 2006). Watson and Jenkins identify this moment as an act of imitation: 'This moving tableau, which sums up well the importance of Julian's words in Gascoigne's treatise, shows Gascoigne subsuming her own death in the visionary death described in *A Revelation*, and practising a form of *imitatio Julianae* in her determination to depend on the image of the dying Christ for her "heven".' In her article questioning whether it was even possible for these counter-Reformation women to 're-enact' medieval 'pieties', Sara Gorman writes: '[The] notion of a direct 'bridge' back to the insular medieval past can scarcely contain the complexities of reading medieval books across the spatial and temporal gap between the composition of these [medieval mystical] works and their consumption by English recusants on the Continent.' Gorman argues that Gascoigne cannot be said to be imitating Julian or directly bridging back to her experience, because she is staring at text attached to the crucifix, not the vision of a bleeding, dying Christ such as Julian saw. See Gorman, '*Imitatio* and Revision? M. Gascoigne, Augustine Baker, and the Reception of Julian of Norwich in Seventeenth-Century Cambrai.' *Moveable Type*. UCL English, No. 4 (2008). [Downloaded 4 September 2009: http://www.ucl.ac.uk/english/graduate/issue/4/articles.html].

There are four extracts from the *Revelation* in the Upholland manuscript, and they treat the central theme of Julian's questioning in her *Revelation*—the paradox of divine love and sin. But Upholland abbreviates hugely Julian's discussion of sin, and selects passages in which the paradox of sin and love is explored through the image of the privity of God. The divine secret deed, the great act by which God shall make all, including sin, well, is 'His prevy conncelle':[27] it is the right of royal lordship, and God's servants must not disturb their lord's peace with questions about what is hidden. Central to Julian's *Revelation* is the paradox of the Christian's 'seeing and seeking', in which we should gratefully contemplate the knowledge we are given but also accept its limitations—the saints exemplify this behaviour.[28] However, as Elisabeth Dutton has demonstrated elsewhere,[29] the Upholland manuscript's interest appears to be more in the secret than in the paradox. The Upholland compiler appears to be interested in knowing, in what can and cannot be known, and in God's will to reveal Himself to us; her/his appreciation of knowing, however, is focussed on the human, rather than the divine, viewpoint.

Baker's numerous writings reveal an interest not in academic knowledge but in mystical 'knowing', a knowing which comes from the direct experience of God:

> No man is able by profoundnesse of his Learning, by ye Subtilty or acutenesse of his Understanding, nor by any meer Human industries, Perfectly to Comprehend or Understand; but it is only Learned & understood by experience by him, to whom ye Divine Goodnesse & liberality shall please to impart ye same experience & knowledg.[30]

---

27. E. Colledge and J. Walsh (eds.), *A Book of Showings to the Anchoress Julian of Norwich* (Toronto: 1978) 2 vols, p. 415, l.13

28. Ibid., *Showings*, vol. 2, chapter 30.

29. Dutton, 'Manuscript Tradition', pp. 135–6.

30. Baker, *Secretum*, p. 1.

To Baker, the image of divine privity is potent, but his focus on human knowledge through experience of God ensures that his discussion of God's secrets, which we may imagine might have drawn him to the *Revelation* passages which appear in Upholland, would surely twist the *Revelation*'s image. The 'secret' in which Baker is interested, then, is not only the mysterious thought of God's mind by which all shall, in the end, be made well; it is also the secret of the mystic's knowing of God.

If we return, then, to his use of the term 'mystic' in his discussion of the title of his treatise *Secretum Sive Mysticum*, we can see that in Baker's hands the divine secrets are the preserve not uniquely of God but rather of a contemplative oligarchy. The treatise is called *Secretum* because of its mystical content ('it Containeth Mystick matters') and because it comments on the writings of 'Mystick Authors'—St Dionysius the Areopagite, who was the *Cloud*-author's source, and others: the other reason for the title *Secretum* is that Baker himself, 'the Author hereof', does not think it suitable in its entirety for any but advanced contemplatives, who 'pursu internall lives.'

Much of Baker's writing is concerned with championing the experiential mystical inner life exemplified in the *Cloud*, against the more prescriptive Jesuit meditative practices propounded by Father Francis Hull, OSB (professed 1616, d. 1645),[31] confessor to the Cambrai nuns. Baker sought to guide the nuns in a mystic way that relied on extensive reading and discernment of their individual spiritual needs and 'call'. This instinct might well lie behind the emphasis on 'knowing' which has been observed in the Upholland manuscript. The Upholland manuscript, by focusing on the theme of 'prive connrelle' but cutting that theme loose from themes of sin, gives the *Revelation*'s exploration of knowing and unknowing a mystical air, and it is the capacity of the mystical way—entirely lacking from the Julian source

---

31. See A. Bellenger, *English and Welsh Priests, 1558-1800* (Bath: Downside Abbey, 1984), p. 74.

text—to open the contemplative to experience of that which is 'mystick' or 'prive'—which may have interested Baker.

Although we believe that Baker's treatment of his medieval texts is complex and at times heavy handed, Baker is also paying his medieval sources the compliment of sustained and serious attention, and his citation of *auctores* in texts dealing with nearer contemporary writers, for example in *Discretion*, is in many ways scrupulous, particularly in its attention to indicating sources and distinguishing citation from Baker's comment upon it. Furthermore, Baker directly embroiled himself in a contemporary authorship controversy, about *The Abridgement of Perfection*, an English translation by Lady Mary Percy, of the English Benedictine nuns at Brussels, of an Italian work by a Milanese woman, Isabelle Christina Bellinzaga. When both the Italian work and its English translation were attributed to Jesuits, Baker supplied 'many arguments or reasons' challenging these attributions: these arguments are recorded in Baker's treatise titled *An Enquiry*.[32]

Baker troubles himself to consider this authorship question, and make so many 'arguments or reasons', because 'I have by a religious father of our Order … bin moved to doe [so]'. It is the Jesuit involvement which has drawn Benedictine attention, and Baker appears keen to attack the Jesuit programme of meditations, Ignatius of Loyola's *Spiritual Exercises*, which he sees as in conflict with the teachings of the 'mystical way'. He is convinced that Jesuit meditation could not create a mystick-author: 'not any of ye said Society [of Jesus] was ye author of ye said book (being a mystick book of good worth).'[33] At the time Baker wrote *The Enquiry*, the storm was already brewing between Baker and Hull, before they were both removed from Cambrai. It would be nice to think, more positively, that Baker was motivated not by this rupture, but at least partly by an interest in female

---

32. Baker, *Discretion*, p. 22. Augustine Baker, *An Enquiry about the Author of the Treatises of the Abridgement and Ladder of Perfection*, in J. Clark (ed.), *Analecta Cartusiana*, 119:33 (Salzburg: 2010), pp. 1–24.

33. Baker, *Enquiry*, pp. 1, 7.

spirituality, and in providing female spiritual models for the nuns among whom he worked,[34] but in any case his endeavours re-establish the roles of two female writers in the creation of *The Abridgement of Perfection*.

Whatever the particular circumstances of the *Enquiry*, its composition demonstrates that Baker attached an importance to authorship which might seem at odds with the occasionally cavalier approach to authorial meaning which characterises at least parts of his treatment of medieval texts. And of course, Baker was not a medieval writer, but an approximate contemporary of Shakespeare, who was born in 1564 and died in 1616; Baker's longer life spanned 1575–1641. The two men were writing in very different contexts, of course, and Baker spent a significant portion of his adult life living in exile on the Continent, but recent Shakespeare scholarship has paid lively attention to the roles and images of the author at the time Baker was writing, and the results are suggestive.

It has come to be recognized that the role of the author was complicated by *collaboration*, understood in various senses.[35] Some of 'Shakespeare's' plays were co-written, with different playwrights working on different scenes; but other plays have survived in forms which are the fruits of less direct collaboration—the adaptations, expansions, abbreviations, or simply mistakes of actors, theatre managers, or printers. Translations, and citations, of source materials can be fruitfully considered forms of atemporal collaboration and this is true of non-dramatic texts as well as plays. Scholars argue for the importance of collaboration in constructing meaning in Renaissance manuscripts: the reader may be guided as much by annotations, marginal commentaries, aspects of *mise-en-page* decided by scribe

---

34. Dutton has made this suggestion elsewhere ('Augustine Baker and Two Manuscripts' p. 336): she seeks here to correct her overemphasis on this possibility.
35. J. Marsten, *Textual Intercourse: Collaboration, Authorship, and Sexualities in Renaissance Drama*, Cambridge Studies in Renaissance Literature and Culture 14 (Cambridge: 1997).

or printer as by any single 'authorial intention'. Jeffrey Marsten has argued persuasively that, in their considerations of 'a period in which textual property was typically not assigned to authors by law or custom', scholars should be aware of the 'inappropriateness of an authorially based canon in this [Shakespeare's] period.'[36] If, as we are suggesting, Augustine Baker is creating a 'mystick-author' based canon, he might seem, at first glance, to be anticipating a movement which scholars have usually located later, in the increasing importance of author-function:

> The historicity of that need [to know 'who is speaking'] is registered in the word *anonymous*, which supports Foucault's contention that the author has a particular point of emergence as a cultural fiction. *Anonymous* does not take on its recognizably modern sense in English ('bearing no author's name; of unknown or unavowed authorship') until the late seventeenth century; earlier, around 1600, the word signifies 'a person whose name is not given, or is unknown', but does not connect persons with texts (OED). Beginning around 1676, however, *anonymous* begins to signal the author-ization of a text, the importance of someone, anyone, speaking. The author's emergence is marked by notice of its absence.[37]

The 'author's emergence as marked by notice of its absence' might rather nicely describe the activities of scholars creating 'the *Cloud*-author' — a nice irony for the most apophatic of English mystical texts — but Baker anticipates this scholarly creation in his treatment of the 'mystick-author' behind his *Cloud*, as we have seen in his *Secretum*.

'Author', with French and Latin roots signifying 'origins' and 'causing growth', is in medieval texts commonly used of the divine — it refers to the person who originates and gives existence. So Chaucer's Parson tells of 'The

---

36. *Ibid.*, pp. 4, 10.
37. *Ibid.*, p. 12.

auctor of matrimonye, that is Crist,'³⁸ and in *Troilus and Criseyde* Chaucer calls on 'Ioue, o autour of nature!'³⁹ With reference to the creation of the natural world, the word 'author' continues to be applied to God at least until the nineteenth century. The medieval sense of an 'author' in a textual setting is rather more complicated than the modern. Chaucer of course repeatedly invokes 'myn auctor', the source texts he claims to be translating or compiling. He is usually playing on medieval distinctions, famously expounded by Bonaventure, which distinguish between the activities of the author, compiler, and scribe, and create a hierarchy among those roles.⁴⁰ These distinctions might appear familiar and sensible to the modern reader, but Chaucer's use of them, for example in the *Canterbury Tales*,

---

38. G. Chaucer, *The Parson's Tale*, 1.808 in L. D. Benson (ed.), *The Riverside Chaucer* (Oxford: 1987). All Chaucer citations are from this edition.
39. Chaucer, *Troilus and Criseyde*, book III, l. 1016.
40. St Bonaventure, *Opera. Proem in primum librum sententiarum, quaestio* iv, Quaracchi edition (1882) i, 14, col. 2. 'Quadruplex est modus faciendi librum. Aliquis enim scribit aliena, nihil addendo vel mutando; et iste mere dicitur scriptor. Aliquis scribit aliena addendo, sed non de suo, et iste compilator dicitur. Aliquis scribit et aliena et sua, sed aliena tamquam principalia, et sua tamquam annexa ad evidentiam; et iste dicitur commentator non auctor. Aliquis scribit et sua et aliena, sed sua tamquam principalia, aliena tamquam annexa ad confirmationem et debet dici auctor.' Minnis translates 'The method of making a book is fourfold. For someone writes the materials of others, adding or changing nothing, and this person is said to be merely the scribe. Someone else writes the materials of others, adding, but nothing of his own, and this person is said to be the compiler. Someone else writes both the materials of other men, and of his own, but the materials of others as the principal materials, and his own annexed for the purpose of clarifying them, and this person is said to be the commentator, not the author. Someone else writes both his own materials and those of others, but his own as the principal materials, and the materials of others annexed for the purpose of confirming his own, and such must be called the author.' A. J. Minnis, *Medieval Theory of Authorship: Scholastic Literary Attitudes in the Later Middle Ages* (London: 1984), p. 94.

to define himself as merely a compiler,[41] makes ironic play of an additional nuance of 'author' as an earlier writer who may be used to lend validity to a text—a nuance now rendered distinct in the etymologically connected 'authority'. The interplay between these senses of 'author'—originator or creator, writer of texts, authority—underlies medieval theories of authorship which have been delineated for modern scholars by Alistair Minnis,[42] and which stem from scriptural exegesis in which God is the prime mover of scriptural texts, and the actual writers of those texts more like scribes, moved by the Holy Spirit. The medieval sense of the 'author' is imbued with a spiritual force, and this heavy-weight understanding of the author's role lies behind the hesitation, whether real or feigned, which medieval writers exhibit in adopting the title.

Augustine Baker is clearly aware of this medieval, exegetical sense of authorship. He writes of his failure to read the Old or New Testament that he was nonetheless 'Enlightend by ye Spirit th^t had penned those books & that still speaketh in them.'[43] He urges that his writings should be given only to readers who will 'admire and honour' them, but 'especially the First Author therof, being God.'[44] He writes of Aspirations in which God is 'Mover, Worker and teacher', and of Motion and Direction from 'ye Author therof, being God.'[45] From this image of the divine Author, Baker perhaps draws a medieval sense of the human author as a divinely-sanctioned figure, acting at the inspiration of,

---

41. Chaucer, *The Canterbury Tales* (A) 3167–3181. The *Canterbury Tales'* narrator presents himself as compiling the tales told by others, and affects to deny responsibility, for example, for the 'yvel entente' of 'The Miller's Tale'. He puts responsibility on the reader to moderate their reading experience by choosing another, less scandalous story from the tales he has compiled: by claiming that he 'moot' tell all the tales he denies his own power of selection and presents himself more as scribe than compiler.
42. Minnis, *Theory*.
43. Baker, *Secretum*, p. 58.
44. *Ibid.*, p. 38.
45. *Ibid.*, p. 40.

in imitation of, the divine Author, and this understanding of authorship puts Baker out of step with his contemporaries. Perhaps, then he is not so much ahead of his time as behind it in his focus on the Author.

On the other hand, Baker's sense of collaboration appears to be of its time, rather than backward-looking. Baker's authors were extremely varied: just amongst his pre-Reformation English writers there was a huge range of experience including varying degrees of education, profession, number of languages spoken and so on. In addition to the English writers, Baker added his translations and discourses on nearer contemporary, often continental writers, including the works of Tauler, Blosius, Teresa of Avila, Constantine de Barbanson and many others. Baker was faced with the need to draw these works together and present a coherent series of practices to his enclosed female readership, which would have allowed them to make good use of their rich library, without feeling confused when encountering different terminologies and methods for achieving mystical union. But of course, this process of distilling a unified idea of how to achieve mystical union—by reconciling terms and ideas from across huge historical and temporal divides—was no easy undertaking. Generally speaking, it appears as though Baker was more comfortable as a translator of contemporary works such as those of Constantine de Barbanson, Benet of Canfield and Teresa of Avila, and was less confident in his treatment of pre-Reformation English texts, particularly the *Cloud*, the language and meaning of which are at times difficult to follow. Perhaps because of this difficulty with pre-Reformation English works, combined with a desire to link the nuns' exiled present to the English Catholic past, Baker felt motivated to establish the unifying concept of the 'mystick-author' as someone possessing qualities of thought and understanding that lead them to union with God: the essence of mystical union itself transcending time and historical circumstances, and the textual remains documenting this union, open to cross-reference and collation, and with the potential to inspire and guide attempts at imitation.

We can see a rationale for this reconciling of different authors and their texts quite clearly in Baker's *Apologie* for his works, written in 1629, approximately four years before the official enquiry into his writings, which took place in 1633. This enquiry arose as a response to suspicions raised by Father Francis Hull, the official chaplain and confessor to the Cambrai nuns. Hull brought Baker's works to the attention of the Benedictine General Chapter, which discussed the orthodoxy of Baker's works, and ultimately approved them. In his *Apologie* Baker writes for a multi-faceted audience: ostensibly his usual female readership, but certainly with an awareness that his writings were likely to be read by those who were less sympathetic. About the difficult situation of 'mystick-authors', and his role as a writer and commentator on their works, he writes:

> ... some scholasticks in these dayes ... are so rigid in censuringe the writings of misticks, that hardly dare any of those mistick[s] sette out any-thinge. And yet those carpers themselues are farre enough from setting out any such misticke matters, as whom it suffiseth they can censure the said doeings of others, & dispose themselues no further. If one of those misticks doe trippe in a tearme that perhaps little or nothinge importeth, they crie out as if the whole world were like to be corrupted & vndone by it.[46]

The 'mystic' is set up in opposition to the 'scholastic', and the 'mystics' seem to be those who might be caught in the act not, as might be expected, of contemplation, but rather of writing. The scholastics, who might be expected to be writing, are rather the figures who prevent the writing of others through rigid censorship, and consequently the achievement of mystical union by readers. The 'carpers', for whom Baker's works are 'mistick' know nothing

---

46. Baker *Apologie*, pp. 59–60.

of what we can call adjectivally 'misticke matters.'[47] Two further passages in Baker's *Apologie* provide us with clear insight into why he copied, translated and expounded on what he deemed to be 'mystic' or 'spirituall' works more generally:

> If you or I should seeke to find out the reason, wherefore amonge such a great number of soules in these daies that haue verie good wills & much aptnesse in their natures, & haue wthall great store of good bookes wch they daylie pervse, scarse any of them, (or at least very few), doe attaine contemplation, or make any true progress in spirit, he shall find the only want to be, that they haue not some

---

47. These matters are clearly differentiated from the 'Mysteries' of Christian Religion, for all that those 'Mysteries' also came by contemplation to 'Apostles, Doctors & other Principall Members & Beginners of ye church.' Baker uses the familiar phrase 'Mysteries of our faith' to mark out what appear to be doctrinal certainties, apparently given once-and-for-all to the early church, as distinct from 'mystick matters', still being revealed to contemplatives. In relation to the Mysteries of the Church, the role of contemplation — here Baker's passive contemplation — is in offering not new insight, but affirmation of faith: 'the wonderfull proofe & Satisfaction th^t a Soul hath of ye Verities of Christian Religion by one of ye said passive Contemplations.' (Baker, *Secretum*, p. 90) Christianity is here defined in opposition to other faiths, although the expected point comparison — of Christian doctrine, Christian 'Mysteries' as distinct from others — does not come: rather, oddly, 'No Religion of Judaïsm, Turcism, Hersy or Heathenism ever did or possibly Can bring One to such a Contemplation' (Baker, *Secretum*, p. 90) — it is not Christian doctrine which is distinguished, but Christian contemplation's capacity to prove Christian Mysteries. *The Oxford English Dictionary* (*OED*) suggests that 'mystery' was used in Baker's time to mean 'A religious truth known or understand only be divine revelation', or 'A doctrine of faith involving difficulties which human reason is incapable of solving.' though both of these definitions might apply, Baker's specific connection of Christian Mysteries to contemplation might possibly indicate more specifically the Fifteen Mysteries of the Church which form the objects of contemplation in the rosary. These Fifteen Mysteries were formalized by Pope Pius V in 1569, but *OED* records the earliest English use of 'mystery' in this sense in Bishop J. Taylor's *Golden Grove*, first printed in 1655. Baker's *Secretum*, once again, anticipates this occurrence by at least twenty years.

> experienced guide that can tell them more then bookes doe, or can teach them how to vnderstand & make right vse of bookes. Who by readinge Aristotle, yea or of his comments allso, comes to be a philosopher, if he haue not besides some liueinge expositor, that can & and will at large explicate the docrine of Aristotle?... And so it is indeed with the vse of spirituall bookes.[48]

When this passage is contrasted with that from the *Apologie* cited above, in which Baker appears to be chastising the scholars for not allowing mystics to get on with their writings and experience, it becomes clear that Baker believes that there is more than one kind of scholar. There are those who 'carpe' and then there are those who write—expounding philosophies for the benefit of others. Baker is clearly designating himself not simply as a scholastic writer, but as an expositor of textual meaning. In what follows, Baker defends his treatises of guidance:

> ...accordingelie haue I (as I hope) behaued my-selfe by wordes & writings, wch hath beene in supplieinge what other writers could not prudentlie doe in their publicke writings. Some of their doeings I haue expounded, no otherwise then they meant, yet perhaps somewhat further then they thought good to expresse; some things w^{ch}... they could not wth prudence sette downe, but passed ouer wth silence, I (my case beinge otherwise), haue beene bold, (& that not wthout necessitie) to vtter vnto you by word or writinge. But [t]hat I doe to you & not publicke to the world, but priuate & proper for you, as I haue aboue signified ...These writers most of all regarded the persons for whom they wrote, beinge all sorts of spiritts, & so doe I regardinge the particularities of those spirits for whom in perticular I write. These publicke writers accommodated themselues to all, I to a few.[49]

---

48. Baker, *Apologie*, p. 62.
49. *Ibid.*

In defence of his writings, Baker declares that he is compiling and commenting on the works of others. However, his additions often serve not to illuminate what his sources provide, but rather to expound his own meanings, and these additions are so extensive and independent of the original texts that in making them Baker is filling an author function.

Baker does not assume the role of the medieval compiler, hierarchically lower than his *auctores*: rather, his treatment of the authors he translates, compiles, and comments upon reflects a sense of himself as working among his equals—indeed his politically oppressed intellectual equals, who, aiming at a larger public readership, had to hold back certain things—'which they could not with prudence sette down'—which Baker, writing for his enclosed audience, could then distill. In this sense, Baker's writings are collaborations, albeit atemporal ones, with Hilton and the *Cloud*-author, as well as with Canfield and de Barbanson, amongst others. The results are collaborative texts, in the rich sense which Renaissance scholars have elaborated, and they are also perhaps slippery texts where an author's original meaning can be subsumed by Baker's own.

Up until now the legacy of Baker's grouping of the 'Middle English mystics' has been lost on members of the English literary academy. Yet simultaneously, and it would seem accidentally, Baker's canon-building project has been preserved, though not identified as such, in the resin of religious interest in Baker as a writer of spiritual guidance works. Discerning if or when Baker's activities came to have a direct impact on the modern canonization of the 'Middle English mystics' is the next task. It is certainly the case that his interest in the works of the so-called Middle English mystics lead to the first printing of Julian's *Revelation* in 1641, and an 1871 edition of the *Cloud* with Baker's commentary, as well as ongoing interest in and preservation of these works within the Benedictine abbeys and monasteries linked to Cambrai, Paris and contemporary Benedictine houses.

Baker's development of a larger group of 'mystick-authors' and religious writers containing the Middle English mystics thoroughly complicates Watson's assertion that the creation of the Middle English mystics canon is a result of twentieth century scholarship with a 'confessional bias'. We have argued that the mystics-grouping develops from a seventeenth-century desire for a pre-Reformation past that could be made to cohere with the seventeenth-century present. Baker's grouping of these pre-Reformation writers with seventeenth-century authors and others suggests an entirely different reading milieu than that proposed by Watson, who argues the mystics must be read alongside seminal works within the Medieval English literary canon as well as a body of 'canonical authors' writing in Latin and Anglo-Norman. Perhaps in order to do these medieval English writers real justice, we must consider them in a vast array of reading contexts, ranging from the medieval through to the modern period. Only then can we begin to understand the rich possibilities of their meanings—and significance to a multiplicity of readers over time—meanings which deepen as these authors and their works are considered with relation to the settings in which they were, are and will be encountered.

8

Towards a Chronology of Father Augustine Baker's Writings

JOHN P. H. CLARK

A key passage which provides a framework for the chronology of Father Baker's writings during the earlier part of his period as confessor to the Cambrai English Benedictine nuns is found in his *Secretum*, part spiritual autobiography, part commentary on 'Cloud of Unknowing', of which the first part was completed on 1st December 1629, and the second part must have been completed early in 1630.[1] In the second part,[2] he says that about six years and nine months after his 'second conversion' to contemplative prayer (which had taken place in Devon in 1620), on a mid-Lent Sunday—this must be 1627—he was give a deepened spiritual awareness which let to a change in his use of time. Up until now he had been spending seven or eight hours a day in mental prayer, and reading spiritual books voraciously. From this point his time spent in mental prayer was much reduced, and his reading gave way to writing, so that in the two years and nine months since that time—he is writing at the end of 1629 or very

---

1. Augustine Baker, *Secretum Sive Mysticum*, in J. Clark (ed.), *Analecta Cartusiana*, 119:7 (Salzburg: 1997), p. 94. I suggested (*Secretum*, p. ii) 'by the end of 1630', for the completion of *Secretum*, Book Two, but now prefer 'early in 1630'.
2. Baker, *Secretum*, 249–50.

early in 1630—he has written forty books[3] of various sizes, few or none of them, he modestly says, very large. Fifteen of these were collections and translations out of other authors; the remaining twenty-five were his own work.

It is not certain which 'books' precisely Baker means here. Several of his books, such as *Directions for Contemplation, Books D, F, G, H*, contain various distinct treatises. And we must allow for possible lost books. Moreover, in the composite books, there is evidence of occasional instability in the contents. There are references to some material in *Book B* which is not found in the only extant full manuscript of *Book B*.[4] Dame Barbara Constable made a careful edition of *Directions for Contemplation*, dated 1645, in which she placed after *Book H* the treatises on saying the Office and hearing Mass, which are located in *Book F* in the copy made by Dom Leander Prichard[5], and are elsewhere quoted as belonging to *Book F*.[6]

With one exception,[7] we rely on copies, not autographs, for Baker's full-length works. This means we cannot in

---

3. The reference to 'forty books' raises a question in connection with *Sancta Sophia* (Douai: 1657), Father Serenus Cressy's distillation of Baker's writings. This is stated on the title-page to have been made out of 'more than forty treatises'. Is this a precise statement, or is it simply a recollection of Father Baker's words in *Secretum*? *Sancta Sophia*, in fact, includes material from works of Baker written after *Secretum*, including *Mirror*, probably the lost treatise of *Reflection*, and the treatise of *The English Mission*.

4. Augustine Baker, *Directions for Contemplation-Book D* in J. Clark (ed.), *Analecta Cartusiana*, 119:11 (Salzburg: 1999), p. 11, 'What a creature is as in respect of the creator. Se (*sic*) in the *Book B*, in the collections out of the 3ᵈ booke of *The Will of God*.' This is supported independently by Baker's reading list; see footnote *ad loc*. Later in *Book D*, (p. 45), Baker refers to other material from Benet Canfield which he specifically says is in his *Book E*.

5. Augustine Baker, *Directions for Contemplation—Book H* in J. Clark (ed.), *Analecta Cartusiana*, 119:14 (Salzburg: 2000), p. ix–x.

6. For example, Augustine Baker, *A Secure Stay in All Temptations* in J. Clark (ed.), *Analecta Cartusiana*, 119:8 (Salzburg: 1998), p. 88.

7. Augustine Baker, *Dicta sive Sententiae Sanctorum Patrum de Praxi Vitae Perfectae*. See J. McCann, 'Ten More Baker Mss.', *Ampleforth*

most cases trace the process of revision and adjustment which Baker himself must have carried out, although there are indications that in at least some texts such adjustment took place. Thus the treatise of *Sickness* quotes a famous passage from Walter Hilton, which is followed by the note: 'But I have since written it wth my own hande in some of our books more intelligiblie for y^r understanding.'[8] In some cases there are mutual cross-references between two of Baker's works, which may be taken as a sign that he was working on them concurrently.[9] But without the autographs, we cannot say which of these books in a pair came first, and which has had the cross-reference added as an afterthought.

Baker not only revised but on occasions expanded his texts, notably some of his composite texts. Thus *Secretum* written, as said, in 1629/30, refers to the treatise *Nothing and Nothing makes Nothing* as to be found in *Remains*,[10] but Baker's final version of *Remains*, bearing the approval of 1634, and in which the first item is dated 4th September 1633[11], contains much material which is explicitly stated to have been written after Baker was moved to Douai in the summer of 1633.[12]

While some of Baker's later treatises, written from 1629 onwards, carry a date, the earlier treatises can only be given an approximate date based on other evidence. Dom Justin McCann, in his great pioneer work[13], proposed dates for the composition of most treatises, based on good evidence.

Journal 63 (1958), p. 81.
8. Augustine Baker, *Sickness with Collections from the Book called Death* in J. Clark (ed.), *Analecta Cartusiana*, 119:32 (Salzburg: 2009), p. 107.
9. See below on *Sickness/Confession; Discretion/Enquiry; Alphabet/Stay.*
10. Baker, *Secretum*, p. 176.
11. Augustine Baker, *Remains* in J. Clark (ed.), *Analecta Cartusiana*, 119:31 (Salzburg: 2008), p. 1.
12. Baker, *Remains*, p. 1.
13. J. McCann, ed., *The Life of Father Augustine Baker, O.S.B. (1575–1641) by Fr, Peter Salvin & Fr, Serenus Cressy* (London: 1933), especially pp. 160–201. J. McCann & H. Connolly (eds.), 'Memorials of Father

Now that texts are available for many treatises, adjustment and refinement may be offered on some points.

Many treatises carry approbations dated at various points from August 17th 1629.[14] It was in this year that Father Francis Hull was appointed chaplain at Cambrai.[15] Disagreements between Father Baker and Father Hull would lead to the vindication of Baker's teaching at the General Chapter of 1633, but with the removal of both men from Cambrai. The date of an approbation only provides, of course, a *terminus ante quem* for the composition of a treatise; a number of treatises approved in 1629 were demonstrably written earlier.

Baker himself states[16] that *Book A*, a collection of teaching on the religious life from various authors, together with some of his mnemonic rhymes, was the first book that he wrote at Cambrai.[17] We may take it that the composite *Book B*, and *Book C* on offices and employments, followed directly; all may be dated to 1627.[18] It might seem natural to place *Books D–H* simply in that order, after *Book C*, *Books D, F, G, H* being *Directions for Contemplation*, with *Book E*, a collection of translations, providing supporting material. In fact, the matter is rather more complex. Justin McCann placed *Book D* 'about 1627', *Books E, F,* and *G* 'about 1628'.[19] *Book H* includes a reference to a meeting between Constan-

---

Augustine Baker and other Documents relating to the English Benedictines' in *Catholic Record Society* 33(1933), pp. 274–293.

14. Baker, *Directions for Contemplation – Book D*, p. 1, approved 17th August 1629.
15. Athanasius Allanson, *Biography of the English Benedictines*, (Ampleforth: 1999), pp. 36, 44.
16. Augustine Baker, *Vox Clamantis in Deserto Animae* in J. Clark (ed.), *Analecta Cartusiana*, 119:22 (Salzburg: 2004), p. 201.
17. Baker would continue to produce mnemonic rhymes, and this facility would remain with him even when his facility for writing dried up at the end of his time at Douai. McCann & Connolly, 'Memorials', p. 123, note 193. McCann, *Life*, p. 193, note 56. McCann, 'Ten More Baker Mss.', pp. 81–82.
18. McCann, *Life*, p. 161, note 1.
19. McCann, *Life*, pp. 170–72, notes 17–19; p. 175, note 26.

tin de Barbanson, the author of *Secrets Sentiers de l'Amour Divin*, and one of the English Benedictines (Dom Placid Gascoigne) at Cologne in April 1628, 'being this yeare of our Lord',[20] so that *Book H* may be dated to that year.

Directions for Contemplation is conceived as a whole. It draws together, in a systematic way, teaching which Baker must have given orally to the nuns for quite some time, between his arrival at Cambrai in 1624 and mid-Lent 1627. While some of his treatises, such as that of *Sickness*, have an air of being written *calamo currente*, with little or no subsequent re-ordering, *Directions for Contemplation* gives the impression of extreme care and economy in composition, with logical progress and avoidance of repetition. Thus, in *Book D*, Baker writes: 'This contemplation may be actiue or passiue; the difference you shall read at lardge in the 3^d part of this treatise'.[21] The reference is to *Book G*.

Prefixed to *Book D* is an author's 'profession' in Latin and in English, submitting what is written to the judgement of superiors. The Latin version has: 'Professio Authoris. Prima Pars', indicating that the 'profession refers to *Book D* specifically, and not to *Directions for Contemplation* as a whole. This is dated 12th May 1628.[22] This date, of course, like those of the various approbations of Baker's writings, only provides a *terminus ante quem* for the completion of the work in question. The approbation for *Book D* is dated 17th August 1629 and was by Fr Leander de Sancto Martino (Jones), and was confirmed on 16th October 1629 by Fr Rudesind Barlow.[23] The approbation for *Book F* by Rudesind Barlow is dated 24th December 1629,[24] that for *Book G*, by Leander de Sancto Martino, is dated 27th August 1629,

---

20. Baker, *Book H*, pp. 18–19. McCann, *Life*, p. 166, note 9.
21. Baker, *Book D*, p. 48.
22. Baker, *Book D*, pp. 2–3. The English is on pp. 4–5.
23. Baker, *Book D*, p. 1.
24. Augustine Baker, *Directions for Contemplation—Book F* in J. Clark (ed.), *Analecta Cartusiana*, 119:12 (Salzburg: 1999), p. 1, with footnote.

and was confirmed without date by Rudesind Barlow.²⁵ The approbation for *Book H* was given on 24th December 1629 by Rudesind Barlow.²⁶ So *Directions for Contemplation* was examined and approved as a totality, some time after it was written.

As noted earlier, *Book E*, a collection of translations, breaks the sequence of a series of books which otherwise are Baker's own *Directions for Contemplation*. The subject-matter of *Book E* is extremely important for Baker and the nuns, for it includes among many other authors, Harphius, Benet Canfield, Joannes a Jesu Maria, and Barbanson.²⁷ We have seen that translations from other authors, whose works were available in Latin but not in English, were an important part of Baker's literary effort after mid-Lent 1627. No doubt here too, he was again doing in a systematic way what he had previously done informally and extempore, as is indicated by Dame Gertrude More's response to the reading by Baker of a passage from Barbanson later in 1625 or perhaps very early in 1626.²⁸ In *Book D*, Baker refers to his translation from Barbanson's *Secret Sentiers*, Part 2, chapters 10–11, which is in *Book E*, though *Book E* is not here named, and a little later he refers to his translation of the passage on active annihilation from the third part of Benet Canfield's *The Will of God* (=*The Rule of Perfection*), which he here explicitly says is in his *Book E*.²⁹ Presumably Baker had

---

25. Augustine Baker, *Directions for Contemplation—Book G* in J. Clark (ed.), *Analecta Cartusiana*, 119:13 (Salzburg: 2000), p. 1.
26. Baker, *Book H*, p. 1.
27. Augustine Baker, *Book E* in J. Clark (ed.), *Analecta Cartusiana*, 119:18 (Salzburg: 2002).
28. Augustine Baker, *The Life and Death of Dame Gertrude More*, in B. Wekking (ed.), *Analecta Cartusiana*, 119:19 (Salzburg: 2002), pp. 37–38. The turning-point for Dame Gertrude's spiritual development came at about All Saints' tide in the year of her profession, which was 1625, in consequence of a consultation with Father Baker.
29. Baker, *Book D*, pp. 42, 45. See note 4 above, on a reference also in *Book D* to material from Benet Canfield which at that time was in Baker's *Book B*.

begun compiling *Book E* as a companion to *Book D*. *Book E* is also mentioned in Baker's early treatise on *Sickness*.[30]

Baker had made other translations by the time that *Directions for Contemplation* was in progress. He had an abiding commitment to Tauler and pseudo-Tauler, as well as to Suso and pseudo-Suso (Rulman Merswin), and to some small items attributed to Eckhart, through the Latin translations of the Carthusian, Laurentius Surius. His translations of Tauler would eventually run to eight volumes.[31] The treatise of *Sickness* mentions 'the translated sermons of Thaulerus'.[32] *Book D* refers to the 'first tome' of Baker's Tauler translations,[33] so there must have been at least two volumes at this time. The second of the three parts of Baker's *Doubts and Calls* refers to the 'fourth tome' of Baker's 'Tauler'[34] The first section of *Doubts* existed by the time that Baker was working on *Book F*, since it is mentioned there.[35] The reading-list included in *Spiritual Alphabet*, which was written in 1629, says there were six parts at that time.[36]

In *Book D*, Baker refers to the catalogue of books at the Cambrai convent for recommended reading 'at the end of this booke'.[37] There are various forms of the reading list.[38] That appended to the edition of *Book H*, from a transcrip-

---

30. Baker, *Sickness*, pp. 32, 113.
31. J. Clark, 'Father Augustine Baker's Translations from the Works of John Tauler in the Latin Version of Laurentius Surius' in *Analecta Cartusiana*, 201 (Salzburg: 2003), pp. 49–51. McCann, *Life*, p. 198, note 64, states that Baker's translation of the pseudo-Taulerian 'Institutions' only received its finishing touches in 1637.
32. Baker, *Sickness*, p. 113.
33. Baker, *Book D*, p. 105.
34. Augustine Baker, *Doubts and Calls* in J. Clark (ed.), *Analecta Cartusiana*, 119:10 (Salzburg: 2009), p. 108.
35. Baker, *Book F*, pp .15, 17.
36. Augustine Baker, *Alphabet and Order* in J. Clark (ed.), *Analecta Cartusiana*, 119:16 (Salzburg: 2001), p. 40.
37. Baker, *Book D*, p. 18.
38. J. T. Rhodes, 'Dom Augustine Baker's Reading Lists' in *Downside Review* 111 (1993), pp. 157–173.

tion of Father Leander Prichard, is the fullest. It includes some material compiled by Baker after *Directions for Contemplation*, such as the *Idiot's Devotion*.[39] *Book D*, at this point in the text, refers especially to the *Spiritual Institution* of Blosius and *Quiet of the Soul* by Bonilla. [40] Baker had a great devotion to Blosius, and the reading-list in its fullest form, includes seven volumes of Blosius in manuscript transcriptions.[41] The voluminous translations of Blosius which are extant in association with undoubted Baker texts are generally taken to be his,[42] but we do not know their chronology. The English version of Bonilla, found in association with Baker texts, is also thought to be his.[43]

The first part of *Doubts and Calls*, which we have seen ante-dates *Book F*, refers to Baker's 'Collections in 4to',[44] which included an extract from the printed English version of the Spanish book *Desiderius*. These 'Collections' may well have been just an anthology of existing texts, not necessarily including any original translations by Baker; they are not known to survive. However, the same first part of *Doubts and Calls* refers explicitly to the Third Part of Baker's *Collections*, a distinct work, consisting of translations, and it repeats a long passage from Joannes a Jesu Maria which is there translated.[45]

---

39. Baker, *Book H*, pp. 82–89.
40. Baker, *Book D*, p. 18.
41. Baker, *Book H*, pp. 82–89. J. Clark, 'Father Augustine Baker's Translations from… John Tauler…', pp. 82–89.
42. McCann, *Life*, pp. 166–67, note 10.
43. McCann, *Life*, p. 167, note 11, dated the translation of Bonilla 'about 1630', but it is likely to be earlier, since it is already mentioned in *Book D* in J. Clark (ed.), *Analecta Cartusiana*, 119:34 (Salzburg: 2011), pp. 113–132.
44. Baker, *Doubts and Calls*, p. 45.
45. Baker, *Doubts and Calls*, pp. 54–56. The concluding remark about the approbation of *Collections III* by Rudesind Barlow must have been added later, since approbations only became an issue in 1629.

Of *Collections*,[46] the first part is entirely from Harphius, the second entirely from Barbanson, and the third from various authors, including Johannes a Jesu Maria, Blosius, Alvarez de Paz, Ruysbroeck, Benet Canfield, and others. Baker also made a translation, in a distinct volume, of the *Twelve Mortifications* from Harphius's *Theologica Mystica*. This again is explicitly mentioned in *Book D*.[47] Justin McCann considered that Parts 1 and 3 of *Collections* were compiled 'about 1629', while Part 2 was compiled 'about 1628'.[48] The evidence of *Doubts and Calls* in conjunction with *Book F* indicates a date not later than 1628 for *Collections III*, and by implication for *Collections I*. As to Part II, it includes a translation of the passage which Baker translated extempore for Dame Gertrude More and other sisters in 1625, and of which Dame Gertrude then begged to have an English translation.[49] The likelihood is again that Baker had begun to assemble, long before mid-Lent 1627, some of the material which found a home, with other material now systematically translated, in *Collections*, and that *Collections* had at least substantially taken shape by 1628.

Baker many times refers to *The Imitation of Christ* by Thomas à Kempis, which was at the time attributed by some to Jean Gerson rather than to Thomas à Kempis, and was available in English translation.[50] But Baker translated a number of Thomas à Kempis' other writings and sermons. Some of these translations are included in the reading-list

---

46. Augustine Baker, *Collections I–III* and *Twelve Mortifications of Harphius* in J. Clark (ed.), *Analecta Cartusiana*, 119:21 (Salzburg: 2004).
47. Baker, *Book D*, p.11. This is in the reading-list in Baker's *Alphabet*, p. 39, and is edited together with Baker's *Collections I–III*.
48. McCann, *Life*, p. 168–170, notes 13–15. The approbation for *Collections II* and for *Alphabet and Order*, (Baker, *Collections I–III*, p. 41), dated 24th December 1629, is, of course, only a *terminus ante quem*.
49. The passage in question is translated in *Collections II* (Baker, *Collections I–III*), p. 47. The translation in *Collections* is different to that given in Wekking, *The Life … of Dame Gertrude More*.
50. Rhodes, 'Reading Lists', p. 168.

in *Alphabet*.⁵¹ Very little of these translations are left.⁵² Apart from Baker's specific translations of particular works, there are very many translations of brief extracts which he made *ad hoc* and incorporated in his various treatises.

At least two significant original treatises by Baker existed by the time he completed *Book D*. *Book D* refers in several places to the treatise of *Confession* as having already been written.⁵³ In turn, *Confession* refers to the treatise of *Sickness* as already written.⁵⁴ But *Sickness* refers to the treatise of *Confession*.⁵⁵ *Sickness* includes treatment of scruples regarding previous confessions already made, so that some of its subject-matter overlaps with that of *Confession*. Baker mentions that he was working on *Sickness* on St Wulstan (of Worcester's) day, 19ᵗʰ January.⁵⁶ Bearing in mind the over-lap of subject matter, as well as the mutual cross-references, we may suppose that Baker was working on *Confession* and *Sickness* concurrently. *Sickness* refers to Baker's *Book C*⁵⁷, and also to *Book E*⁵⁸, and so must post-date these. It also speaks much of mortifications and resignation to the will of God, matters which are taken up more systematically in *Book D* and *Book G* respectively. Justin McCann says cautiously that *Sickness* was written 'in 1629

---

51. Baker, *Alphabet*, p. 40. The same items are found in the fuller reading-list copied by Dom Leander Prichard, see *Book H*, p. 87.
52. Augustine Baker, *Letters and Translations from Thomas à Kempis in the Lille Archives and elsewhere;The Devotions of Dame Margaret Gascoigne* in J. Clark (ed.), *Analecta Cartusiana*, 119:28 (Salzburg: 2007). See also the Addendum in Augustine Baker, *Idiot's Devotion—Directions: Parts One and Two* in J. Clark (ed.), *Analecta Cartusiana*, 119:29 (Salzburg: 2008), p. 144.
53. Baker, *Book D*, pp. 15, 83, 85.
54. Augustine Baker, *Five Treatises; The Life and Death of Dame Margaret Gascoigne; Treatise of Confession* in J. Clark (ed.), *Analecta Cartusiana*, 119: 23 (Salzburg: 2006), p. 133.
55. Baker, *Sickness*, p. 80.
56. Baker, *Sickness*, p. 91.
57. Baker, *Sickness*, p. 18.
58. Baker, *Sickness*, pp. 32, 113.

or earlier'.⁵⁹ In fact, if we take it that *Confession's* reference to *Sickness* is original to the treatise, *Confession* and *Sickness* may both be placed no later than 1628.⁶⁰ *Doubts and Calls* deals with the discernment of, and obedience to, the will of God, the distinction between ordinary and extraordinary calls, and the relation of such calls to obedience to monastic authority. We have seen that at least the first part of *Doubts and Calls* was written by the time that Baker completed *Book F* (in 1628).⁶¹ Justin McCann dated *Doubts and Calls* to 1628-29.⁶² Whether the composition of *Doubts and Calls* was prolonged from 1628 to 1629 is a moot point.

We have seen that the completion of *Book H* may be placed in 1628. By this time, Baker had apparently written *Anchor of the Spirit*, to which he refers in *Book H*.⁶³ *Anchor* includes, intermingled with itself, *Remedies against Temptations*, a modernisation of the third and last (and printed) version of the book of that name which is now known to have originated in a treatise by the Augustinian friar, William Flete, though in Baker's day it was attributed to Richard Rolle.⁶⁴

---

59. McCann, *Life*, p. 196, note 61. McCann notes that some additional matter is dated 6ᵗʰ July 1632 (Baker, *Sickness*, p. 127).
60. McCann, *Life*, p. 170, note 16, where *Confession* is placed 'probably in 1628'.
61. See above, note 35.
62. McCann, *Life*, pp. 174–75, note 25.
63. Baker, *Book H*, p. 30. *Anchor* was approved on 11ᵗʰ November 1629, and *Book H* on 24ᵗʰ December 1629, but these are only *termini ad quem*, For *Anchor*, see Augustine Baker, *The Anchor of the Spirit; The Apologie; Summarie of Perfection* in J. Clark (ed.), *Analecta Cartusiana*, 119:30 (Salzburg: 2008). The approbation for *Anchor* is found on p. 1.
64. Baker, *Anchor*, p. 16, note 1. McCann, *Life*, p. 193, note 55, states there is uncertainty as to whether Baker wrote a distinct treatise *Remedies*, as distinct from the *Remedies against Temptations* incorporated with *Anchor*. Augustine Baker, *A Secure Stay in all Temptations* in J. Clark (ed.), *Analecta Cartusiana*, 119:8 (Salzburg: 1998), p. 105, states: 'The book of *Remedies* is for this purpose also, and so is all the later part of *The Anchor of the Spirit*.' This is ambiguous. No separate treatise *Remedies* by Baker is known to exist.

Prefixed to Baker's treatise of *Discretion* is his 'Profession' concerning his writings, in which he submits them to the judgement of his superiors. This is dated 10th August 1628 or perhaps 1st August 1628.[65] *Discretion* itself was approved on 24th December 1629.[66] *Discretion* refers to another treatise planned but not yet written, concerning the Jesuit, Hieronymus Platus' book on the religious life. This would be included in due course.[67]

Baker makes recurrent reference in his books to *The Abridgment of Perfection*, a book which was the fruit of collaboration between the lay-woman, Isabella Christina Bellinzaga of Milan and her Jesuit director, Achille Gagliardi. The English version was made by Lady Mary Percy, Abbess of the English Benedictine nuns at Brussels, and was first printed in 1612. In the edition of 1625 the book was attributed to Gagliardi rather than to Isabella Bellinzaga, and the translation to the Jesuit Anthony Hopkins rather than to Abbess Percy. The edition of 1628 reinstated Abbess Percy as the translator, while still attributing the book to Gagliardi. Baker's *Enquiry*, resolving both these matters, is dated 1st February 1629.[68] At the beginning of this treatise, Baker speaks of a promise that he made earlier in *Discretion* to deal with this topic.[69]

However, in the text of *Discretion* as we have it, Baker says on this point: 'I have made a distinct treatise of it in a

---

65. Augustine Baker, *Discretion* in J. Clark (ed.), *Analecta Cartusiana*, 119:9 (Salzburg: 1999), pp.1–3, with date of 10th August 1628. Likewise, Colwich Abbey ms. 5. But Ampleforth Abbey ms. 136 gives: 1° August 1628 (information received from Dame Benedict Rowell, Colwich Abbey, and Dom Anselm Cramer, Ampleforth Abbey).

66. Baker, *Discretion*, p. 1.

67. Baker, *Discretion*, p. 90–91. Baker's treatise on Platus' book is *Five Treatises*, pp. 34–40.

68. Augustine Baker, *An Enquiry about the Author of the Treatises of the Abridgement and Ladder of Perfection; The Mirror of Patience and Resignation; Love of Enemies; All Virtues in General; Spiritual Emblems* in J. Clark (ed.), *Analecta Cartusiana*, 119:33 (Salzburg: 2010), p. 23.

69. Baker, *Enquiry*, p. 2.

book... called *An Enquiry*...⁷⁰, an indication that Baker was still working on *Discretion* and *Enquiry* concurrently.

The *Spiritual Alphabet*, which may be placed in 1628–1629,[71] was approved on 27th August 1629.[72] Among other Baker texts to which it refers are *Discretion*,[73] and the treatise on meditation on the Passion which is the second of five items in *Book H*.[74] *Alphabet* is described on the title-page as being 'for the use of beginners'.[75] It may be understood as a sequel to *Directions for Contemplation*, covering more basic ground, and well adapted to the training of novices. Baker's *Apology*, a defence of his spiritual teaching as intended specifically for contemplative nuns, and not for general readership, has no indication of date, but refers to *Discretion* as already written.[76] Justin McCann thought that it was probably written in the early part of 1629.[77]

Five Treatises must have been completed in 1629.[78] It was approved on 30th October of that year.[79] We saw earlier that one of the five treatises had been promised in *Discretion*. In *A Secure Stay*, there is a reference to the treatise of *Scandals*, as one of the five treatises in this book.[80] The second, and last, part of *Stay* was completed by Baker on 19th October 1629,[81] later than the date when *Alphabet* was approved. The first part of *Stay* was approved on 14th November that year.[82]

70. Baker, *Discretion*, p. 22.
71. McCann, *Life*, p. 162, note 4.
72. Baker, *Alphabet*, p. 1. The approbation was renewed on 4th April 1634.
73. Baker, *Alphabet*, pp. 13–14.
74. Baker, *Alphabet*, p. 8 (=Baker, *Book H*, pp. 6–25).
75. Baker, *Alphabet*, p. 1.
76. Baker, *Apology*, p. 68.
77. McCann, *Life*, pp. 164 65, note 7.
78. McCann, *Life*, p. 179, note 32, places it '1627–29'. No doubt the various treatises were written over a period of time.
79. Baker, *Five Treatises*, p. 1.
80. Baker, *Stay*, p. 68.
81. Baker, *Stay*, p. 153.
82. Baker, *Stay*, p. 1.

Just as there is an overlap in cross-references between *Discretion* and *Enquiry*, so there is between *Alphabet* and *Stay*. Thus *Stay* remarks that *Alphabet* and *Confession* have both already been approved by superiors.[83] But the existing text of *Alphabet*, referring to a particular point, says: 'You shall find it best expressed in the later end of the second part of the *Stay*'.[84] So either *Stay* was already well in progress when this was written, or else there has been a subsequent adjustment in the text of *Alphabet*. *Order of Teaching* was approved on 24th December 1629.[85] In it, Baker refers the reader to *Alphabet* and to 'other treatises'. The treatise was left unfinished, but was rounded off with a reference to the teaching on aspirations in *Book G*.[86] Justin McCann suggested that the short piece on the *Library* should also be placed 'about 1629',[87] and the treatise on *Admittance* 'about 1630'.[88]

A number of substantial treatises or compilations belong to the period 1629/30 – 1633, the later part of Baker's time at Cambrai. *Secretum*, as we have said,[89] was begun towards the end of 1629 and finished early in 1630. This marks a new development in Baker's writing, and also a movement towards the diffuseness which we find in a number of his

---

83. Baker, *Stay*, p. 108. *Alphabet* was approved on 27th August 1629, *Confession* on 17th September 1629.

84. Baker, *Alphabet*, p. 6.

85. Baker, *Collections I–III*, p. 41. The approbation for *Collections II* includes *Order*, which is said to be 'added to the said *Collections*'.

86. Baker, *Order*, p. 80 and p. 63, where the copyist further refers the reader to Baker's *Book D*.

87. McCann, *Life*, p. 186, note 44. Anselm Cramer, '"The Libraries of this Howse". Augustine Baker's Community and their Books', in *'Stand up to Godwards': Essays in Mystical and Monastic Theology in honour of the Reverend John Clark on his Sixty-fifth Birthday*, in J. Hogg (ed.), *Analecta Cartusiana*, 204 (Salzburg: 2002), pp. 103–110, for an edition with introduction.

88. McCann, *Life*, pp. 161–62, note 2. 'Certeine Collections out of y[e] book of *Admittance*' in J. Clark (ed.), *Analecta Cartusiana*, 119:34 (Salzburg: 2011), pp. 104–112.

89. See above, note 1.

later productions. Hitherto, he had been busy, in addition to his original compositions, with making English versions of Latin texts; now he sets out to produce a commentary on the *Cloud of Unknowing*. We do not know when Baker first had access to the manuscript of the *Cloud*. There is a reference to the *Cloud* in *Book H*, but since the text continues directly with a reference to Baker's exposition of the *Cloud*, presumably as this is found in his *Secretum*,[90] which was only written, or at any rate completed, at the end of 1629 or early in 1630, it would appear that this reference is an addition to the text made later by Baker. The *Cloud* is not included in the reading-list in *Alphabet*,[91] but this could possibly be because it was considered unsuitable for beginners. The *Secretum* sets out to provide a commentary on a potentially difficult text, and one which, as Baker points out, anticipates some of the teaching of Alphonsus of Madrid, Benet Canfield, and Barbanson, on which he has been drawing.[92] In the event, Part One of the *Secretum* includes much material for Baker's spiritual autobiography, while the commentary on the *Cloud*, only touching on selected points, is found in Part Two. Material from the *Abridgement* and from Angela of Foligno is appended to Part One; material from Blosius and Barbanson follows the commentary in Part Two, followed by an extended discussion by Baker of spiritual aridity and contemplation, with more autobiographical material.

A further major undertaking at this time was the compilation of *Idiot's Devotion*, a great collection of spiritual exercises and prayers. This was originally planned to be in thirteen parts, but eventually rose to sixteen.[93] Justin

---

90. Baker, *Book H*, p. 25. But the text continues, 'And this poynt I haue more fully expressed in my exposition vpon the said *Clowde*'.
91. Baker, *Alphabet*, pp. 39–40.
92. Baker, *Secretum*, pp. 6–9.
93. Augustine Baker, *Idiot's Devotion: Directions; Parts One and Two* in J. Clark (ed.), *Analecta Cartusiana*, 119:29 (Salzburg: 2008), pp. ii–iii. In addition to this edition of *Ideot's Devotion Parts One and Two*, with *Directions*, there is Augustine Baker, *Ideot's Devotion—The Penitent* in J. Clark (ed.), *Analecta Cartusiana*, 265 (Salzburg: 2008), pp. 52–94.

McCann proposed[94] that the book of exercises, *Idiot's Devotion A*, was compiled 'in and around 1630'. This is no doubt true. We should suppose, however, that the collections of exercises and prayers had been in formation for some time. Baker specifically says that the Second and Third Parts owe much to Dame Gertrude More.[95] The *Directions for Idiot's Devotion (Idiot's Devotion B)*, a substantial piece in its own right, is dated 1st July 1630.[96]

It was probably around 1630 that Baker compiled his *Examples*, a large work in at least six parts, consisting of translated extracts from *Vitae Patrum*, Cassian's *Collationes*, and other sources.[97] Appropriately, following so much work already done for the Cambrai nuns, Baker in 1631 compiled his *Exposition* of St Benedict's *Rule*, another large undertaking. The dedicatory letter, addressed to Abbess Catherine Gascoigne, is dated 28th June 1631.[98] In this, Baker says that the work has taken him five months -another intensive effort.

Baker's *Collections out of the book called Death*, in which he speaks of himself as seriously ill and faced with the possibility of death, is dated 6th July 1632.[99] This date may refer to the date when he excerpted the book, rather than to when he first wrote it. The fact that these *Collections* are asssociated with *Sickness* in the manuscript tradition does not in itself mean that the two works were written at, or about, the same time; the association could well be due to the link in subject-matter.

Vox Clamantis was conceived as an introduction to Walter Hilton's *Scale of Perfection*, of which, with the same author's *Mixed Life*, Baker was making at the time a modernised ver-

---

94. McCann, *Life*, p. 183, note 39.
95. Baker, *Life ... of Dame Gertrude More*, p. 45.
96. Baker, *Idiot's Devotion*, p. 67.
97. McCann, *Life*, p. 177, note 29. McCann & Connolly (eds.), 'Memorials', p. 122, note 185, states that it was compiled at Cambrai.
98. Augustine Baker, *St Benedict's Rule* in J. Clark (ed.), *Analecta Cartusiana*, 119:24 (3 vols.) (Salzburg: 2005), vol. 1, p. 1.
99. Baker, *Death*, (see note 8), p. 127.

sion from the early printed edition.[100] This version is in two parts, the first dated 28th August 1632, and the second, 22 December of the same year, so that *Vox Clamantis* may be dated to the second part of 1632.[101] Baker's use of the *Scale of Perfection*, for which, like the *Cloud*, he had a high respect, goes further back: the famous passage of the pilgrim going to Jerusalem is discussed in *Sickness*[102], and a transcript of it forms the conclusion to *Stay*.[103] This passage, as a distinct unit, is also in the reading-list in *Alphabet*.[104] In the event, the use made of Hilton in this treatise is small. The treatise is substantially devoted to showing how St Benedict's *Rule* provides careful legislation for the exterior life of a religious community, precisely with a view to fostering that interior docility to the Spirit which Baker sought for himself and for the nuns: in some measure it follows on from *Doubts and Calls*. Less happily, the controversy with Father Francis Hull was looming in the later part of 1632. The two statements in defence of Baker's teaching and practice, addressed to the President of the English Benedictine Congregation, are to be found in *Vindication*,[105] the first signed by Baker, Abbess Catherine Gascoigne, and Dame Gertrude More, and the second by Baker alone, are dated 6th September 1632 and November 1632 respectively. The two short *Protestations*, of which the first is a defence of the doctrine of the divine call in *Vox Clamantis*, were composed in connection with the same controversy, leading up to the meeting of the General Chapter in August 1633.[106]

---

100. Baker, *Vox Clamantis*, p. 1.
101. McCann, *Life*, pp. 181–82, note 37, pp. 199–200, note 67.
102. Baker, *Sickness* pp. 105–107.
103. Baker, *Stay*, pp. 144–152.
104. Baker, *Alphabet*, p. 39.
105. McCann, *Life*, p. 199, note 66. Selections from *Vindication* are printed in Baker, *Life ...of Dame Gertrude More*, pp. 366–78.
106. McCann, *Life*, p. 190, note 52. The two *Protestations* are printed in Baker, *The Life...of Dame Gertrude More*, pp. 347–350, and Baker, *Vox Clamantis*, pp. 205–07.

After Baker was moved to Douai in 1633, there is a change in his writings, reflecting the changed circumstances in which he was placed. Father Leander Prichard, Baker's biographer, heard him say at Douai that he would now find it impossible to write the sort of instructions on contemplation which he had formerly written for the nuns.[107] He was now writing for men, or was at any rate surrounded by men. There is more appeal to the intellect and to reasoning, and Baker is more defensive and argumentative. Prichard says that some time before Baker left Douai for England in 1638, his facility for writing had dried up.[108]

Baker's *Remains*, consisting originally of occasional pieces written for the Cambrai nuns, continued to be expanded at Douai. The opening piece was completed on 4th September 1633, and the whole received approval on 4th April 1634.[109]

Dame Gertrude More had died at Cambrai on 17th August 1633, shortly after Baker's departure. After her death, her devotional papers were passed to Baker at Douai. He arranged them, presumably in 1634, and gave them the title *Confessiones Amantis* (known as *More B*).[110] This would eventually be published under the editorship of Dom Francis Gascoigne in 1658. Baker also worked on Dame Gertrude's *Life* (known as *More A*). In the earlier part of this work, he refers to the date when she took the habit, which was in December 1623, stating it was nearly twelve years ago, so the *Life* cannot have been finished before 1635.[111]

In his *Life* of Dame Gertrude, Baker several times refers to a treatise by Brother Ricerius of Marchia, and expresses

---

107. McCann & Connolly, ed., 'Memorials', p. 122, note 185.
108. McCann & Connolly, ed., 'Memorials', p. 123, note 193.
109. See notes 11–12 above. Baker, *Sickness*, p. 27, also has an item in *Remains*.
110. McCann, *Life*, pp 188–89, note 50. Augustine Baker, *Confessiones Amantis: The Spiritual Exercises of ... Dame Gertrude More*, in J. Clark (ed.), *Analecta Cartusiana*, 119:27 (Salzburg: 2007).
111. McCann, *Life*, p, 188, note 49. Baker, *Life ... of Dame Gertrude More*, p. liii, note 58; Chapter 4, p. 15.

his intention of appending it to her collected papers.[112] A considerable fragment of an English version exists, which may be his.[113]

Justin McCann though it probable that Baker's translation of the *Relation of Fr Balthasar Alvarez* to the Jesuit General concerning his prayer was made at Douai about 1635.[114] In fact Baker had been familiar with Luis de la Puente's *Life* of Alvarez for some years before his; there is a reference to it already in *Vox Clamantis*.[115] His *Life* of Dame Gertrude More has a reference to this work, on the controversy that arose within the Society of Jesus over Father Alvarez's form of prayer,[116] and there is another reference to it in *Spiritual Emblems*.[117]

Baker's *Mirror of Patience and Resignation* is specifically dated 30th July 1635.[118] This was a sequel to the now lost treatise of *Refection*.[119] Associated with *Mirror* in the manuscript tradition are *Love of Enemies* and *All Virtues*.[120] Justin McCann thought that *Spiritual Emblems* was written 'probably in 1636'. One passage was being written on St Matthew's feast (21st September).[121] But in one place, clearly referring to *Mirror*, it refers to it as 'the precedent treatise'.[122] This might mean that *Mirror* was written immediately before it in time, or it might alternatively mean that

---

112. Baker, *Life ... of Dame Gertrude More*, pp. 286–87.
113. McCann, *Life*, pp. 193–94, note 57. *The Words of Brother Ricerius of Marchia* in J. Clark (ed.), *Analecta Cartusiana*, 119:34 (Salzburg: 2011), pp. 133–138.
114. McCann, *Life*, p. 163, note 5. J. Clark, *Dom Augustine Baker's Translation of the 'Relation' of Fr Balthasar Alvarez* in *Analecta Cartusiana*, 236 (Salzburg: 2005), pp. 5–14.
115. Baker, *Vox Clamantis*, p. 97.
116. Baker, *Life ... of Dame Gertrude More*, pp. 140–146.
117. Baker, *Spiritual Emblems*, p. 124. (See note 68).
118. Baker, *Mirror*, p. 70. (See note 68).
119. Baker, *Mirror*, p. 29. McCann, *Life*, pp. 190–91, note 53.
120. McCann, *Life*, p. 186, note 45, p. 162, note 3.
121. McCann, *Life*, pp. 175–76, note 27. Baker, *Spiritual Emblems*, p. 140.
122. Baker, *Spiritual Emblems*, p. 91.

it is because of its similarity in subject-matter at this point that Baker is referring back to it. The treatise on the *Fall and Restitution of Man*, written at Douai, is dated 14th August 1635.[123] The *Treatise of the English Mission* (known as *Mission A*) may be dated 1635–36.[124] Baker also wrote his treatise *Concerning his own Life* (known as *Autobiography*), to which are prefixed *Rythms*. The *Rythms* are specifically dated July 1636.[125] There is also his long and rather unwieldy *Conversio Morum*, emphasising the obligation of mental prayer in the monastic life; a note appended to this specifically places this treatise in 1636.[126] Dame Margaret Gascoigne, a younger sister of Abbess Catherine Gascoigne, died on 16th August 1637. It is to this year that Baker's *Life and Death of Dame Margaret* (known as *Gascoigne A*), and his arrangement of her *Devotions* (known as *Gascoigne B*) may be ascribed.[127] The lengthy *Flagellum Euchomachorum*, continuing the defence of mental prayer made in *Conversio Morum*, is dated 15th December 1637.[128] The *Introduction* to the *Treatise of the English Mission* (known as *Mission B*), in which Baker was unwise enough to make a barely veiled personal criticism of President Rudesind Barlow, and which led to his being sent on the English Mission, was finished a few days before Lent 1638.[129] His last work written at Douai, the brief *Summary of Perfection*, dedicated to the Abbess of

---

123. McCann, '*Ten More Baker Mss.*', p. 81.
124. McCann, *Life*, p. 187, note 47.
125. McCann & Connolly, ed., 'Memorials', p. 3. McCann ascribed the writing of *Autobiography* to the winter of 1637–38 (*Life*, p. 165, note 8), but this is not certain.
126. Augustine Baker, *Conversio Morum* in J. Clark (ed.), *Analecta Cartusiana*, 119:25, 2 vols. (Salzburg: 2007), p. 341.
127. McCann, *Life*, pp. 180–81, notes 34–5. Baker, *Life and Death of Dame Margaret Gascoigne*, (see note 54). Baker, *Devotions of Dame Margaret Gascoigne*. (See note 52).
128. McCann, *Life*, pp. 179–80, note 33. Baker, *Conversio Morum*, p. 341, has an additional note, dated 3rd December 1637, which refers to *Flagellum* as already written.
129. McCann & Connolly (eds.), 'Memorials', p. 141, note 242.

the English Poor Clares at Aire, is dated 10th April 1638.[130] Father Baker's *Dicta sive Sententiae sanctorum Patrum*,[131] a compilation in centuries of instructions from patristic and mediaeval writers, is all in Latin, and so cannot have been made for the Cambrai nuns. Its wide range indicates access to a good theological library, and so it may be assigned to Father Baker's time at Douai, though the date of its compilation is unclear.

A PROVISIONAL CHRONOLOGY FOR DOM AUGUSTINE BAKER'S WRITINGS TO 1629

1627

Book A
Book B
Book C

1627/1628

Tauler Part 1 – and more
Bonilla – Quiet of the Soul
Blosius: Spiritual Institution – and more?
Harphius: Twelve Mortifications

1628

Sickness
Confession
Book D
Book E
Collections I–III (Harphius, Barbanson, etc.).
Tauler Part 4
(Collections in Quarto)
Doubts and Calls Part 1 (+ Parts 2 and 3)
Book F

---

130. Baker, *Apologie*, p. 102, (see note 63).
131. McCann, *Life*, p. 173, note 23. McCann, 'Ten More Baker Mss.', p. 81.

Book G
Anchor of the Spirit/Remedies against Temptations.
Book H
Discretion

1628/1629

Translations from Thomas à Kempis
Spiritual Alphabet

1629

Enquiry (about the authorship of *The Abridgement of Perfection*)
Apology
Five Treatises
A Secure Stay in all Temptations
Order of Teaching
Library(?)
Secretum Part 1 – 1st December
Secretum Part 2 – end of 1629/early 1630

The dates indicated are those for completion; some of the composite works, notably collections of translations, and books containing more than one treatise, may have been some time in the making. One treatise in *Remains* is mentioned in *Secretum*, but material in this volume was still being added in 1633 after Baker was moved to Douai.

9

Abbot Blosius and Father Baker

J. T. RHODES

François Louis de Blois, or Ludovicus Blosius (1506–1566), was of noble birth and was just fourteen when he entered his local Benedictine Abbey of Liessies, near Avesne-sur-Helpe, some 35 miles south-east of Cambrai. In about 1522 he was sent to Ghent for further studies and two years later he went on to the famous Collegium Trilingue at Louvain, although he does not seem to have taken any degree. He returned to Liessies in 1530 to succeed Abbot Gilles Gippus, who had served since 1499 and he remained there as abbot until his death, despite offers of preferment, including Archbishop of Cambrai. The abbey had been in decline for many years: observance of the Rule was very lax, monks were involved in many activities outside the cloister, spirituality was tepid and the financial state insecure. But the monks were comfortable and there was no appetite for change. The young abbot set a personal example of strict observance, but it was not until the upheavals caused by the resumption of war between France and Spain in 1537 that Blosius was able to act. The abbey was in unsafe border territory, so most of the monks dispersed to other (equally lax) houses; just three of them chose to accompany their abbot to live in strict observance of the Rule. A few others joined them and by the time they returned to Liessies reform became a possibility. But it was a mitigated observance that Blosius set out in his *Liber Statuorum* for the abbey, which was approved in 1545. These Statutes were subsequently adopted by other Benedictine communities in Hainault and elsewhere and influenced several others;[1] Blosius had obviously got the balance right. The observance of choir Offices was central and priests were encouraged to say Mass daily; the transcription of manuscripts was recommended for manual work. The management of Liessies was greatly improved, far more was given in alms, new buildings were provided, library resources improved and perhaps it was at this time that the famous collection of paintings, including a series of religious founders, was begun.[2]

Despite his influence on Benedictine reform it was as a spiritual writer that Blosius became famous in the mid-sixteenth century, and his works have remained in print until our own times.[3] From his first publication, *Speculum monachorum* in 1538 under the pseudonym Dacryanus until his death, at least forty-three editions of his works were published. Of these the *Speculum monachorum* and the *Institutio spiritualis* were the most popular; Lamennais declared the former to be superior even to the *Imitation of Christ*.[4] A collected edition of his works by his confrère, Froius, appeared in 1568, going through nine editions up to 1626; the definitive edition of his *Opera* appeared from the Plantin offices in Antwerp in 1632, edited by another Abbot of

---

1. G. de Blois, trans. Lady Lovat, *A Benedictine of the sixteenth century (Blosius)* (Dublin & London: 1878); A. Baudrillart, A. De Meyer, Et. Van Cauwenbergh (eds.), *Dictionnaire d'histoire et de géographie ecclesiastique*, vol. ix, cols. 228–242 (Paris: 1937); M. Viller (ed.), *Dictionnaire de spiritualité* (Paris: 1937), vol. I, cols. 1730–738.
2. Most were dispersed or destroyed in 1792 but a few are said (by Wikipedia) to survive in local churches.
3. e.g. Blosius, *Comfort of the afflicted* (London: 2000) by the St Austin press.
4. Baudrillart et al, *Dictionnaire*, ix, col 231, for Lamennais' French translation of 1820.

Liessies, Antonius de Winghe. Blosius' works were also published with other popular works, thus his *Enchiridion parvulorum* was added to the 1580 Lyon edition of the *Theologia mystica* (previously known as the *Theologia germanica*) and his *Brevis regula* was appended to the Cologne 1582 and later editions of the *Imitatio Christi* and to J. Pomière's *Traité de la vie contemplative*, (Paris 1605). His own works were also anthologised, notably the *Igniarium divini amoris seu precationes piae ex operibus V. P. Ludovici Blosii... excerpta*, published from the Plantin office at Antwerp in 1635; the selection was probably made by Antonius de Winghe, since like the *Opera* it is well organised with useful indices. It refers to the subject divisions of the larger work and comes from the same printer. It provided a pocket-sized digest of his works for devotional use. Even more concise was J. B. Mayer's *Calendarium Benedictinum, id est sententiae selectae ex libris ... Ludovici Blosii ... collectae & pro singulis totius anni diebus distributae*, (Salzburg: 1664).

During the sixteenth century Blosius' Latin works were published in France, Flanders, Germany, Italy and Spain, but it was not until 1859 that a *Manuale vitae spiritualis continens Ludovici Blosii* was printed in London, edited by the President of Ushaw College, Charles Newsham, for the use of his students;[5] the preface by Cardinal Wiseman waxed lyrical in praise of Blosius. Similarly, French, Dutch, German and Italian translations of his works were available by 1562 with Spanish titles from 1587. The earliest English translations were all selections added onto other publications. The 1584, and later editions, of Loarte's *Exercise of a Christian life*[6] included 'certaine very devout exercises and prayers' from Blosius; Henry Garnet SJ included the rosary from *Conclave animae fidelis* in chapter 5 of the editions of

---

5. See the 'In memoriam' to Wilberforce's translation of Blosius' *The sanctuary of the faithful soul* (Westminster: 1905).
6. A. F. Allison & D. M. Rogers, *The Contemporary Printed Literature of the English Counter-Reformation between 1558 and 1640. Volume II: Works in English* (Aldershot: 1994), hereafter *ARCR* II, 64–66.

his *Societie of the rosary*, 1593–4, 1596-7, 1624;[7] 'Thirteene short precepts' from his *Brevis regula* were appended to *Desiderius*,[8] 1604, and 'An epistle of Ludovicus Blosius, written to an especiall friend, upon the perfecting and publishing of his work entitled *The Parlour of the Soule*' was included in Richard Brathwaite's fascinating collection, *A spiritual spicerie*, London, 1638.[9]

The abbot of Liessies was famous throughout Europe. The Emperor Charles V is said to have read the prayers of the *Cimeliarchio* daily, and his son, Philip II, was apparently reciting one of its prayers on his deathbed. Jesuit novices were recommended to familiarise themselves with his teachings. Blosius had helped the Jesuits establish themselves in the Low Countries in 1542, and in 1552, together with some of his confrères, he made the Exercises in Louvain and thereafter expected his novices to have some experience of them. Bellarmine praised the *Institutio spiritualis*, as did Francis of Sales, and in 1632 the life of Louis de Blois was included in the Bollandists' *Acta sanctorum*.

One can speculate as to why Blosius' works did not appeal to English publishers and translators, whereas his contemporary, Luis de Granada, 1505–1588, had ten English titles in some thirty-four editions c.1580–1634, with twenty of them published in London.[10] Like Blosius, Granada encouraged the practice of prayer, the cultivation of virtue, contempt for the world and personal mortification; he also cited the Rhineland mystics, especially Tauler, as well as Catherine of Siena. But Granada's emphasis was on a godly and virtuous life; prayer, or rather meditation, was only one facet of this, with equal emphasis being placed on obedience to the commandments, use of the sacraments,

---

7. *ARCR* II, 319–321.
8. *ARCR* II, 889.
9. A. W. Pollard & G. R. Redgrave, ed, *A Short-Title catalogue of Books Printed in England, Scotland, & Ireland*, Vol. I (2nd ed, London: 1986), hereafter *STC* 3586, pp. 290 – 303. It is not obviously translated from Blosius' *Conclave animae*.
10. *STC* 16899.3 – 16922a.7.

reading and good works. Blosius' main focus was on the interior life, devotion to the Person of Christ, especially his Heart[11] and his Passion, the renunciation of all self-will; religious were to live up to their profession, and above all, his readers were encouraged to seek an ever closer intimacy with God. The abbot was perhaps too redolent of the medieval spirituality that England had abandoned at the Reformation and not sufficiently 'regulated' to appeal to recusant translators.

Blosius was part of an ongoing tradition which kept alive the teachings of earlier mystics and visionaries. The Brethren of the Common Life had recommended the works of Suso and Ruusbroec and kept their writings in circulation.[12] In 1513 Jacques Lefèvre d'Etaples published his *Liber trium virorum et trium spiritualium virginum* which made available Hildegard's *Scivias*, Elizabeth of Schonau's visions and Mechthild's *Flowing Light of the Godhead*. The Carthusians of Cologne probably did most to keep the medieval mystical authors in circulation: Lanspergius published St Gertrude in 1536 and Fr Baker was much helped by his *Speculum perfectionis*[13] but Surius was the most prolific translator and editor, dedicating his edition of Suso to Blosius.[14] The abbot maintained this tradition since many of his publications were as much quotation as original, although in the sixteenth century that was not considered a weakness. His *Psychagogia* was culled from the works of Saints Augustine and Gregory and St John Chrysostom (which he had translated from the Greek in

---

11. J. Bainvel, *Devotion to the Sacred Heart of Jesus* (London: 1924), traces development of the devotion through Mechtild, Gertrude and Tauler to Lanspergius and Blosius, pp. 175, 178–82.
12. J. Van Engen (ed.), *Devotio moderna: basic writings*. Classics of western spirituality (Mahwah: 1988), pp. 80, 82, 83.
13. P. Salvin & S. Cressy, *The Life of Father Augustine Baker O.S.B.* in J. McCann (ed.), *Analecta Cartusiana*, 119:20 (Salzburg: 1997), p. 86.
14. Latin editions of works by Tauler, Ruusbroec, Suso and Herph translated and edited by Surius were published at Cologne between 1548 and 1588.

his student days), the *Dicta quorumdam patrum aurea* was drawn from Tauler, Ruusbroec, Alonso of Madrid and others. In the preface to *Canon vitae spiritualis*, (Louvain, 1539), he tells his dedicatee, Cardinal Francisco de Quignones (of the reformed breviary): 'totum opusculum nihil aliud est quam farrago quidam piorum documentorum'. The *Institutio spiritualis* had been *compiled* originally for his own use and he told Florentius a Monte that the appendix was 'drawn almost entirely from different places in the works of Doctor John Tauler. I have not always quoted his exact words, but I have taken care to give the sense of what he writes'.[15] He must have had access to a considerable library and one wonders how much was inherited and how much he did to improve the library at Liessies. Indeed, Fr Baker himself probably had access to it, for in *Conversio Morum*[16] he says of a citation of Florens Radewijns, (a founder of the Brethren of the Common Life): 'the booke out of which I so extracted it pertaining to Laesiensis Abbie,[17] and is not commonlie found in other libraries (as I thinke)'. Fr Peter Salvin, Fr Baker's younger contemporary, certainly visited Liessies and the fonds Liessies at Lille includes seventeenth-century English translations of Blosius' *Rule of a spirituall life* and *The life of St Michtilde*.[18] Access to the library at Liessies would have been an invaluable resource for Baker, and one not too far distant from Cambrai.

But what of Blosius and English readers? Although nothing by Blosius was published in England until 1593–94[19] and translations were meagre, he was not unknown to sixteenth- and seventeenth-century English readers. John Bateman and Miles Buckley who both died in 1559 both

---

15. B. A. Wilberforce, trans., *A book of spiritual instruction... by Ludovicus Blosius* (London: 1925), p. 151.
16. Augustine Baker, *Conversio Morum* in J. Clark (ed.), *Analecta Cartusiana*, 119: 25 (Salzburg: 2007), p. 324.
17. Laesiensis does not appear in place-name dictionaries I have consulted, but Laetiensis = Liessies where Blosius was Abbot.
18. Lille, archives départmentales du nord, 9 H 35, 9 H 36.
19. *ARCR* II, no. 319, Garnet's *The Societie of the rosary*.

possessed a copy of the *Psychagogia* of 1549, while Andrew Perne who died in 1589 had the *Consolatio pusillanimium* of 1570.[20] The 1606 Cologne *Opera Omnia* was given to Thomas Brudenell by his brother John between 1610 and 1612.[21] Various editions of the *Opera* were in English cathedral libraries, as well as a few other works, but it is not clear when they were acquired.[22] The Jesuits at Holbeck also had the 1606 Opera as well as the *Igniarium* of 1635.[23] It seems that Blosius was known in the circle of Lady Falkland (1585/ 86–1639) who translated some of his works.[24] Among the English abroad, John Ramridge had the 1570 *Brevis regula*, which is rather strange since he was murdered in 1568.[25] The 1702 library catalogue of the English Benedictines of St Edmund's, Paris: lists seventeen works by Blosius in Latin, French and Spanish. The library at Colwich contains ten editions in Latin, French and English. I am sure that other copies of Blosius were available in England during the late sixteenth and seventeenth centuries and that many more were to be found in the libraries of exiled English communities.

It seems likely that Father Baker became acquainted with Blosius before he went to Cambrai in 1624. In *Book G* he tells us, and Dr Clark suggests this is autobiographical:

> I also knew a man who, findinge or conceavinge that he could not meditate, & having a good will, he tooke in hand the plaine exercise of acts that is taught & sett downe by Blosius in the *Institution*

---

20. See E. Leedham-Green, *Books in Cambridge inventories*, 2 vols (Cambridge, 1986).
21. N. Barker & D. Quentin, *The library of Thomas Tresham and Thomas Brudenell* (Roxburghe Club: 2006), p. 134.
22. D. J. Shaw et al (eds.), *Cathedral libraries catalogue*, vol. II, pt. 1 (London: 1998), #B.1843–48.
23. H. Dijkgraaf, *The library of a Jesuit community at Holbeck* (Cambridge: 2003), pp. 136, 159.
24. H. Wolfe (ed.), *Elizabeth Cary. Lady Falkland. Life and Letters* (Cambridge: 2001), pp. 106, 207, 221.
25. C. Coppens, *Reading in exile* (Cambridge: 1993), pp. 72, 100.

> (Cap. 10) & he therein continued (but with some great corporall mortification...) very constantly, & at length (after some time) came to an exercise of aspirations wherein he continued but a very short space, beinge called & taken out of them in a passive contemplation...²⁶

Aspirations were characteristic of Blosius' teachings (also of Lanspergius).²⁷ Again, in *The order of teaching* Baker refers to Blosius' teaching on the exercise of acts:

> And so doth Blosius plainly signify, by the exercise of acts which he hath in his *Institution*, the xth, xith, xiith chapters. In which xth chap: he affirmeth, that the exercise of acts, (being but one and the selfsame, without any variety), which he there had set down, being seriously prosecuted, together with the practice of mortification, would bring the soul to mystick union, and to perfection. But yet I understand Blosius, that the partie must not retain propriety in his said exercise of acts, but must leave it when he is called to an higher, as is the exercise of proper aspirations. And I do assure myselfe that the doctrin of Blosius in this point is true. For I know another, (to whom I would herein give as much credit as to Blosius), who in his own experience upon himselfe, found it to be true. I mean, that both Blosius and the said other experienced person do intend, that the exercise of acts (without any precedent use of meditation) being undertaken upon ones first entry into a spirituall life, and being prosecuted with the exercise of mortification, will bring the soul to perfect contemplation.²⁸

One wonders whether Baker's first encounter with the Rhineland mystics and visionaries such as St Gertrude was

---

26. Augustine Baker, *Directions for Contemplation: Book G* in J. Clark (ed.), *Analecta Cartusiana*, 119:13 (Salzburg: 2000), p. 29, perhaps the period 1619–21. Salvin & Cressy, *Life*, p. 86.
27. For example Lanspergius, *Pharetra divini amoris* (1533 etc.).
28. Augustine Baker, *Alphabet and Order* in J. Clark (ed.), *Analecta Cartusiana*, 119: 16 (Salzburg: 2001), p. 75 (contractions silently expanded).

also through Blosius. In *Confession* he comments: '& to this effect doth Rusbrochius write & reprehend, as you find his words in Blosius'.[29] Perhaps the most telling comment on the importance of Blosius to Baker is to be found in the provision of the works of Blosius for the nuns of Cambrai:

> Blosius his workes. Written hande, bound in 7. generall bookes, whereof thes I most comende vnto you: his spirituall Institution...his Mixture or Compounde, and his spirituall table, his looking glasse for monkes. The other bookes contain also good matter for you. But some things in them are not for your use, namely those that concerne the controversies of thes daies. Allso his Psigagoie... will be little or nothing for your use.[30]

The reference to 'written hande' is a reminder that in the sixteenth and seventeenth centuries 'publication' was not confined to print.[31] It was, of course, mainly in manuscript that translations of Blosius circulated among the exiled communities of nuns.

Baker was an active translator, as surviving manuscripts indicate. There is also the Upholland Anthology with its two extracts from Blosius. But he was not the only translator of Blosius' works, and the extent of his translating activity is by no means clear. For instance, the Blosius items in Ampleforth MS 86 are all in Fr Batt's translation. He was professed at Dieulouard in 1615 or 1616, held various positions in the Congregation, but from 1642 until his death in 1651 he lived as a simple monk at St Edmund's, Paris.[32] They are included in: 'The workes of ye thrice

---

29. Augustine Baker, *Treatise of Confession* in J. Clark (ed.), *Analecta Cartusiana*, 119: 23 (Salzburg: 2006), p. 140, see p. 112, n.1.

30. J. T. Rhodes, 'Augustine Baker's reading lists' in *Downside Review* 384 (July 1993), pp. 159–60.

31. See in general: H. Love, *Scribal publication in seventeenth-century England* (Oxford: 1993).

32. Salvin & Cressy, *Life*, pp. 166–67, and J. Clark, *Father Baker's translations from the works of John Tauler in the latin version of Laurentius Surius* in *Analecta Cartusiana* 201 (Salzburg: 2003), pp. 82–89; M. Truran, 'Two

renowned Prelate D. Lewis Blosius Abbot of Lessie in ye Low Countries Monke of ye Holy Order of S. Benet faithfully translated into English by ye Rd Father Batt, Monke of ye English Congregation'.[33] These two volumes were copied by Dom Thomas Witham, professed at St Gregory's 1685, dying in 1729. They belonged to the English Benedictine nuns of Our Lady of Good Hope in Paris where Mother Maura Witham died in 1700 and Mother Christina Witham in 1740. More work is needed on the translations of Blosius. Does the translation of *A solace for such as are sad* copied (perhaps translated?) by Elizabeth Collingwood in 1679 match any other translation? She entered Cambrai in 1677 aged eighteen, but later 'went away'.[34]

Interest in Blosius was not confined to his own order. *His looking glace for the religious* has been among the manuscripts of Syon Abbey since their Lisbon days.[35] In addition to Garnet, other Jesuits who made use of Blosius included Costerus and Arias who also included his rosary among their works. The Poor Clares of Rouen (or Aire) had a late seventeenth-century manuscript: *The spirituall institution out of Blosius*[36] and another manuscript in the same collection[37] contains the whole of the *Institution* together with

---

extracts from the Writings of Blosius in *The Upholland Anthology'*, in *'Stand up to Godwards'*: *Essays in mystical and monastic theology in honour the Reverend John Clark on his sixty-fifth birthday* in J. Hogg (ed.), *Analecta Cartusiana*, 204 (Salzburg: 2002), pp. 157–61; D. M. Rogers, 'Anthony Batt: a forgotten Benedictine translator' in G. A. M. Janssens & F. G. A. M. Aarts (eds.), *Studies in seventeenth-century English literature, history and bibliography*, (Amsterdam, 1984), pp. 179–193.

33. Paris: Bibliothèque Mazarine, MSS 1121–1122, respectively 990 + 92 pages and 1135 + 89 pages.
34. The manuscript is at Ushaw College, Durham.
35. R. Whitford, *A looking glace for the religious* in V. Lawrence (ed.), *Salzburg studies in English literature*, 92: pt. 18, volume 1 (Salzburg & Lewiston: 1991).
36. Durham University, Special Collections, Poor Clares of Darlington, MS 10.
37. Durham University, Special Collections, Poor Clares of Darlington, MS 62.

part of his *Speculum monachorum* as well as Baker's *Matters of confession* and the *Twelve mortifications* of Harphius, some 'instructions from Dr Perin's book' and the 'Instructions of Master Eccardus... lying on his death bed', also associated with Baker but the Eccardus at least is not his translation.[38] It is interesting to find Baker and Blosius both being copied by Franciscans. Some of Baker's principal sources were drawn from the Franciscan family: Harphius, Benet Canfield and Bonilla, whose *Short treatise of the quiet of the soul* of 1658 and 1700 was Baker's only published translation[39] and he wrote the *Summarie of perfection* 'principallie for the Abbesse of the Poor Claires of Ayre'.[40]

Blosius' spiritual works were highly regarded throughout Europe from the mid-sixteenth century. His spirituality was grounded in Scripture, in the church fathers and medieval mystics and visionaries whose works were being published, especially by the Carthusians of Cologne from the 1530s. His extensive citation of these authorities served to make them available to others within the context of his particular understanding of religious life and the development of a personal life of prayer. He gave his readers plenty of practical examples of prayer, particularly the affective 'aspirations' rather than the more formal meditations that became increasingly dominant in the later sixteenth century. The *Institutio spiritualis* and *Speculum monachorum* were his most carefully structured works, as they were his most popular; the majority of Baker's references to Blosius were to his *Institutio*, and especially its final chapter 12. On

---

38. Augustine Baker, *Confession*, for the Baker material. Augustine Baker, *Collections I–III and The Twelve Mortifications of Harphius* in J. Clark (ed.), *Analecta Cartusiana*, 119:21 (Salzburg: 2004), for Harphius. Rhodes, 'Lists', p 163, for Perin. Augustine Baker, *Doubts and Calls* in J. Clark (ed.), *Analecta Cartusiana*, 119:10 (Salzburg: 1999), p. 53, for Eccardus.
39. D. M. Rogers, 'A first check-list of additions and corrections to Clancy's *English Catholic Books, 1641–1700*', *Recusant History*, 13, 2, October 1975, p. 149.
40. Augustine Baker, *Summarie of Perfection* in J. Clark (ed.), *Analecta Cartusiana*, 119:30 (Salzburg: 2008), p. 90.

occasion Blosius sounds almost like St John of the Cross as he describes the joy of the mystical union which both he and Baker saw as the goal of the spiritual and religious life:

> Now the powers of the soul shine like stars and the soul itself is fit to contemplate the abyss of the Godhead with a calm, simple and joyful intuition, without any imagination and without any reflections in the intellect... Hence the soul which contemplates that bright cloud or dark light, leaving itself and flowing into God, is made one spirit with him in the inward essence of the soul and, generated with the eternal Word of God, whom the heavenly Father there shows or brings forth, is renewed in a wonderful manner, and is rendered fit for every good work and exercise.[41]

PUBLICATIONS OF LUDOVICUS BLOSIUS

The publications of Ludovicus Blosius have been culled from many, often obscure, sources and contemporary references, including the 1632 Antwerp edition of his works. What follows is probably the most complete listing available.

1538	*Speculum monachorum* (2 editions)	Louvain
1539	*Canon vitae spiritualis*	Louvain
1540	*Canon vitae spiritualis*	Louvain
1540	*Paradisus animae fidelis*	Antwerp
1548	*Den spieghel der gheestelijcker menschen*	Antwerp
1549	*Psychagogia*	Louvain
1549	*Collyrium haereticorum*	Louvain
1549	*Canon vitae spiritualis*	Louvain
1549	*Cimeliarchion piarum precularum*	Louvain
1549	*Enchiridion parvulorum*	Louvain

---

41. Ludovicus Blosius, *A book of spiritual instruction*, trans. B. A. Wilberforce, edited by a Benedictine of Stanbrook Abbey (London: 1955), Ch. 12, pp. 83 and 95.

1549	*Psychagogia*	Louvain
1549	*Speculum monachorum*	Louvain
1549	*Sacellum animae fidelis*	Louvain
1550	*Den Spiegel der religiosen* (2 editions)	Antwerp
1551	*Institutio spiritualis*	n.p
1553	*Institutio spiritualis*	Louvain
1553	*Institution spirituelle*	Louvain
1554	*Den reghel des geestelijcx levens*	Louvain
1554	*Den reghel des geestelijcx levens*	Antwerp
1554	*Miroir de religion*	Louvain
1554	*Institution spirituelle*	Louvain
1555	*Den rhegel des geestelijcx levens*	Louvain
1555	*Margaritum spirituale*	Louvain
1555	*Brevis regula tyronis spiritualis*	Louvain
1555	*Institutio spiritualis*	Louvain
1555	*Consolatio pusillanimium*	Antwerp
1555	*Consolation pour les pusillanimes*	Antwerp
1558	*Conclave animae fidelis*	Antwerp
1559	*Consolatio pusillanimium*	Antwerp
1560	*Psychagogia*	Antwerp
1560	*Psychagogia*	Louvain
1560	*Vertroostinge der cleynmoedigher...* (incl. Blosius)	Brussels
1562	*Instituzione spirituale*	Florence
1562	*Vertroostinge der cleynmoedigher...* (incl. Blosius)	Brussels
1562	*Faculam illuminandis haereticis*	Louvain
1563	*Augensalblyn vor die eygensinnigen christen*	Cologne
1563	*Cabinet de l'ame fidele*	Louvain
1563	*Speculum monachorum*	Louvain
1564	*Livret elegant & consolable... la regle de la vie spirituelle*	Paris
1564	*Conclave animae fidelis*	Antwerp
1564	*Petit flambeau propre pour illuminer les heretiques*	Louvain

1565?	*Sacellum animae fidelis* Louvain	
1560	*Opera* Brussels	
1568	*Opera omnia* Louvain	
1568	*Vertroostinghe der cleynmoedighe* Brussels	
1569	*Regel des geistlichen Lebens* Dilingen	
1570	*Ein geistlichs Schatz kammerlin der glaubigen Seel* Dilingen	
1570	*Institution spirituelle* Louvain	
1570	*Brevis regula Tyronis spiritualis* Louvain	
1571	*Brevis regula Tyronis spiritualis* Dilingen	
1571	*Opera omnia* Cologne	
1571	*Pusillanimium consolatio* Venice	
1571	*Chrystliche Bildscule oder Wegweiserin* Dilingen	
1572	*Opera omnia* Cologne	
1572	*Petitie table spirituelle* Paris	
1573	*Miroir spirituel* Paris	
1575	*Sacellum animae fidelis* Louvain	
1576	*Miroir spirituel* Paris	
1576	*Consolation des pusillanismes* Liege	
1580	*Fasciculum sacrarum* Cologne	
1580	*Fasciculus piarum precationum* Cologne	
1580	*Theologia mystica (incl. Enchiridion parvulorum)* Lyons	
1582	*Imitatio Christi (incl. Regula brevis)* Cologne	
1583	*Cabinet de l'ame fidelle* Douai	
1583	*Tabella spiritualis (= Sacellum animae fidelis)* Padua	
1585	*Le miroir des religieux et religieuses* Paris	
1585	*Psychagogia* Rome	
1585	*Canon vitae spiritualis* Ingolstadt	
1587	*Psychagogia* Rome	
1587	*Instruccion espiritual y regle breve* Madrid	
1587	*Esperon d'amour divin* Antwerp	
1587	*Extrait de Apologia pro Thaulero* Paris	
1587	*Canon vitae Christiani spiritualis: das ist Rechtschur...* Ingolstadt	

1588	*Breve regola d'un novitio spirituale* n.p
1589	*Opera omnia* Cologne
1589	*Espeio esspiritual* Alcala de Henares
1590	*Vertroostinge der cleynmoedighe* Antwerp
1594	*Vertroostinge der cleynmoedighe* Brussels
1595	*Speculum corona; Monile scriniolum* Douai
1595	*Opuscula quaedam spiritualia* Douai
1596	*Cabinet de l'ame fidelle* Douai
1597	*Obras* Seville
1598	*Obras*Madrid
1598	*Opuscula quaedam spiritualia* Douai
1598	*Opera omnia* n.p
1599	*Institution spirituelle* Douai
1600	*Petite table spirituelle* Paris
1600?	*Collyre pour les heretiques* Antwerp
1601	*Consolation des pusillanimes* Paris
1602	*Obras* Paris
1605	*Obras* Madrid
1605	*Instruction breve* (in J. Pomere, *Traite de la vie contemplative*) Paris
1606	*La concolation des pusillanimes* n.p
1606	*Opera omnia* Cologne
1606	*Obras* Madrid
1606	*Epistola di Dacriano* (in *Imitatione di Christo*) Rome
1607	*Le cabinet de l'ame fidele* Douai
1607	*Specchio de monachi* Genoa
1608	*Las Obras* Madrid
1609	*Fasciculus mellifluorum precatiorum* Cologne
1609	*Obras* Barcelona
1609	*Thresor ou coffret spirituel* Douai
1609	*Consolatio pusillanimum* (in Italian) Venice
1609	*Fasciculus sacrarum* Cologne
1611	*Vertroostinghe der cleynmoedighe* Brussels
1612	*Le miroir des religieux et religieuses* Lyons

1613	*Obras*	Valladolid
1613	*Ibras de Lodovico abad Leainse*	Valladolid
1614	*Obras*	n.p
1615	*Opera omnia*	Cologne
1616	*Miroir des religieux et religieuses* (3 editions)	Lyons
1617	*Le consolation des ames scrupuleuses* (anthol. Ed. Gazet)	Atrecht
1617	*Geistliche Unterweisung*	Cologne
1617	*Psychagogia*	Passau
1618	*Opera omnia*	Cologne
1619	*Las Obras*	Gerona
1619	*Las Obras*	Madrid
1620	*Fasciculus mellifluarum*	Cologne
1620	*Opera omnia*	Antwerp
1622	*Opera omnia*	Paris
1624	*Tabella spiritualis*	Padua
1625	*Opera omnia*	Cologne
1625	*Las Obras*	Pamplona
1626	*Opera omnia*	Augsburg
1628	*Institution spirituelle*	Paris
1629	*Institution spirituelle*	Douai
1630	*Opera et Margaritum spirituale* (2 sep. edns?)	Antwerp
1632	*Opera omnia*	Antwerp
1633	*Opera omnia*	Antwerp
1634	*Bourdon des ames devotes*	Douai
1634	*Preculae ad modum piae*	Douai
1635	*Igniarium divini amoris*	Antwerp
1636	*Himmlischer Seelentrost*	Munich
1636	*Vierslagh der goddelycker liefden*	Antwerp
1638	*An Epistle in R. Brathwait, A spiritual spiceries*	London
1640	*Prieres tres devotes et entretiens interieurs*	Mons
1640	*Prieres tres devotes*	Douai
1641	*Prieres tres devotes*	Antwerp
1641	*Vierslagh der goddelycker liefden*	Antwerp

1641	*Fasciculus mellifluorum praecationum* Paris	
1642	*Institutio spiritualis* (2 editions) Paris	
1642	*Institution spirituelle* Paris	
1643	*Vierslagh der goddelycker liefden* Antwerp	
1643	*Epitome passionis Domini.... Ex ea quam habet Blosius* Brussels	
1646	*La spirituelle et sainte institution* Mons	
1647	*Preculum ad modum piae* n.p	
1650	*Speculum monachorum* (ed. J. Bollandus) Antwerp	
1650	(before, n.d) *Rosarium ex Blosio* Munich	
1651	*Recueil de quelques points de Blosius* Paris	
1653	*Das Leben unser ... Herrens... Iesu Christi* Cologne	
1653	*Monile spirituale* Cologne	
1654	*Dominicae passionis explicatio* Cologne	
1655	*Monile spirituale* Munich	
1655	*Theologia mystica* (includes *Enchiridion parvulorum*) Lyons	
1657	*Institutio spiritualis, das ist Geistliche Vnderweisung* Cologne	
1660	*Consolatio pusillanimium* Cologne	
1663	*Canon vitae... das ist Richschur...* Cologne	
1663	*Geistliche Taffel* Cologne	
1663	*Regel dess geistlichen Lebens* Cologne	
1663	*Certaine devout prayers* Douai	
1664	*Calendarium Benedictinum, sententiae selectae* Salzburg	
1665	*Prieres tres-devotes et entretiens interieurs* Mons	
1665	*Les regles de la vie spirituelle* n.p	
1665	*Handtbuchlein der kleinen... Seelen* Cologne	
1669	*Vertroostinge der cleynmoedige* Louvain	
1670	*Les regles de la vie spirituelle* Mons	
1670	*Soete versuchtingen tot Jesus* (*Sacellum animae*) Antwerp	
1672	*Opera omnia* Campidonae	
1672	*Instruccion de religiosos /Garcia de Cisneros, Blosius etc* Salamanca	

1675   *Troost der zielen* Bruges
1675   *Troost der zielen* Brussels
1676   *Mirrour for monkes* (2 editions) Paris
1678   *Fournice of divine love* Cambrai
1683   *Regel courte et facile* Paris
1685   *Troost der zielen* Ghent
1686   *Troost der zeilen* Brussels
1686   *Furnace of divine love* London
1686   *Seven exercises* London
1689   *Calendarium Benedictinum: das ist Ausserlesne...* Salzburg
1690   *Vertroostinge der kleinmoedige* A'dam
1691   *Obras* Barcelona
1693   *Consolatio pusillanimium: geistlicher Trost* Cologne
1694   *Dominicae passionis: ...Ausslegung dess Leydens* Cologne
1694   *Consolation des affligez...* Mons
1694   *Preculae ad modum piae* Mons
1694   *Speculum monachorum* Mons
1695   *Troost der zielen* Antwerp
1696   *Inwendighe aensprake* Bruges
1696   *Geestelycke onderwysing* Louvain
1697   *Vertroostinghe der kleyn-moedighe* Antwerp
1697   *Explicacion muy excelente de la Passion del Senor* Madrid
1718   *Entretiens spirituels* Liège

The Works of Ludovicus Blosius, as arranged by Antonius de Winghe, Antwerp, 1632

I *PARADISUS ANIMAE FIDELIS*

(i) *Canone vitae spiritualis*
(ii) *Cimeliarchio piarum precularum*
(iii) *Medulla psalmodiae sacrae*
(iv) *Officio horarum de Jesu et Maria*

II *PSYCHAGOGIA seu animae recreatio cum appendice*
Addita est Comparatio Regis et Monachi ex... D. Chrysostom

III *SACELLUM ANIMAE FIDELIS*
(i) *Tabello spiritualis*
(ii) *Preculae admodum piae*
(iii) *Dicta quorumdam patrum vere aurea*

IV *INSTITUTIO SPIRITUALIS, quatuor adduntur appendices:*
(i) *Ex libris Joannis Tauleri & aliorum*
(ii) *Corollarium exercitionem institutionis spiritualis*
(iii) *Piae precationes*
(iv) *Apologia pro Joanne Thaulero*

V *BREVIS REGULA & exercitia quotidiana tyronis spiritualis*

VI *CONSOLATIO PUSILLANIMIUM: cui annectitur Paraclesis divina ex sacris litteris*

VII *MARGARITUM SPIRITUALIA: sex partes dividitur*
(i) *De incarnatione & vita Domini Nostri Jesu ex Thaulero & Rusbrochio*
(ii) *Epitome vitae Christi ex quatuor Evangelistis*
(iii) *Dominicae Passionis explicatio, fere ex Thaulero*
(iv) *Farrago utilissimarum institutionum, potissimum ex Rusbrochio*
(v) *Articuli vitae Christi*
(vi) *Divini amoris igniariolum*

VIII *CONCLAVE ANIMAE FIDELIS in quatuor partes distinctum*

(i) *Speculum spirituale*
(ii) *Monile spiritualis*
(iii) *Corona spiritualis*
(iv) *Scriniolum spirituale*

IX *INSTRUCTIO VITAE ASCETICA qui titulus est novus*

(i) *Speculum monachorum* (by Dacryanus)

(ii) *Enchiridion parvulorum, libri duo, cum precatiunculis &* doxologies
(iii) *Septem exercitia seu meditations pro religiosis tyronibus*

X *POLEMICA, seu defensio vera fidei*
(i) *Collyrii haereticorum libri duo, cum appendice*
(ii) *Facula illuminandis & ab errore revocandis haereticis, cum appendice*
(iii) *Epistole Blosii Gallice scripta iam Latine versa, ad nobilem matronam per haereticos a vera fide seductam*

10

The Spiritual and the Philosophical Quest: Augustine Baker and René Descartes

JOHN COTTINGHAM

It might appear at first sight that the spiritual and even mystical quest on which Augustine Baker was engaged bears little relation to the purely intellectual and theoretical inquiries which occupy philosophers. But in some of my previous writings I have argued that the domains of philosophy and spirituality are not as far apart as they are often represented as being,[1] and this led me to suspect, when I was asked to contribute to this volume,[2] that there might be some interesting links between the religious meditations of Augustine Baker and the philosophical meditations of his famous contemporary, René Descartes.

---

1. See for example J. Cottingham, 'Descartes as Sage: Spiritual Askesis in Cartesian Philosophy', in C. Condren, S. Gaukroger and I. Hunter (eds.), *The Philosopher in Early Modern Europe* (Cambridge: 2006), Ch. 8, pp. 182-201; reproduced in J. Cottingham, *Cartesian Reflections* (Oxford: 2008), Ch. 14.

2. I am most grateful to Abbot Geoffrey Scott for inviting me to participate in the Augustine Baker Symposium held at Douai Abbey on 3 September 2009, and thereby providing me with the stimulus to delve into the writings of Baker, of which I was previously woefully ignorant. From the papers given by the other participants at the Colloquium I learnt a great deal, though I am conscious of how much I still have to learn about 'that mysterious man'.

Both men were born at what we now see as the threshold of the modern age, a half-century or so after the death of Copernicus and not too long after the birth of Galileo. Baker was the older man by some twenty years: he died of the plague in 1641, the year Descartes published his metaphysical masterpiece, the *Meditations on First Philosophy*; Descartes died of pneumonia on an ill-fated visit to Sweden ten years later.

Near contemporaries: yes. But did they have anything else in common? Some people might find it outrageous to mention life of the venerable Benedictine father in the same breath as that of the 'French cavalier'[3] who ushered in the modern philosophical era. Certainly, the former was a paradigm of religious devoutness, while the latter was a champion of independent scientific thinking. But why, on reflection, should these two modes of thought be supposed to be in conflict? To assume that there is, or must be, such a conflict is, in my view, one of the major errors that blights our contemporary intellectual culture. Descartes was, to be sure, a philosopher, and (though he would not have used the modern term) a scientist; but he was also a committed theist. The aim of this paper will be to explore some significant points of contact which can be seen in the way the search for God is conducted in Baker and Descartes respectively. But before we begin, it may be useful to say a brief word about Descartes's modern reputation, which can, I think, seriously prejudice the way we interpret him.

1. The prejudice against Descartes

Descartes was one of the inaugurators of the scientific revolution which laid the foundations of modernity: his conception of a universal template for science, based on clear and distinct mathematical principles, remains one

---

3. The phrase is that of Charles Péguy: 'Descartes, dans l'histoire de la pensée, ce sera toujours ce cavalier français qui partit d'un si bon pas.' *Oeuvres en Prose 1909-1914* (Paris: 1957), p. 1303.

of the corner stones of physics. What is perhaps less well known is that he was a devout Catholic, who placed God at the very centre of his philosophical system. Historically, the Catholic Church, of which Descartes was all his life a member, has been highly suspicious of Cartesian philosophy, regarding it as unorthodox and potentially subversive of the faith. Soon after his death, Descartes's writings were placed by the Church on the 'Index' of prohibited books; and in the succeeding centuries 'the image of Descartes as an anti-clerical and indeed anti-religious force', even though 'deeply contrary to his actual disposition'[4] has proved remarkably resilient. The factors behind this erroneous ecclesiastical view of Descartes as a danger to religion are many. In the first place, he was associated with Galileo as a supporter of the 'new', sun-centred cosmology that was *prima facie* in conflict with biblical statements apparently implying a fixed and central Earth; and although Descartes prudently refrained from publishing his treatise on 'The Universe' (*Le Monde*) following the condemnation of Galileo by the Inquisition in 1633, and despite the fact that he concluded his eventually published major textbook *The Principles of Philosophy* [1644] with a statement of submission to the authority of the Church, his manoeuvres could not entirely shield him from suspicion in the tense and confrontational religious climate of the seventeenth century.

Nowadays, of course, the Church has no problem with a sun-centred planetary system; but, for all that, the received ecclesiastical image of Descartes remains, in many quarters, distinctly negative. In a set of reflections published in the year of his death, the late Pope John Paul II pointed to a period of moral disintegration that had characterized much of the twentieth century, with first the rise of totalitarianism, and later the erosion of traditional family values; and, perhaps surprisingly, he went on to trace the philosophical roots of this moral collapse to some of the central ideas put

---

4. B. Williams, *Descartes: The Project of Pure Enquiry* (Harmondsworth: 1978, repr. 2005), p. 24.

forward by Descartes. The rot started, he maintained, with the way Descartes constructed his philosophy, basing it on the foundation of individual self-awareness, the famous *Cogito ergo sum* ('I am thinking, therefore I exist'):

> In the [philosophy of] the pre-Cartesian period [for example in Aquinas], God as fully self-sufficient being was considered as the indispensable support every created being, and hence for man. The *cogito ergo sum* carried within it a rupture with this line of thought ... The *ens cogitans* (thinking being) became primary. After Descartes, philosophy became a science of pure thought: all that is *being*—the created world, and even the Creator, is situated within the ambit of the Cogito, as contents of human consciousness.[5]

It would indeed be sinister to give primacy to individual consciousness in a way that threatens the existence of an objective basis for reality, value and meaning. But (though some twentieth-century philosophers took this route)[6] it is anachronistic to retroject this conception back on to Descartes himself.

Descartes, to be sure, did begin his search for truth by establishing the indubitable certainty of his own existence.[7]

---

5. Pope John Paul II, *Memory and Identity* (London: 2005), p. 9
6. The orientation alluded to here, centred on the contents of personal consciousness rather than an independent external reality, is indeed one prominent strand in twentieth-century philosophical thought. found most notably in the school of 'phenomenology' founded by Edmund Husserl, whose *Cartesian Meditations* (1931) had argued that 'By my living, by my experiencing and acting, I can enter no world other than the one that gets its sense [*Sinn*] and validity [*Geltung*] in and from me, myself. E. Husserl, *Cartesian Meditations* [*Kartesianische Meditationen*, 1931], trans. D. Cairns (Dordrecht: 1988), Ch. 1, §8.
7. As Descartes puts it in Part Four of his intellectual autobiography, the *Discourse on the Method* [*Discours de la méthode*, 1637], 'seeing that this truth, *I am thinking therefore I exist*, was so firm and sure that even the most extravagant suppositions of the sceptics were incapable of shaking it, I decided that I could accept it without scruple as the first principle of the philosophy I was seeking' (AT VI 32:

Yet it simply does not follow that the 'I' is 'primary' for Descartes, in the sense that it no longer needs the support of a self-subsistent creator, on which traditional theology had insisted. On the contrary, whenever Descartes discusses his 'Cogito' argument, he stresses the frail, temporary nature of his self-awareness: 'I am, I exist—that is certain. But for how long? For as long as I am thinking. For it could be that were I totally to cease from thinking, I should totally cease to exist' (Second Meditation).[8] Not only is such self-awareness a tiny flickering candle of certainty that could be extinguished at any minute, but Descartes soon proceeds to use this very fragility of his thinking as a decisive indicator of his complete dependence on a power greater than himself:

> A lifespan can be divided into countless parts, each completely independent of the others, so that it does not follow from the fact that I existed a little while ago that I must exist now, unless there is some cause which as it were creates me afresh at this moment—that is, which preserves me (Third Meditation).[9]

In the *Meditations*, Descartes expects the reader to follow him along a subjective path of discovery: he begins his meditations 'quite alone', asks what if anything he can be certain of, arrives at the indubitable Cogito. But this almost immediately leads him beyond himself. His very awareness of his ignorance, and other many defects, immediately leads him to measure himself against the idea of something higher and greater. 'For how could I understand that

---

CSM I 127). In this chapter, 'AT' refers to the standard Franco-Latin edition of Descartes by C. Adam & P. Tannery, *Œuvres de Descartes* (12 vols, revised edition, Paris: 1964-76); 'CSM' refers to the English translation by J. Cottingham, R. Stoothoff and D. Murdoch, *The Philosophical Writings of Descartes*, vols I and II (Cambridge: 1985), and 'CSMK' to vol. III, The Correspondence, by the same translators together with A. Kenny, (Cambridge: 1991).

8. René Descartes, *Meditationes de prima philosophia*, (1641), AT VII 27: CSM II 18.
9. AT VII 49: CSM II 33.

I doubted or desired—that is lacked something—and that I was not wholly perfect, unless there were in me some idea of a more perfect being which enabled me to recognize my own defects by comparison?' The priority of the self over God is simply an *epistemic* priority—it simply comes first in the order of discovery, not in the order or reality. So far from initiating a 'rupture' with tradition, Descartes follows a traditional line, going back to Aristotle, and further articulated by St Thomas in the thirteenth century, when he distinguished matters that were 'prior from our point of view' (*priora quoad nos*) from those that were 'prior in themselves' (*priora simpliciter*).¹⁰ As Descartes makes clear in the Third Meditation, the infinite substance that is God is logically, causally and ontological prior—it has 'more reality' that a mere finite substance such as myself. Everyone knows Descartes's famous *Cogito ergo sum*—'I am thinking therefore I exist'. But in the mind's very reflection on itself, the implicit presence of God is presupposed from the outset. As Descartes put it in an earlier work, the *Rules for the Direction of our Intelligence*, in a Cartesian maxim that deserves to be just as well known as its more famous cousin: 'I am, therefore God exists', '*Sum, ergo Deus est*'.¹¹

But what, to conclude these introductory comments on Descartes, shall we say of John Paul II's remark, quoted earlier, that in Descartes's philosophy even the Creator is situated 'within the ambit of the Cogito'? Epistemically that is quite right, in so far as the Cartesian meditator reviews the ideas he finds within himself, and isolates one, the idea of God, for special inquiry. But Descartes's method in the Third Meditation is precisely to focus on the content of that idea as demonstrating that it could *not* have been constructed from his own resources as a thinking ego, but requires the real existence of a self-sufficient author, who 'in creating me, placed this idea in me to be, as it were, the mark of the craftsman stamped on his work' (AT VII

---

10. St Thomas Aquinas, *Summa theologiae* [1266-73], I, q. 2, a. 2.
11. Descartes, *Regulae ad directionem ingenii* [c. 1628], Rule XII (AT X 421: CSM I 46).

51: CSM II 51). The whole procedure is explained by Descartes with great precision in his later work, the *Principles of Philosophy* (1644), where the ontological primacy of God is made crystal clear:

> There is a great advantage in proving the existence of God by this method, that is to say, by means of the idea of God. For the method enables us at the same time to come to know the nature of God, *in so far as the feebleness of our nature allows*. For when we reflect on the idea of God which we were born with, we see that he is eternal, omniscient, omnipotent, the source of all goodness and truth, the creator of all things, and finally, that he possesses within him everything in which we can clearly recognize some perfection that is infinite or unlimited by any imperfection (*Principles*, Part I, art. 22).[12]

2. The interior path to God

It is now time to attempt some comparisons between the Cartesian search for God, just outlined, and that which Augustine Baker describes in such meticulous detail in *Sancta Sophia*. There are, as will already have emerged, some obvious points of contact. Descartes's path to truth is a solitary one: he begins the *Meditations* by observing *solus secedo* — 'I withdraw, on my own'. Baker's path to spiritual purification is self-evidently an interior one: his writings abound in instruction about internal prayer, private contemplation, and the practice of meditation, along with what he calls 'solemn and rigorous retirements', designed to separate us (secular as well as religious) from the 'many

---

12. AT VIIIA 13: CSM I 200. The reason for the (supplied) emphasis will emerge in section 3. For more on the importance of God in Descartes's system, see J. Cottingham, 'The role of God in Descartes's Philosophy', in J. Cottingham (ed.), *Cartesian Reflections* (Oxford, 2008), Ch. 13, on which this section of the present paper draws.

distractive employments and studies' of our day-to-day activities.[13]

These are not mere accidental quirks in the two thinkers, as if they happened to share some curious, idiosyncratic quasi-autistic approach to the projects they had set themselves. The interior, contemplative tradition is of course an integral strand in Christian spirituality. Baker's formation was a Benedictine one, and in Treatise II he praises solitude 'Whatsoever spiritual employment a soul hath, and whensoever she desires to have any conversation with God, solitude is the state most proper for it.'[14] And he goes on to follow St Benedict in quoting Hosea: *ducam eam in solitudinem et loquar ad cor illius* (' I will lead her [the soul] into solitude and speak to her heart' (2:16).[15] Descartes, for his part, was taught by the Jesuits, at the College of La Flèche, near Poitiers, and the decision to write his masterpiece in the form of a six-day programme of personal meditations draws evident inspiration from the *Spiritual Exercises* of the order's founder, Ignatius, originally composed in Spanish in the 1520s.[16]

---

13. Augustine Baker, *Sancta Sophia*, compiled by S. Cressy, (Douai: 1657, repr. Oxford: 2007), Treatise III, Section 2, Ch. 4, §3 (p. 260). References by Treatise, Section, Chapter and Paragraph number are given in this style in all subsequent references to the *Sancta Sophia*, with the page number of the Oxford 2007 reprint supplied in brackets.
14. Baker, *Sancta Sophia*, Tr. II, Sectn i, Ch 6, § 12 (p. 134).
15. Anima ('soul') is a feminine noun in Latin (and many other languages). It is interesting (as Abbot Edmund Power points out in Chapter 1 of the present volume) to see how Baker, writing in English, always follows the 'Latin' rule and uses the feminine pronoun ('she', 'her') when referring to the soul; as Power suggests, this may predispose him to an excessively dualistic or incorporealist view of our human nature. See also section 4 of the present chapter, below.
16. St Ignatius Loyola, *Spiritual Exercises* [*Ejercicios espirituales*, [c. 1525], transl. J. Munitz and P. Endean (Harmondsworth: 1996). A copy of Ignatius' original Spanish manuscript was first published posthumously, in 1615, but there is a Latin translation, dated 1551, probably made by Ignatius himself; and another more polished Latin version, was published in Rome, with papal approval, in 1548, under the title *Exercitia Spiritualia*. Baker's own view of the Jesuits, incidentally, was

The path of solitude and interiority has a long prior history, going back at least to St Augustine's maxim in his treatise *On True Religion*: '*Noli foras ire, in teipsum redi; in interiore homine habitat veritas.*' ('Go not outside, but return within thyself; in the inward man dwelleth the truth.').[17] But why should the truth dwell within us? It is not as if the outside world is devoid of traces of its creator: *Caeli enarrant*, says the Psalmist: the heavens declare the glory of God (19 [18]:1). And St Thomas is quite happy to construct his famous five proofs of God on the basis of inference from features found in the world around us, the outside world. In contrast to this, the interior approach of Augustine, takes its cue from Genesis I, 27: man is made in the image of God, and since God is spirit, not body, it must be above all the structure of the human *mind*, so reasons Augustine, that provides us (albeit in vastly imperfect form) with some insight into the nature of the divine. This theme is taken up, over the centuries, by many spiritual writers. The Franciscan St Bonaventure in his own 'journey of the mind towards God', the *Itinerarium mentis in Deum* (1259), directly harks back to St Augustine when he declares: 'let us return to ourselves, into our mind, so as to reveal the *lux veritatis in facie nostrae mentis*—the light of truth shining in our minds, as through a glass, in which the image of the Blessed Trinity shines forth'.[18]

In this tradition, then, interiority is the path to a greater understanding of God. It is clear enough why this notion should appeal to someone like Baker, who is committed to the religious life, but perhaps less clear what it has to do with the Cartesian programme for establishing new foundations for knowledge. Yet, in a series of reflections often downplayed by modern secular philosophical commentators, Descartes establishes those foundations of knowledge by meditating (as we have seen) on the idea of God he finds

---

a critical one; see Chapter 8 by E. Dutton and V. Van Hyning, 'Augustine Baker and the Mystical Canon', in this volume.

17. St Augustine of Hippo, *De vera religione*, xxxix, 72.
18. St Bonaventure, *Itinerarium mentis in Deum*, III, 1.

directly within himself—an idea whose immeasurable content he quickly realizes he could not have constructed from his own resources, and which must therefore have been placed in him by his creator. The ancient metaphor, comparing God to *light*, with its roots in Plato and in the Fourth Gospel, and so very prominent in Augustine and Bonaventure, now bursts forth in a passage of striking devotional fervour, at the end of Descartes's Third Meditation: 'here let me pause for a while and gaze with wonder and adoration on the beauty of this immense light, *insofar as the eye of my darkened intellect can bear it'*.[19] And directly following on from this, at the start of the Fourth Meditation, Descartes announces that 'from the contemplation of the true God, in whom all the treasures of wisdom and the sciences lie hidden,' he thinks he can see a way forward to the knowledge of other things.

The phrase just quoted, is, in the Latin wording of Descartes's original text, an almost exact citation from the Bible. In his letter to the Colossians (2:3), St. Paul had talked of 'the mystery of God and of the Father and of Christ, *in whom are hid all the treasures of wisdom and knowledge*' (*in quo sunt omnes thesauri sapientiae et scientiae absconditi*). Descartes, many of whose contemporary readers would have instantly recognized the reference to the Vulgate, subtly changes the singular *scientiae* ('knowledge') to the plural *scientiarum* ('sciences'). For St. Paul, God (in Christ) is the mysterious source of all wisdom; for Descartes, reaching knowledge of God opens the path to 'the sciences'—to true scientific understanding. But the journey begins with the mind's delving into itself. And the same applies to Baker's spiritual journey. As he puts it in the *Sancta Sophia*, 'the foundation of all ... must be (1) a true knowledge of ourselves, and (2) of the all-sufficiency, universal being, infinite perfections, and incomprehensible beauty and goodness of

---

19. Descartes, *Third Meditation*, final paragraph (AT VII 52: CSM II 36). The reason for the (supplied) emphasis will emerge in section 3.

God, who is to be the only object of our contemplation and love.'[20]

3. The struggle from darkness to light.

We discern the light of God by withdrawing to the interior domain of our own reflections. Important though this link between Descartes and Baker may be, the critic may at this point be inclined to question just how far the comparison has got us. Admittedly, there is a general framework of interiority in many spiritual writers, and some of this may have rubbed off in the way Descartes constructed his philosophical meditations. But for all that, are not the two projects, of Baker and Descartes respectively, irreducibly distinct—the one oriented towards personal sanctity—moral and spiritual purification—while the other is directed towards constructing a system of scientific knowledge? Descartes may have revealed elements of his Ignatian upbringing in the style of his writing and thinking, but was not his goal utterly different from Baker's, namely, as he put in the final part of his scientific manifesto, the *Discourse on the Method* (written in French in 1637), securing practical technological benefits that would be *utiles à la vie*—improve the lot of mankind here on earth?

The last point cannot be denied. Solitary reflection is not an end in itself, for Descartes, but a means to an end. But notice that Baker makes precisely the same point. Interiority is not to be sought for its own sake, since it can have deleterious effects. It may be used 'not with a design the more freely to seek God, but instead to study and enrich the mind with knowledge; and then there is always the

---

20. Baker, *Sancta sophia*, Tr. II, Section, i, Ch 1, §3 (p. 112).'The foundation of all our spiritual duties must be a true knowledge (1) of ourselves, our own nothing, our unprofitableness, vileness, and misery, which is to be the object of our aversion and hatred; and (2) of the all-sufficiency, universal being, infinite perfections, and incomprehensible beauty and goodness of God, who is to be the only object of our contemplation and love.'

danger that it may 'puff up the mind with pride', and actually end up being hurtful to the soul.'[21]

Yet this in turn appears to lead us to an even starker point of contrast: for Baker, what is paramount is the moral and spiritual quest; for Descartes, it is the quest for knowledge. For Baker everything is subordinate to the soul's struggle to perfect itself so that it may ultimately be united with God; for Descartes, metaphysical meditation is primarily a means, as he says in the opening paragraph of the *Meditations*, towards the goal of 'establishing something in the sciences that is stable and likely to last.' Without denying this divergence in their primary aims, I want to argue in this third section that the strategy employed by Baker and Descartes for reaching those goals is remarkably similarly, especially in the basic conception of *human nature* which it presupposes.

The key point of comparison lies in two phrases from Descartes which I have already quoted In his quest for knowledge, the Cartesian meditator sees the way forward to God: 'in so far as the feebleness of our nature allows'; or again 'in so far as the eye of my darkened intellect can bear it.'[22]

Both phrases might have come straight from Baker. It is impossible to read either Baker or Descartes without being given a keen sense that the quest for the divine is a *struggle*—a struggle out of darkness towards the light—and one that is hampered from the outset by the flaws in our human nature. Self-knowledge, as we have already seen, is for Baker the first element in the spiritual path, but it is centred on awareness of our own 'nothing, our vileness, unprofitableness and misery'.[23] The theme goes back at least as far as St Augustine, and the doctrine of original sin. Leaving aside the theological complexities involved in interpreting the story of the Fall, what emerges very clearly

---

21. Baker, *Sancta Sophia*, Tr. II, Section i, Ch. 6, §7 (p. 132).
22. See texts cited above, at notes 11 and 18.
23. See above, footnote 19.

from St Augustine's account is that we are all subject, as human beings, to two inherent defects: the darkening of the intellect, and the perversion or enfeeblement of the will.[24] Following this tradition, Baker speaks of 'ignorance and concupiscence' as the 'bitter fruits of original sin'.[25] The concept of sin seldom if ever figures in modern analytic moral philosophy, and many of my philosophical colleagues would raise very sceptical eyebrows if anyone in the seminar room were to dare to mention notions like the Fall; but in fact one does not have to be a Christian to acknowledge the all-too-obvious facts of our inherent human liability to error, both intellectual and moral—our tendency to fail, or turn aside, in our search for the good and the true. Yet the Augustinian line (one that runs like a thread through many Christian writings, including those of that other great contemporary of Baker and Descartes, Blaise Pascal) is that by divine grace we are able, in spite

---

24. See for example *De Natura et Gratia* [413-5], Ch. 24; cf. Confessions, Bk. VII.

25. Baker, *Santa Sophia*, Tr. II, Section 2, Ch. 15, §9 (p. 205). See St Thomas Aquinas, *Summa theologiae*, I^{a}II^{ae} q. 85, a. 3. Aquinas is more precise in specifying four 'wounds' that are the result of original sin, corresponding to the four (Platonic) cardinal virtues that are impaired: 'There are four of the soul's powers that can be the subject of virtue, as stated above [Qu. 61, art. 2] viz. the reason, where prudence resides, the will, where justice is, the irascible [or 'spirited' part of the soul], the subject of fortitude, and the concupiscible [or appetitive], the subject of temperance. Therefore in so far as the reason is deprived of its order to the true, there is the wound of ignorance; in so far as the will is deprived of its order of good, there is the wound of malice; in so far as the irascible [or spirited] is deprived of its order to the arduous, there is the wound of weakness; and in so far as the concupiscible is deprived of its order to the delectable, moderated by reason, there is the wound of concupiscence. Accordingly these are the four wounds inflicted on the whole of human nature as a result of our first parents' sin. But since the inclination to the good of virtue is diminished in each individual on account of actual sin, as was explained above [art.1], these four wounds are also the result of other sins, in so far as, through sin, the reason is obscured, especially in practical matters, the will hardened to evil, good actions become more difficult and concupiscence more impetuous.'

of these defects, to have some hope of a way out. As Pascal put it in the *Pensées* (the notes for his never-to-be-completed *Apologie de la religion Chrétienne*) the twin pillars of the Christian faith are the corruption of our nature and the possibility of redemption; the wretchedness of humanity without God, and the blessedness of humanity with God.[26]

The way Augustine Baker explores this theme is via the vivid image of 'two internal guides'. He observes that

> There are two internal lights and teachers, to wit, (1) the spirit of corrupt nature; (2) the Divine Spirit, both which, in all our deliberate actions, do offer themselves, and even strive for mastery, contending [which] of them, with the exclusion of the other, shall lead us in the ways proper and pleasing to each ... For the spirit of corrupt nature only teaches us such things as are for the present pleasing or profitable to our carnal desires or sensual and secular designs, but pernicious to the soul or spirit; the which, following the light of nature, runs into endless errors and labyrinths, all which lead us from God and true happiness unto eternal misery. On the other side, the Spirit of God, discovering unto us the folly and danger of following *so blind and pernicious a guide as nature* is; teaches us that our happiness consists in forsaking such a wandering guide, and treading paths quite contrary; in renouncing present sensual pleasures and commodities so far as they are a hindrance ... to our knowing of God and spiritual things ...[27]

This idea of two contradictory guides, two 'internal lights and teachers', which draw us in opposite directions, is a powerful way of expressing the essential conflictedness of our human nature. Again, this is something which contem-

---

26. B. Pascal, *Pensées* [1670], ed. L. Lafuma (Paris: 1962), no. 427: 'La foi chrétienne ne va presque qu'à etablir deux choses: la corruption de la nature, et la redemption de Jésus Christ.' Compare no. 6: 'misère de l'homme sans Dieu; félicité de l'homme avec Dieu.'
27. Baker, *Sancta Sophia*, Tr. I, Section ii, Ch. 1, §2 (p. 28), emphasis supplied.

porary secular rationalism is very apt to ignore, or to deny, but it seems to me that it is a plain fact that any sound philosophy must acknowledge. We are not angelic creatures, who only have to perceive the good and the true to follow it. On the contrary, as is explored time and again in the great classics of Western literature, and as the course of history, even of our supposedly enlightened modern times, makes all to clear, we are a *flawed species*. In the telling phrase of the author of the Fourth Gospel, men often 'prefer the darkness to the light'.[28]

Though the conflictedness of our human nature may be well supported by the facts of history and of daily observation, Baker's harping on our 'vileness and misery' can sometimes (at least on my first untutored reading of the text) appear extraordinarily bleak and grim, and (to my ear at least) his long and stern catalogue of temptations and mortifications at times seems to verge on the relentless.[29] As a result, the general reader may be tempted to put his arguments to one side, as relevant only to members of religious orders who are committed to a very special and demanding type of life, and conclude that Baker has little to say to the world at large. But Baker's explorations of human conflictedness do connect up with what I have already suggested is something deeper and more universal about our human predicament, whether secular or religious; and here it is, I think, interesting to see a closely similar framework emerging in the very different context

---

28. Or, as Paul famously put it the letter to the Romans, 'Woe is me! The good that I would, that I do not, and the evil that I would not, that I do' (Rm 7:19).

29. To mitigate this, it is important to note that Baker in (*Sancta Sophia*, Tr. II, Scctn 1, Ch 5 (p. 128)) explicitly distinguished between voluntary mortifications (about which he did had many reservations) and involuntary ones, which are simply the 'crosses' and 'afflictions' that we unable to avoid, such as 'sickness, want, disgraces, loss of friends, temptations, desolations', and in general the trials and burdens associated with one's state of life. See M. Durkin, 'Augustine Baker and Evelyn Underhill' in M. Woodward (ed.), *That Mysterious Man: Essays on Augustine Baker* (Abergevenny: 2001), p. 177.

of Descartes's philosophical meditations, with its very different set of problems.

The key to grasping this is the term 'nature', perhaps one of the most interesting and under-researched concepts in the philosophical lexicon. When Baker speaks of 'nature' as a 'pernicious' guide, he means, of course, our fallen nature, corrupted by sin. This is very different from the typical use of the term 'nature' by typical present-day writers, where it is more or less equivalent to the sequence of natural, scientifically observable, facts that make up the empirical world, or the set of actual traits which happen to be found in our species. Here, 'nature' is entirely value-free notion, neither good nor bad, but simply 'there'. Yet alongside these two notions, fallen nature, and empirical nature, there is a third notion of 'nature', with a long philosophical history, which we find in the middle ages, in such Thomistic phrases as the *lex naturae* or *lex naturalis*, the 'law of nature';[30] or, again, in the phrase found in many medieval and renaissance writers, and prominent in Descartes, the *lux naturae* (or *lumen naturale*), the natural light. Like Baker's concept of nature this is not purely descriptive, but stems from an evaluative moral framework; but its connotations are *positive*, so that it means something exactly opposite to the dangerous light of corrupt nature that leads us astray. (To see how potentially confusing these three historically and conceptually quite different senses of 'nature' and 'natural' can be, consider a phenomenon like paedophilia: in one sense it is a *natural* impulse in Baker's negative sense—arising from of a damaged nature, stained by corruption; in a second sense it is 'natural' in the purely descriptive modern usage—that is to say, it is something that, as a matter of statistical fact, is found in a certain percentage of the population; and in the third, Thomistic sense, it is 'unnatural', contrary to the

---

30. The notion actually goes back to pre-Christian writers, notably the Stoics, as summarised by Cicero, *De Re Publica* [51 BC], III, 33, in A. Long and D. Sedley (eds), *The Hellenistic Philosophers* (Cambridge: 1987), Section 67S.

'natural law', or the moral order, which flows ultimately from the *lex divina*, the law of God.[31])

When Descartes uses 'natural', in such phrases as the 'natural light', he is referring to something entirely uncorrupted– one of the authentic gifts God has bestowed upon us. In many of his writings (and it is this which often makes him seem more cheerful and optimistic than Baker), he is at pains to underline the beneficial side of our human nature—our innate endowment of reason, that 'best distributed thing in the world', as he called it in the *Discourse*. Although our intellects are imperfect, in that they are finite and extremely limited in what they can grasp, they remain, for Descartes, albeit to a very restricted extent, mirrors of the divine intellect. For God has endowed the human mind with certain clear and distinct ideas, such as the basic truths of logic and mathematics; and if we focus on these ideas carefully and attentively, we cannot doubt their truth.

---

31. The various senses of 'natural' continued to cause problems throughout the seventeenth and eighteenth centuries. In the second of his Fifteen Sermons (1726), Joseph Butler talks of various 'natural principles' in man, including that whereby 'man approves or disapproves his heart, temper and actions'. But Butler then makes a crucial distinction between principles that are natural merely in the sense of being prevalent, or commonly occurring, and those which are natural in the sense that they carry an authoritative or (as philosophers now say) a 'normative' force. We may have natural dispositions to kindness and compassion, but 'since other passions [such as anger] ... which lead us ... astray, are themselves in a degree equally natural, and often most prevalent ... it is plain the former considered merely as natural ... can no more be a law to us than the latter.' But alongside such naturally occurring impulses, there is 'a superior principle of reflection or conscience in every man ... which pronounces some actions to be in themselves just, right, good; others to be in themselves evil, wrong, unjust.' The deliverances of conscience, then, are not to be regarded as simply one group among the many competing internal principles which may motivate us, but have a special authoritative status, which enables them, in Butler's phrase, to 'be a law to us'. Butler concludes that 'it is by this faculty [of conscience], natural to man, that he is a moral agent ... a faculty in kind and in nature supreme over all others, and which bears its own authority of being so' (Sermon II, §8, emphasis supplied).

If humans have an innate capacity for the truth, how come we so often go astray? Here Descartes unmistakably shows the Augustinian and Thomistic heritage he shares with Baker; for he introduces an epistemic analogue of original sin—the preconceived opinions or prejudices (*praejudicia*) which we inherit from our parents and teachers, and which obstruct the natural light. Many of these damaging elements, are not merely historically and culturally acquired (like the mistaken, earth-centred view of the planetary system), but are virtually inseparable from our human makeup: for example, we often rely on the senses, and precipitately accept what they seem to tell us (for instance that the sun is roughly the same size as the moon), when it would be more prudent to withhold judgement. Our sensory nature (another Augustinian theme) is the source of much error and confusion. So while our nature, in so far as it is created by God, contains what we need to reach the truth, our nature, corrupted by cultural prejudices and rash reliance on precipitate judgements, leads us astray.

This brings me to my final point of contact between Baker and Descartes, namely their approach to the question of how we *deal* with the flaws of our nature. What is the way out for human beings, given our inherent defects? Here again the common Augustinian heritage is telling. Baker, in his 'Anchor of the Spirit', a guide he composed for the nuns under his instruction, sums it up in a mnemonic quatrain:

> In free will
> Is all the skill;
> Use it rightly
> & be happy.[32]

---

32. Augustine Baker, *The Anchor of the Spirit* in J. Clark (ed.), *Analecta Cartusiana*, 119:30 (Salzburg: 2008), p. 1. Baker explains [Anchor, p. 2]: 'I call it an Anker, by reason that, as a shippe, by the means of an anker (to which it is fast tied) is preserved against all storms, tempests and perils or shipwracke, so the doctrine of this brief treatise, being well observed in practice, will secure a soul in all temptations

Just as the will must be exercised, for Baker, in mortifying our sinful nature and turning the soul towards God, so, for Descartes, the will must be exercised in resisting the '*praejudicia*', the prejudices or inherited preconceived opinions that cloud our judgement; that done, we must use the will to keep focused on the clear deliverances of the natural light that will reveal the truth. The recipe, for Descartes, is resolutely to avoid giving our assent to any proposition where the truth is not clear. For the essence of error, like the essence of sin, says Descartes, is 'the incorrect use of free will' (Fourth Meditation). But it is not easy, given the hold that our sensory nature has over us. We humans are not disembodied inquirers after truth and goodness, we are embodied creatures, subject to the passions—and these can have a powerful effect in turning us away from the good and the true. The divine light, says Baker, can be 'for a time wholly extinguished', or its efficacy 'weakened' by 'sensual ends and interests'.[33]

Descartes, in fact, is interested as a philosopher not just in the pursuit of truth but also in the pursuit of goodness, and the obstacles in its way. In his last work, the *Passions of the Soul*, written in French in 1649, he discusses techniques which will enable the passions to be controlled and managed. Here his work as a scientist comes into play: his physiological investigations with animals had led him to an early version of what we now call the theory of the conditioned response, and his idea was that if it is possible to alter the reactions of animals with suitable training, reprogramming, as it were, their conditioned pathways, similar techniques might be developed in humans with a view to controlling the passions.

This might seem sinister—replacing morality with mere conditioning. But technology is only sinister if it is cut off (as is much of today's technology is) from a vision of the good. For Descartes, scientific knowledge of the workings

---

and perils that may occur in spiritual life, and will hold her fast to God.'

33. Baker, *Sancta Sophia*, Tr. I, Section ii, Ch. 1, §4 , p. 28.

of the body, and of the passions, is not some free-floating aim; it has to be harnessed to a clear conception of the good, which stems ultimately (like all truth and reality) from knowledge of God. Descartes the scientist is here ultimately subordinate to Descartes the metaphysician, and to the quest for God in the *Meditations* which I described earlier. And in the Fourth Meditation, underlining the ultimate basis for the avoidance of error, whether intellectual or moral, he describes our freedom as consisting in submission to the God-given natural light of truth and goodness, whose brightness is such that as soon as we glimpse it properly, we cannot but follow it: *ex magna luce in intellectu sequitur magna propensio in voluntate* from a great light in the intellect there follows a great inclination in the will.[34]

So the various ways of controlling passions, whether the spiritual techniques and mortifications of Baker, or the scientific techniques and conditioning programme of Descartes, are always to be put to the service of a metaphysical vision. As Descartes puts it in the *Meditations* we need to 'pause for a while, and spend time in the contemplation of God ... and gaze with wonder and adoration at the beauty of this immense light';[35] or as Baker puts it in the *Holy Wisdom*, 'the stream of holy affections doth freely flow by loving, admiring, adoring, congratulating, resigning, and offering the soul to God contemplated with the eye of faith, as in the saying of St Denys the Areopagite, *Converte te ad radium* 'Turn thyself to the beam of divine light.'[36]

4. Coda: Withdrawal or integration?

I hope I have shown that, for all the obvious divergences in their interests, their programmes, and their goals, the Benedictine sage and the French philosopher share a certain framework, a kind of structural template, which condi-

---

34. AT VII 59: CSM II 41.
35. See above, at footnote 18.
36. Baker, *Sancta Sophia*, Tr. III, Section ii, Ch. 7, §18, p. 241.

tions the way they conceive of the good and the true, and the way they think that human beings should pursue these divinely sourced goals. Yet it would be too tidy to leave it there, without pointing, before we close, to one very significant difference.

Baker, when all is said and done, is an ascetic. He deeply mistrusts the senses, and his whole programme seems informed by the desire to escape from the sensory domain to pure mental contemplation of God. As his puts it in the *Anchor of the Spirit*,

> You have it still
> Believe that will
> Above in *mens*
> Though not in sense[37]

That is to say, the path to blessedness lies entirely via the pure mind or intellect (*mens*), and not in any part of our sensory nature. Or as he says in another poem, 'What I find, I shall not mind; what I mind, I shall not find'. In other words, whatever I find in the world I am not to mind, or care about; and what I should care about (God) I shall not find in anything experienced via the senses. Baker explains that we shall not find God in this life, but the most that we shall find is 'but some image and representation of him, which is a creature, & a gift of his, but not the creator whom we look after'. Or again 'We must ever distinguish between God himself (in whom only we are to rest) & his works or gifts, which we are only to use, and not to enjoy or rest in'.[38]

This is not without its problems. I'll very briefly and schematically mention just five which come to mind. I should add that I claim no great originality in raising these points, nor am I trying to bring this paper to a close by indulging in some random sniping at Baker; the purpose is simply to flag some issues arising from his work that might repay further philosophical or theological reflection.

---

37. Baker, *Anchor of the Spirit*, pp. 1, 2, 13-14.
38. *Ibid.*, p. 4.

(1) To begin with, there seems to be a worrying slide in the closing injunction. To say we are not to 'rest in', that is, finally rest content with, the gifts of the senses is one thing; but it is not clear why this entails the strict asceticism which prohibits our *enjoying* them.

(2) With regard to the slogan 'in *mens*, though not in sense' we should I think be on our guard against a kind of Platonic or Augustinian fallacy which would move from 'God is not corporeal' or 'God is not an object of the senses', to 'God is *incorporeal*', or 'God is apprehended *purely* intellectually.' God, to be sure, transcends the corporeal world, but as far as I can see that does not entail that we can confidently declare, just like that, that he is to be apprehended only intellectually, let alone that he some kind of disembodied spirit. Better to say, more cautiously, as Nicolas Malebranche did a few decades after Baker and Descartes, that 'just as He includes the perfections of matter without being material, so He includes the perfections of created spirits without being spirit—at least in the manner we conceive spirit.'[39]

Here, though, it should be added that the mystical or apophatic strand in Baker would probably lead him to concur with the gist of this Malebranchian point: in the closing sections of the *Holy Wisdom* he comes close to saying that *nothing whatever* can be said of God—indeed that the union of the soul with God is a 'union of nothing with nothing'; and that in the final state the soul, freed from 'all sensible operations and 'all express intellectual operations' 'seeks nothing that either sense or understanding can fix upon'. Yet despite its long ancestry in the Western Christian tradition, going back to St Denys, or 'Pseudo-Dionysus' (to whom Baker explicitly refers),[40] this pure apophaticism of course presents serious theological problems, though it is outside the scope of this paper to broach them here.[41]

---

39. N. Malebranche, *Recherche de la Vérité* (Paris: 1674), Bk. 3, Ch. 9.
40. See above, at note 33.
41. For a fascinating study of some of the issues, see D. Turner, *The Darkness of God* (Cambridge, 1995). See further J. Cottingham, *The*

(3) In denying we can have sensory knowledge of God, Baker is in one way, simply following the standard Thomistic line that no property found in the empirical world can give us knowledge of God (except by analogy). St Thomas's conception of God as *ipsum esse* or 'pure Being' (God 'only *is*', as Baker puts it a the start of his 'Anchor' poem, p. 1) indeed entails that God is not to be identified with any created object, or anything that can be grasped or sensed in the empirical world: that would be idolatry. But this surely cannot mean that God is to be thought of as a *nuda et occulta substantia*—some kind of wispy 'naked and hidden' substrate to whom no predicate can be attached.[42] This would reduce 'pure being' to a mere existential quantifier ('there is an X such that ...) with nothing to complete the formula. On the contrary, God, if he exists, must have properties.

(4) One may agree that these properties are not the kinds of property we can grasp or observe in the empirical world, but arguably this should not be taken to mean that God is wholly abstracted from his creation, so that there is no relation between what we observe and the nature of God. On the contrary, to believe in a creator God is surely to believe that the creation must carry at least some traces or marks of its divine origin. Indeed, by describing the things in the world ('what I find') as *gifts* of God, Baker surely concedes that there is *something* divine about them (even though they may only offer us analogous and not direct understanding of his nature).

(5) For Christians, the doctrine of the Incarnation must surely make a difference. If Christ was fully God and fully human, a visible 'icon' or image of the invisible God (Colossians 1:15), then his life on earth presumably gives us some

---

    Spiritual Dimension (Cambridge, 2005), Ch. 8, §3, and Idem, *Why Believe?* (London, 2009), Ch. 3.

42. The Latin phrase is from Pierre Gassendi's criticism of the idea of a substance wholly abstracted from its predicates. See Gassendi, *Fifth Set of Objections to Descartes's Meditations* (AT VII 273: CSM II 191). The 'Objections and Replies' were published with the Meditations in 1641.

genuine and significant insight into the divine nature; and conversely, a result of the Incarnation is that our human nature is in some way taken up, divinized; the image of God, marred in Adam, is restored in Christ.[43]

In sum, both philosophical reflection and Christian theology seem to point in the same direction: God conceived of as pure Being ('I am that I am') should not be thought of as something flat and colourless, a merely quantificational place-holder or a pure abstract intellect; the pure Existence that is God is something, for the believer, that 'stands out', bursts forth to be the light of the world, full of grace and truth (John 1: 14). God is not only the mysterious source of all truth, goodness and beauty, but is manifest in the human world.

What of Descartes's position on all this? Since he is famous for his mind-body dualism, one might have expected him to follow the anti-sensory line found in Baker, drawing on his Platonic and Augustinian roots. But, unexpectedly, he goes a different route. Despite the unfair label 'ghost in the machine' which is so often used to tag his views on the mind-body relation,[44] Descartes is at pains to stress in the *Meditations* that we are not merely present in an alien body, as a sailor might be present in a ship, but that, on the contrary, we are 'very closely joined and intermingled with it'. To borrow a theological concept, the mind for Descartes, is genuinely and fully *incarnate* in the body, so to make up what he called '*le vrai homme*' — the real

---

43. Cf. 1 Corinthians 15:22. A stimulating critique of Baker from the perspective of 'Incarnational Theology' is offered in D. J. Power, *The Christian Anthropology of Augustine Baker's Holy Wisdom* (PhD Dissertation, Kings College London: 1991). For some of the issues relating to 'Incarnational Theology', see J. Svartvik, 'Forging an Incarnational Theology Two Score Years after Nostra Aetate' in *Studies in Christian-Jewish Relations*, 1.1 (2005) at http://escholarship.bc.edu/cgi/viewcontent.cgi?article=1011&context=scjr.

44. The pejorative phrase was originally coined by G. Ryle, *The Concept of Mind* (London: 1949), Ch. 1.

human being.⁴⁵ As a result, our sensory human nature, created by God, cannot entirely be written off as bondage to sin. On the contrary, the sensations and passions we experience are given us by God to indicate what is beneficial and harmful to the mind-body composite, so that, as Descartes says in the Sixth Meditation, 'there is absolutely nothing to be found that does not bear witness to the power and goodness of God'.⁴⁶

This is why Descartes insisted (when advising Princess Elizabeth of Bohemia) that 'the pleasures of the body should not be despised, nor should one free oneself altogether from the passions.'⁴⁷ And he goes on in *The Passions of the Soul* to offer a ringing endorsement of the affective dimension⁴⁸ which arises from the inescapably corporeal side to our humanity:

---

45. Descartes, *Discourse*, Part Five, AT VI 59: CSM I 141. For the intermingling of mind and body, see Sixth Meditation, AT VII 81: CSM II 56.
46. Descartes, *Sixth Meditation*, AT VII 87: CSM II 60).
47. Descartes, *Letter to Elizabeth* of 1 September 1645 (AT IV 287: CSMK 265). Contrast the antihedonistic orientation of the Stoics: vera voluptas voluptatum contemptio. ('True pleasure is to despise the pleasures.') Seneca, *De vita beata* [c. AD 58], IV, 2.
48. It should in fairness be added that Baker's theology, though resolutely incorporealist, is not blind to the affective dimension: the goal of union with God involves not just a colourless mental apprehension but depends on love. As Baker puts it, the soul 'endeavouring to contemplate Him in the darkness and obscurity of a blind and naked faith, void of all distinct and express images, will by little and little grow so well disposed to Him, that she will have less need of forcing herself to produce good affections to Him, or of prescribing to herself determinate forms of acts or affections; on the contrary, divine love will become so firmly established in the soul, so wholly and only filling and possessing it, that it will become, as it were, a new soul unto the soul, as constantly breathing forth fervorous acts of love, and as naturally almost as the lungs do send forth breath.' *Sancta Sophia*, Tr. III, Section 2, Ch. 1, §12, p. 249. There is evidently a mode of affectivity envisaged here; words like 'fervorous' seem to imply more than an abstract movement or engagement of the soul; but it is not very clear how the notion of 'fervour' can have any purchase abstracted from any corporeal context in terms of which we usually understand it. For more on the affective dimension in

> The pleasures common to soul and body depend entirely on the passions, so that persons whom the passions can move most deeply are capable of enjoying the sweetest pleasures of this life. It is true that they may also experience the most bitterness when they do not know how to put these passions to good use… But the chief use of wisdom lies in teaching us to be masters of our passions and to control them with such skill that the evils which they cause are quite bearable, and even become a source of joy.[49]

The message is one of reconciliation and integration, not of withdrawal to a higher plane. It would, I think, be a truly fascinating project to explore which of the two recipes for ultimate fulfilment, Baker's or Descartes's, is closer to the authentic Christian vision of human flourishing. Or perhaps we do not need to choose, since the Christian vision, despite its universality, surely does not reduce us all to a single type, but allows scope for different kinds of life, and different kinds of vocation. But addressing those questions is a task for another day.

Baker's theology, see P. Tyler, 'Theological Writing as *Theologica Mystica*', in the present volume.

49. René Descartes, *Passions of the Soul* [*Les passions de l'âme*, 1649], art. 212. See further J. Cottingham, *Philosophy and the Good Life: Reason and the passions in Greek, Cartesian and Psychoanalytic Ethics* (Cambridge: 1998), Ch 3.

11

Baker's Critics

Geoffrey Scott

In his survey of the English Benedictines from their restoration until 1688 David Lunn rounds up his study of Augustine Baker in these words:

> Like Galileo, Baker could not object to any opposition to his doctrines by the authorities at the top, since his ideas and methods were officially and fully endorsed. In his mind the danger lay in the redefinition of his ideas by the authorities to be used as a bomb to shatter rebel missionaries. Stranded and disorientated by the realisation that he had been manipulated, perhaps at Cambrai, certainly at Douai, Baker retreated into himself. After his death, the congregational officials and his followers continued the work of channelling him into conventionality. No one, however, whether friend or enemy, has succeeded in capturing the real Augustine Baker, who advocated a style of prayer that could be lived in any walk of life but refused to be confined to any closed system. This prayer is anarchic; it places its persevering practitioners in direct relationship to God, without benefit of clergy.[1]

Baker was not only 'anarchic' in prayer but in manner and life and attitudes also, which helps to explain why

---
1. D. Lunn, *The English Benedictines 1540–1688* (London: 1980), p. 217.

some abbots and priors occasionally took a dislike to him, although some abbesses and prioresses, it has to be said, approved of him.

In this chapter I hope to look at Baker's contemporary, and best-known, critics among the monks and nuns who disapproved of him and his teaching. But before I deal with Baker's contemporary monastic critics, I would, out of interest, like to look briefly at some of his later non-Benedictine critics. After Baker's death in 1641, students were rarely able to avail themselves of exact copies of his manuscript works. That lacuna is now being filled by John Clark's *travail Bénédictin* in editing all Baker's extant works in the *Analecta Cartusiana* series. Because they did not know this extraordinary character personally, later scholars were introduced to Baker principally through his published works, that is, mainly through Serenus Cressy's abridgement of Baker's spiritual teaching, *Sancta Sophia,* (Douai: 1657), and the *Apostolatus Benedictinorum in Anglia,* (Douai: 1626), the historical work which sought to establish the legitimate lineage of the restored English Benedictines in their descent from the medieval English Benedictine Congregation. Although President Clement Reyner is the reputed author of this work, Baker seems to have been its main compiler. Because of the abundance of documents preserved in this volume and its accurate historical assessment, the *Apostolatus* had few seventeenth-century critics. It was not only employed in Serenus Cressy's (1605–1674) *The Church-History of Brittany*, (Rouen: 1668), but also in the Anglican historian, Henry Wharton's (1664–1695) *Historia Sacra*.[2]

---

2. S. Cressy, *The Church-History of Brittany* (Rouen: 1668), pp. 287, 313, 349, 382, 413. Only the first volume of Cressy's *Church-History* was published. The second volume remains in manuscript in the Bibliothèque Municipale in Douai. See also H. Wharton, *Anglia sacra, sive, Collectio historiarum partim antiquitus, partim recenter scriptarum, de archiepiscopis & episcopis Angliae, a prima fidei Christianae susceptione ad annum MDXL* (London: 1691), p. 789 (marginal note). Baker was also responsible for collecting and editing the published works of Dame Gertrude More, *The Holy Practises of a Devine Lover or the*

Wharton's work was published in the context of a liberal Anglican apologetic amplified by recourse to scientific and rationalist arguments to demonstrate the reasonableness of Anglicanism over against the obscurantism and foolish superstitions of the Church of Rome. Surprisingly, Wharton's *The Enthusiasm of the Church of Rome Demonstrated* (London, 1688) in which he argued that the 'extraordinary Illuminations' of Catholic saints like St. Ignatius of Loyola testified to the irrationalism and fanaticism of the Roman church, as opposed to the 'rational piety' of Anglicanism included no criticism of Baker or his school.[3] However, Baker was used to defend the Church of Rome by his disciple Serenus Cressy who crossed swords with Edward Stillingfleet (1635–1699). Thus Stillingfleet's responses represent the first major criticism of Baker's teaching since Baker's death in 1641. It is well known that the 1650s witnessed the appearance of large numbers of publications relating to Baker, including *Sancta Sophia* itself, and Cressy seems to have been mainly responsible for keeping the master's memory alive in the three decades following his death. Cressy's varied career as a member of the Great Tew Circle of intellectuals, later as an Anglican divine, and as a Benedictine monk (professed in 1649) who acted as a royal chaplain, did not detract from his continued interest in mysticism. Cressy was known in Port Royalist circles; he had originally felt his vocation was to the Carthusians, and later, as an English Benedictine, he was to edit a number of mystical treatises, including the first edition of Julian of Norwich's *Revelations* (1670). This last was published some thirteen years after his edition of *Sancta Sophia*. After his

---

Sainctly Ideots Devotion (Paris: 1658), and *The Spiritual Exercises... and Ideots Devotions... Confessiones Amantis. A Lovers Confessions* (Paris: 1658).

3. H. Wharton, *The Enthusiasm of the Church of Rome Demonstrated* (London: 1688), p. 15; L. Okie, 'Wharton, Henry (1664–1695)' in *Oxford Dictionary of National Biography* (Oxford University Press: Sept 2004); online edition, Oct 2008 [http://www.oxforddnb.com/view/article/29167, accessed 20 July 2009].

conversion in 1646, Cressy published *Exomologesis* (1647, and later editions), which was a response to William Chillingworth's (1604–1644) *The Religion of Protestants as a Safe Way to Salvation* (1638). *Exomologesis* represented a preliminary skirmish before Cressy engaged in a similar contest with Stillingfleet, and in this work he demonstrates he was already aware of the importance of Baker, the 'very sublime contemplative' he called him, whose teachings had brought about his own conversion: 'I found myself pressed to hasten my reconcilement to the Church, because I thirsted to become capable of practising those heavenly instructions.'[4]

In the preface to his edition of *Sancta Sophia*, Cressy was clearly aware of criticisms of Baker which must have still been circulating in 1657. He explained that Baker's doctrine of God's internal guidance 'is the very soul of Christianity', and the accusation that this guidance 'should prejudice the authority of superiors' was caused by 'a mere jealousy'. Cressy sought to defuse accusations that Baker's teachings encouraged 'the frantic enthusiasts of this age', meaning presumably contemporary radical English Puritans, and he admitted that his *Sancta Sophia* was primarily designed to help 'a few contemplative persons' since Baker's doctrine was inevitably 'above the reach of vulgar capacities'. Finally, he admitted that practitioners of Baker's way always remained obedient to superiors and to the magisterium of the Church. Stillingfleet, on the other hand, insisted that Cressy's preface gave little help to understanding of Baker's knotted prose; for all the help (which) Mr Cressy gives in his Preface, he exclaimed, 'we may as well hope to understand the *Quakers Canting* as Mr. *Cressy's (Preface)*.'[5]

Stillingfleet's war against Cressy was continued during the 1670s, through the medium of published responses

---

4. S. Cressy, *Exomologesis or a Faithful Narration of the Occasion and Motives of the Conversion unto Catholique Unity* (Paris: 1653), pp. 445–446.

5. N. Sweeney (ed.), *Sancta Sophia* (London: 1871), Preface, pp. 8–11; E. Stillingfleet, *A discourse concerning idolatry* (London: 1671), p. 328.

from each combatant. Both acted as apologists for their separate churches. Stillingfleet's particular criticism of Baker's mystical teachings arose from his interest in natural theology and from his scornful attack on Romish and monastic 'enthusiasms and raptures'. In the following century, the study of natural theology and the use of rational arguments against religious superstition and enthusiasm were to be major concerns. The popularity of natural theology and attraction of scientific enquiry also affected English monks in this period and partly explains why, thanks to these fashionable intellectual pursuits, there was such a complete lack of interest among Benedictines in Baker's teaching throughout most of the eighteenth century. Stillingfleet was renowned for the breadth of his knowledge and for his painstaking research, and his appreciation of Baker and the specific mystical concepts he employed suggest he had read *Sancta Sophia* very carefully. Bakerism was most systematically demolished in Stillingfleet's *Discourse on Idolatry* (1671) which elicited Cressy's two responses, *Fanaticism Fanatically Imputed* (1672), and *An Answer to Mr. Cressy's Epistle* (1674).[6]

Stillingfleet's attack was rational, Anglican, and moderate. He noted that Cressy, 'after his many turnings and changes of opinions sits down at last (as appears by his publishing *Mother Iuliana's* revelations and the *Preface* to *Sancta Sophia*) with the deserved Character of a *Popish Fanatick*'. Having kept the bible out of the hands of the people, he went on, the Roman Church had 'gratified the

---

6. E. Stillingfleet, *A discourse concerning the idolatry practised in the Church of Rome and the danger of salvation in the communion of it in an answer to some papers of a revolted Protestant : wherein a particular account is given of the fanaticism and divisions of that church* (London: 1671); Serenus Cressy, *Fanaticism fanatically imputed to the Catholick church by Doctour Stillingfleet and the imputation refuted and retorted by S.C. a Catholick* (1672); E. Stillingfleet, *An Answer to Mr. Cressy's Epistle apologetical to a person of honour touching his vindication of Dr. Stillingfleet* (London: 1675). See also S. Cressy, *A Collection of Several Treatises in Answer to Dr. Stillingfleet* (1672), and his *An Epistle Apologetical of S.C.* (1674).

earthy dulness of a *superstitious* temper, and the airiness and warmth of the *Enthusiastical*. For the former, they are abundantly provided by a tedious and ceremonious way of external devotion as dull and as cold as the earth itself; to the other they commend *abstractedness of life, mental prayer, passive unions, a Deiform fund of the soul, a state of introversion, divine inspirations,* which must either end in *Enthusiasme* or madness.' As we shall see, the search for the 'fund (or basis or essence) of the soul' was central in Baker's squabble with Rudisind Barlow, his fellow English Benedictine. Stillingfleet went on to note that Baker's attainment of 'union with God' could only come about '*in the way of unknowing,* (for nothing so dangerous as the *use of reason)* and *self-annihilation* (which) makes it difficult to give any account of such unintelligible stuffe, for we must only grope in obscurity and profound darkness, and draw a *Night piece* without lights.' He took exception to Cressy's dismissal of the value of 'external and imaginary exercises of Prayer... (since) Christ *and his* Apostles *did, who used this low dispensation of* praying *to the last! But alas, they never understood these* passive unions *with* God *in the* fund of the spirit, *they taught men a plain and intelligible way of serving God, and bid them look for perfection in another world'*. Baker's 'Union of nothing with nothing', through which 'the soul comes to a feeling of her not being, and by consequence of the not being of creatures', Stillingfleet treated as 'intolerable nonsense'. '*The plain effect of such* Enthusiastick *fooleries is to make Religion laughed at by some, despised by others, and neglected by all, who take no other measures of it, than from such confounded Writers. If once an unintelligible way of practical* Religion, *become the standard of* devotion, *no men of sense and reason will ever set themselves about it, but leave it to be* understood *by* mad-men *and* practised *by* Fools'.

Baker's admission that 'divine inspirations' should take priority over 'external work' was in direct contradiction to apostolic example, protested Stillingfleet, for if the apostles' had followed it, they would *'never done much good in the World, or been such eminent examples of holy life and actions.'*

Cressy's riposte to Stillingfleet's barrage of criticism was fairly weak. He called Stillingfleet's ideas *'bouffoneries'*, and sought to demonstrate the great fruit produced by *Sancta Sophia*. Cressy defended the historical pedigree for 'the prayer of contemplation' which, he argued, stretched back at least to John Cassian. Stillingfleet's answer to Cressy in *An Answer to Mr. Cressy's Epistle* was lighter and more humorous than his earlier offensive. He asked that if mystic contemplation was without understanding, how might it be explained or understood in the first place, and if all workings of the soul ceased, how therefore could one give an account of the state of non-being? If such 'supernatural communications' such as Baker's were so sublime and could only be described with great difficulty, why write of them and publish about them in the first place. As Stillingfleet himself had experienced no 'mystical unions' he himself had to be relegated, according to Baker's criteria, to becoming merely a 'sensual man' and *'uncapable of understanding the things of the Spirit of God.'* Stillingfleet concluded that Baker and Cressy were like other extreme enthusiasts in that all of them 'talk Non-sense, or unintelligible Canting; and I dare say, they speak nothing more *unintelligible* than ,this *Mystical Divinity*.' He collected an armoury of Catholic devotionary writers who were apparently on his side through their insistence that frequent 'Divine Raptures' had natural, rather than supernatural causes, for they were merely products of 'distemper in the head', 'Melancholy' etc. He ended his scathing attack by some amusing anecdotes: '*What of* Br Gyles, *mentioned both by* Bona *and* Scacchus, *that thought it so easie to fall into* raptures, *that if any one spake the word* Paradise, *he fell into an Ecstasie; insomuch that the Boyes of* Perusium, *as* Scacchus *relates it, would come behind him and cry* Paradise, *on purpose to make him immediately fall down in a* Trance: *must we acknowledge this to be from God? But what shall we say to*

Br Roger, *mentioned by* F. Baker *out of* Harphius, *that* had a hundred Raptures in a Mattins?[7]

Stillingfleet died in 1699, just before the opening of the new century during which interest in Baker had all but disappeared by 1720. The tradition of transcribing Baker's works, particularly Baker's translations of spiritual authors, seems to have declined rapidly, although it it seems to have lingered on in the English Benedictine abbey of Lambspring, near Hildesheim, and among the English Benedictine nuns in Cambrai and Paris.[8] For modern scholars, and for those who seek to define English Benedictine spirituality principally or even absolutely as Bakerite, this is a curious phenomenon, for it suggests that monks and nuns had lost interest in Baker. No one seems to have solved the conundrum of this drying up of Baker studies. Father Placid Spearritt glossed over the causes of this 'lull in Baker studies'. 'Its decline', he maintained, 'set in about the time of the Quietist controversy, when contemplatives became less popular candidates for canonization; and within the English Congregation the eighteenth century brought an almost total shift of influence in favour of the apostolic labours of the mission'. Dame Margaret Truran admitted that 'the dearth of evidence for the rest of the eighteenth century makes it difficult to assess how far Father Baker's teaching continued to be actively propagated', and Professor Tom Birrell sought, not too convincingly, to persuade his readers that it was those who reacted against the age of reason and strove to rediscover the religion of the heart who kept Bakerism alive in the eighteenth century. These were, in his eyes, more often Puritans, Protestants, and Presby-

---

7. Stillingfleet, *A discourse*, pp. 327, 328, 332–336; Cressy, *Fanaticism*, pp. 38, 59; Stillingfleet, *An Answer*, pp. 29–32, 34, 85.
8. J. McCann & H. Connolly (eds.), 'Memorials of Father Augustine Baker and other documents relating to the English Benedictines' in *Catholic Record Society* 33 (London: 1933), pp. 274–293; M. Truran, 'Spirituality: Fr Baker's Legacy' in A. Cramer (ed.), *Lamspringe. An English Abbey in Germany* (Ampleforth: 2004), pp. 83–95.

terians, than Roman Catholic monks and nuns.⁹ Baker had never been condemned as unorthodox, but he had become unfashionable. No further editions of *Sancta Sophia* were published until the revival in the writings of the mystics during the second half of the nineteenth century, and in all my own research of eighteenth-century material relating to the English Benedictines, I have found no mention of Baker in any correspondence, sermons, or conferences. Certainly his published and manuscript works must have continued to lie on convent shelves, but they gathered dust. It is a measure of Baker's unpopularity that in the widely disseminated, and perhaps obligatory, course of novitiate and juniorate studies for monks, compiled c.1764 by the monk and bishop, Charles Walmesley, a mathematician and astronomer, Baker is not mentioned as compulsory reading for novices. This seminal document defined the two ends of the English Benedictine life as, firstly, the acquisition of the Spirit of Religion 'so essential to the Monastick Profession' and, secondly, the development of qualities needed to undertake the labour of the Mission.¹⁰

Any understanding of the development of eighteenth-century Christian spirituality will reveal why interest in Baker and his teachings ebbed. As the fascination for natural science developed, hinted at already in Stillingfleet's works, so did the need to analyse the relationship of religious faith to science grow. Mysticism was about the

9. P. Spearrit, 'The Survival of Mediaeval Spirituality among the exiled English Black Monks' in M. Woodward (ed.), *That Mysterious Man. Essays on Augustine Baker* (Abergavenny: 2001), pp. 28, 32. Truran, 'Spirituality', p. 95. T. A. Birrell, 'English Catholic Mystics in Non-Catholic Circles' in *Downside Review* 94 (1976), pp. 60–64, 70–81, 99–117.

10. H. Aveling, 'The Education of Eighteenth-Century English Monks' in *Downside Review* 79 (1961), pp. 135–152. In the Douai Abbey Archives, a manuscript copy of this course ascribes it to Walmesley. Novices are encouraged to read the Rule and Constitutions, St Gregory's Dialogues, *The Imitation of Christ*, Jerome Piatti SJ on the religious life, and even Stillingfleet was recommended to these English Benedictine theological students. Although he has no mention in the course, Baker would have taken some comfort in seeing Cassian and St Bernard listed as useful authors for novitiate reading.

immeasurable and had no place here; it belonged to the introverted world of the seventeenth century, not the extrovert world of the eighteenth. It is a striking feature of the pattern of the history of theology that sometimes interest in mysticism and its associates tends to appear when theology and faith find themselves under threat from scientific enquiry and research, as, for instance, in the late nineteenth century, for the conceptual framework of mysticism was arguably outside scientific understanding and calibration, as Stillingfleet had insisted. For much of the eighteenth century science seemed to be the lap-dog of theology, and scholarly monks of this period were enthusiastic for marrying theology and faith to geology, astronomy, Newtonian physics, and biblical chronology rather than pursuing Bakerite *arcana*. Thus, it was not merely busy involvement in apostolic missionary endeavour in England which pushed Baker out of the English Benedictine frame.

Although it deserves more research than can be attempted here, we can see the crisis for Bakerism developing in microcosm by way of the seventeenth-century debates over varying concepts of the soul which are found in Baker's writings and in those of later scholars. It is common knowledge that some of the Benedictine critics of Baker opposed the elitism of his spiritual 'way', or objected to his attack on the active missionary apostolate in England, or were convinced that he was a divisive influence in a monastery, instilling among the young disobedience to their superiors in spiritual matters. Traces of such these criticisms as these are to be found in the biography of his disciple, the Cambrai nun, Dame Gertrude More (1606–1633), who had initially been unable to cope with the transcendent simplicity of his teaching. Another critic was his successor at Cambrai, Dom Francis Hull (died 1645), who seems to have preferred Jesuit-type hagiography as the basis for inculcating Christian and Benedictine spirituality rather than Baker's 'illuminism', but Hull might have simply been jealous of Baker's success with his female disciples. Finally, a key opponent of Baker was President Rudisind Barlow (1585–1656), the garrulous theology professor at St Gregory's, Douai, who had been initially sympathetic to Baker. Barlow later took issue with Baker over what, firstly, constituted precisely the *fundus animae*, the basis or essence of the soul, which was, after all, a doctrine which represented the kernel of any mystical tradition, and, secondly, the related question as to 'whether the will acted with little or no dependence on the imagination and the intellect'. The term *fundus animae* occurs in many of the works of the spiritual masters of the Catholic Reformation and doubtless through their teaching found its way into Baker's own work. Barlow took exception to the use of it in Baker since it encouraged thoughts that a soul, having a basis [*fundus*] and thus depth and quality and corruption, would thus be essentially mortal. Baker responded by qualifying his terms and recommended recourse to common sense.[11]

The controversy reappeared, however, when Edward Stillingfleet crossed swords with Serenus Cressy over the use of *fundus animae* in the latter's preface to *Sancta Sophia*. He poured scorn on a 'Deiform fund of the soul, a state of introversion, divine inspirations, which must either end in Enthusiasme or madness'. For him, finding God '*in the pure fund of the Spirit*' was hocus-pocus and he was clear that Cressy scored an own goal by admitting he himself had some difficulty explaining it: '*very few do know that hidden fund of their souls, or believe that they have such a thing within them.*' Certainly, Stillingfleet

---

11. Lunn, *Benedictines*, p. 207. N. Birt, *Obit Book of the English Benedictines* (Edinburgh: 1913), p. 28, for Hull. See also M. Lunn, 'William Rudesind Barlow, O.S.B' in *Downside Review*, 86 (1968), pp. 238–246; J. McCann (ed.), *The life of Father Augustine Baker, O.S.B. (1575-1641) by Fr. Peter Salvin & Fr. Serenus Cressy* (London: 1933), pp. 187–88. McCann & Connolly, 'Memorials', pp. 132–135. For the understanding of the term in mystical writers who influenced Baker, such as Eckhart, Tauler and Harphius, see L. Reypens, 'Ame' in M. Viller et al (eds.), *Dictionnaire de Spiritualité*, vol. 1 (Paris: 1937), cols. 449–464. See L. J. Woodward, 'Verb Tense and Sequential Time in the *Cantico Espiritual* of San Juan de la Cruz' in *Forum for Modern Language Studies* 27 (1991), p. 153, for John of the Cross's and Baker's teachings on the *fundus animae*, here defined as that hidden essence of the soul which survived after almost all the faculties had withered and which was taken over by Christ.

stressed, Christ and the apostles had no understanding of *'these* passive unions *with* God *in the* fund of the spirit'. Stillingfleet's exception to the term heralded the great controversies over the 'essence of the soul' in the eighteenth century when 'love of solitude and meditation was likely to seem eccentric, self-denial rather useless and morose'. The nature of the soul especially exercised sensationalist philosophers of this period who believed the mind was 'nothing but a receptacle for experience', and who focused on the question whether the soul was related in some way to matter. It had 'a physical or at least a physiological basis'. The predominant opinion was thus developed that the soul was physical and 'took form through sensations' even if perhaps it was constituted of 'subtle matter'. All this made Baker's crucial doctrine of the soul's central function in mystical prayer even less likely to be influential in the eighteenth century.[12]

The nineteenth century, however, saw a revival of interest in mysticism, and Baker returned, riding on the wave of a renewed fascination with the English mystical writers. The causes of this renaissance are many and various and can only be summarized here. They included a rejection of the previous century's rationalism in favour of a philosophical Traditionalism which respected Christian spiritual and cultural development as essential elements in the living stream of human history. This Traditionalism was an integral part of that Christian romanticism which manifested itself in an influential neo-medievalism. Catholic Emancipation in 1829 encouraged the English Catholic community to provide itself with its own literary culture. Thus the tradition of compiling manuscript copies of Baker's works emerged again at the beginning of the century, briefly and quietly, and *Sancta Sophia*'s bi-centenary was celebrated in a new edition, albeit in New York, in 1857. Baker studies were to be pursued with a new intensity at Belmont Priory in 1859 which was to become the central

---

12. Stillingfleet, *Idolatry*, pp. 327, 329, 332, 333. Sweeney, ed., *Sancta Sophia*, p. 19. R. R. Palmer, *Catholics & Unbelievers in eighteenth-century France* (New York: 1961), pp.12, 113–114, 133.

novitiate of the English Benedictines. Here, Dom Norbert Sweeney, a disciple of Baker who published another edition of *Sancta Sophia* (1876) as well as a *Life* of Baker 1861), was prior (1859–62). He agreed with the first novice master at Belmont, Dom Laurence Shepherd (1859–1861) to introduce the novices to Baker. Hence began a tradition which lasted into the twentieth century and had a profound effect on English Benedictine formation.[13]

Present at the consecration of Belmont's church in September 1860 was Abbot Prosper Guéranger, who had revived the French Benedictines at Solesmes. His closest English disciple was Dom Laurence Shepherd, novice master at Belmont. Guéranger, in contrast to Shepherd, was to be surprisingly critical of Baker. Guéranger's fame stemmed from his insistence that the liturgy had a central place in the church's life, and he favoured only those mystical writers like St Gertrude the Great (1256–1302) whose spirituality was formed through the liturgy. He objected to Baker's seemingly subordinating the liturgy into becoming merely one prop among many for personal prayer. Valiant efforts have been made to demonstrate Baker's attachment to the church's liturgy, but they are not very convincing. In a letter of 17 June 1863 to Shepherd, Guéranger insisted that his major work, *L'Année Liturgique* whose major theme was the mystery of the incarnation of the Word, provided an 'antidote' to Baker. With a hint of sarcasm, he hoped he might free all Benedictines and Catholics from the clutches of Baker whom he believed stood condemned for Quietism:

> As to myself, I have a horror of him. If I had a translation of this philosopher, I would crush it under

---

13. McCann & Connolly, 'Memorials', VI. Catalogue of Baker MSS., pp. 275, 282, 283, 284, 291, 292, 293. For more on the decline of interest in Baker in the eighteenth century and a revival of his teaching in the nineteenth century, see my chapter in the forthcoming Belmont Abbey centenary volume, 'Something of the struggle for Belmont's soul, 1859–1909'.

the weight of those condemnations of the Holy See against heterodox spiritual teachers.[14]

If Belmont was to stir up long-lived tensions in the English Benedictine Congregation between monastic life in the cloister and that on the mission, perhaps Baker himself would have been struck by another enduring tension, encouraged here by Guéranger. What was to be central to the English Benedictine spiritual tradition in the twentieth century, liturgical worship or private prayer?

---

14. 'Pour moi, je l'ai en horreur. Si j'avais une traduction de ce philosophe, je l'écraserais sous le poids des condemnations portées par le Saint-Siège contre les héterodoxes en spiritualité.' T. Barbeau, 'Préface de Dom Guéranger á l'*Enchiridion Benedictinum* [1872]' in Abbey of Solesmes, *Mélanges Dom Guéranger* (Solesmes: 2005), pp. 267–268 (quotation). D. Hayes & H. Defos du Rau, *In a Great and Noble Tradition. The Autobiography of Dom Prosper Guéranger* (Leominster: 2009), p. xv.

12

Father Augustine Baker in the Nineteenth-Century English Benedictine Congregation

ALBAN HOOD

In 1795, monks and nuns of the English Benedictine Congregation were among many of their fellow compatriots who arrived on English shores having escaped from revolution-torn France. The losses the Congregation had suffered as a result of the revolution were colossal. In the light of these, especially the loss of their monastic buildings, it was perhaps inevitable that the essential English Benedictine temperament in the following decades was activist, rather than contemplative. Catholic spirituality in the early nineteenth century, as in the eighteenth century, was likewise heavily influenced by practical concerns. The spiritual works of the Counter Reformation continued to dominate and were favoured because of their activist dynamic, works like Alfonso Rodriguez' *Practice of Religious Perfection*, and Lorenzo Scupoli's *Spiritual Combat*. Editions of these works continued to be published after 1800 and were to be found in the libraries of Benedictine monks and nuns.[1] Moreover, such works were also

---

1. For example A. Rodriguez, *The Practice of Christian and Religious Perfection* (Kilkenny: 1806, and Dublin: 1840–43), 3 vols.; L. Scupoli, *The*

standard textbooks for early nineteenth-century English Benedictine novices such as the future bishop, Bernard Ullathorne, who in his autobiography recalled reading both Rodriguez and Scupoli, as well as Gobinet's *Instruction of Youth*.[2] At Ampleforth several collections of books are preserved, belonging to early nineteenth-century Benedictine missioners in which the works already mentioned are well represented, together with other well-known Counter Reformation authors such as St Francis de Sales, whose pastoral guidance was evidently drawn upon by generations of nineteenth-century Benedictine missioners.[3]

It has been claimed that the revival of interest in Father Augustine Baker among the monks of the English Benedictine Congregation began in earnest after 1850, but I think there is evidence of the beginnings of this revival much earlier in the nineteenth century, when there was an explosion in English Catholic publishing, with mystical writers such as Baker again coming into vogue. As early as 1812, the English Cisalpinist Charles Butler quoted in his *Essay*

Spiritual Combat (Birmingham: 1769, and London: 1846).

2. L. Madigan (ed.), *The Devil is a Jackass: Being the dying words of the autobiographer William Bernard Ullathorne* (Downside Abbey: 1995), pp.39–45; C. Gobinet, *Instruction of Youth in Christian Piety* (Newcastle: 1783, and Dublin: 1793 & 1821).

3. Gobinet, *The Instruction of Youth in Christian Piety*, for instance, is featured in the collections of a number of Benedictine missioners, notably Father John Fisher (1710–1793) and Father John Turner (1765–1844). Another favourite work was *The Spiritual Entertainments of St Francis de Sales… translated from the original French by William Henry Coombes* (Taunton: 1814). I am grateful to Father Anselm Cramer, the archivist at Ampleforth, for bringing these collections to my attention. For the influence of de Sales, see M. Xavier Compton, 'Saint Francis de Sales and John Bede Polding OSB' in *Tjurunga. An Australasian Benedictine Review* 7 (1974), pp. 9–18. Later in the nineteenth century at the purpose-built English Benedictine monastery and house of studies at Belmont near Hereford, the spirituality of the saint was actively promoted by the future bishop, Cuthbert Hedley. See G. Scott, 'The English Benedictine Mission and missions' in D. H Farmer (ed.), *Benedict's Disciples* (Leominster: 1995), p. 314.

on *Mystical Theology* that Baker was very popular in England.[4] However, given that Baker's work was not published in England from 1657 until 1876, Butler's claim seems to be a surprising one. Geoffrey Scott contends that although interest in Baker declined in the English Benedictine monasteries, 'many Bakerite missioners carried their strain of Bakerism into Catholic households where it was discreetly refashioned to suit a lay audience,' so this may explain Butler's comment.[5]

The 1784 Constitutions of the English Benedictine Congregation, which continued to be re-published intermittently during the nineteenth century until the new constitutions of 1889, repeated the traditional obligation for monks, whether conventual or missioner, to spend half an hour a day in mental prayer. There was no mention of the prayer of affections, desolations and consolations that had been included in the 1661 Constitutions, no doubt as a result of the influence of Father Augustine Baker. Given that the late eighteenth century favoured a more utilitarian spirituality, this is hardly surprising. In the eyes of several early nineteenth-century commentators, such as Charles Butler, it was not the Enlightenment, but the effects of the earlier Quietist controversy that 'had brought devotion itself into discredit, and thrown ridicule on the holiness of an interior life'.[6]

Father Baker's writings had diminished in popularity during the eighteenth century among his fellow monks.[7] Although the spiritual formation of the earliest monks of St Gregory's was firmly centred on Baker's teaching, through

---

4. C. Butler, 'An Essay on Mystical Theology' in *Miscellaneous Tracts* (1812), np.

5. G. Scott, 'The Image of Augustine Baker' in M. Woodward (ed.), *That Mysterious Man. Essaus on Augustine Baker OSB 1575–1641*, (Abergavenny: 2001), pp. 92–122.

6. J. P. Chinnici, *The English Catholic Enlightenment. John Lingard and the Cisalpine Movement 1780–1850* (Shepherdstown: 1980), p. 183.

7. G. Scott, *Gothic Rage Undone. English Monks in the Age of Enlightenment* (Bath: 1993), pp. 127–128.

his disciples Peter Salvin and Serenus Cressy, Baker's influence had long been in decline in that community by the time of its migration to England. Bakerism had not lost its appeal for the nuns, despite the fact that the community founded in Cambrai lost most of its precious Baker holographs and books at the French Revolution. The English nuns of the Community of Our Lady of Good Hope, who settled at Colwich in 1834, succeeded, in spite of the Revolution, in maintaining their strong spiritual tradition of Bakerism. Many Baker manuscripts were still in the community's possession when they settled in England, and interest in Baker's teaching endured due to the determination of Mother Teresa Catherine Macdonald.[8] The Colwich nuns were responsible for passing on the Baker tradition to their chaplain, Father Benedict Dullard, who, according to Bishop Bernard Ullathorne, had the spirit of Father Baker.[9] Dullard (1795–1863) had been professed at St. Edmund's, Douai, for the revived Lambspring community at Broadway, and he and two other monks from this community can be said to have preserved the Baker tradition that was active at Lambspring right through until the mid-nineteenth century. In the nineteenth century also, Father Wilfrid Price (1819–1878) made a copy of Baker's manuscript edition of the Rule of St Benedict in 1838. This copy is now at Stanbrook, where Father Anselm Kenyon (1770–1850), the last surviving monk professed at Lambspring, ended his days. Among his papers after his death in 1850 were discovered some fragments of spiritual verse belonging to Father Dunstan Hutchinson (died 1730), once novice master and prior at Lambspring, who had been a

---

8. B. Rowell, 'Baker's influence on Benedictine nuns', in Woodward, *Mysterious* Man, pp. 87–88.
9. Idem, 'Absent Brethren: The Monastery of Our Lady of Good Hope and the English Benedictine Congregation', unpublished paper given to the English Benedictine History Symposium, April 2000.

Baker disciple and had made a copy of Baker's edition of the Benedictine rule.[10] Evidence of a slow revival of Baker can be detected in the communities of St Gregory and St Laurence during the first part of the nineteenth century. In 1823 Prior Bernard Barber (1790–1850) of Downside wrote to a confrere to request a copy of Baker's *Sancta Sophia*.[11] Barber was probably responsible for encouraging William Bernard Ullathorne to read Father Baker. The bishop noted that when visiting Australia in 1840, among the 'valuable ascetic writings' he took with him, was *Sancta Sophia*.[12] Barber, later President of the English Benedictines, ended his days as chaplain to the nuns at Stanbrook. There, a copy of Cressy's *Life* of Baker has been preserved, which is inscribed with the name of Barber and the date of 1824.[13]

The community of St Laurence, to which Baker himself had belonged, had kept a copy of *Sancta Sophia* on the open shelves in the library at Dieulouard, but 'judging from the number of copies which have survived' at Ampleforth, 'it was quite, but not very, widely read'.[14] It was only in the 1830s that a revival of interest in Baker in the community at Ampleforth came through Father Anselm Cockshoot (1805–1872), who, according to Dom Justin McCann, made a copy of a 1678 Baker manuscript in 1837.[15] As Prior at Ampleforth, Cockshoot actively worked to improve the

10. Augustine Baker, *St. Benedict's Rule* in J. Clark (ed.), *Analecta Cartusiana*, 119:24 (Salzburg: 2005), p. iii; M. Truran, 'Spirituality: Fr Baker's Legacy' in A. Cramer (ed.), *Lamspringe. An English Abbey in Germany*. Saint Laurence Papers VIII (Ampleforth: 2004), p. 95.
11. Downside Abbey, Birt Papers, F32 (14 April 1823), Luke Barber to Anselm Lorymer.
12. Madigan, *Devil*, p. 205.
13. J. McCann & H. Connolly (eds.), 'Memorials of Father Augustine Baker and other Documents relating to the English Benedictines' in *Catholic Record Society* 33 (1933), pp. 274–293; Stanbrook Abbey Archives, Baker MS 12.
14. A. Cramer, *Ampleforth. The Story of St Laurence's Abbey and College*. Saint Laurence Papers VI (Ampleforth: 2001), p. 196.
15. McCann & Connolly, 'Memorials', p. 275.

quality of monastic observance, and in 1845 he sent Brother Austin Bury (1827–1904) and Brother Laurence Shepherd (1826–1885) for studies to Parma in Italy. Cockshoot was also a founding father of the neo-Gothic monastery at Belmont, of which more later. It is also likely that Cockshoot was responsible for introducing the young Shepherd to Baker when Shepherd was appointed novice master at Ampleforth after his return from Italy. Shepherd recalled:

> When I was entrusted with my first real set of five promising young novices, I began in all good earnest to train them. I took every book I could lay hands on. One of the elders warned me against Father Baker: but I took him from the Library, and became enamoured by his style...I epitomised *Sancta Sophia* and passed it thus to my novices.[16]

Shepherd believed that Baker 'was the holiest man that ever belonged to our Congregation',[17] but he was 'warned off' him probably because of opposition to Baker's view that no man should enter the Congregation with a view to going on the mission, or should desire or even think of it after entering monastic life, and should even resolve, as far as his vow of obedience should allow, 'to prevent such an employment'.[18] Although later Baker added a preface to his major treatise on mission to tone down its anti-missionary stance, there was little doubt that he disapproved of monks living away from their monasteries, which in the 1850s most, of course, still did.

Father Baker's writings found a new audience and incited fresh controversy when, in 1859, a new monastic house was established at Belmont near Hereford. St Michael's Priory was founded as a common Novitiate and House of Studies for the English Benedictine Congregation and it was normal thereafter for all aspirants to the three

---

16. Stanbrook Abbey Archives, B. Anstey, MS *Life of the Rev. Dom L. Shepherd* (1897), p. 18.
17. Stanbrook Abbey Archives, Anstey, p. 30.
18. Augustine Baker, *Sancta Sophia*, edited by S. Cressy and N. Sweeney (London: 1876), pp. 187–9.

houses of monks to be sent there immediately. St Michael's was intended to provide a more organised and efficient formation for monks, following complaints to General Chapter that junior monks in monasteries annexed to schools were continually distracted from their studies. An allied motive was a more rigorous preparation of monks for the Benedictine mission, but ironically, by bringing a large group of young men together under a dedicated staff, monks destined for the mission came away with more of a monastic, rather than a missionary formation, for at Belmont they were detached from the secular world and grew attached to community life, carefully performed liturgy, study and silence.[19]

Among the founding fathers of the new priory were a number of monks who held Baker in high regard, namely Laurence Shepherd, Cuthbert Hedley, and Anselm Cockshoot, all of Ampleforth, and Norbert Sweeney of Downside, Belmont's first superior. Shepherd's tenure of the post of Junior master at Belmont lasted only two years, so it was left to others to promote the teaching of Father Baker.[20] In 1861, Norbert Sweeney, the first Prior of Belmont, published *The Life and Spirit of Father Augustine Baker* which was dedicated to the Stanbrook and Colwich nuns. Sweeney spoke of Baker being 'conversant with our solid old English ascetical writers,' and someone who se instruction was of great value in opposing the restlessness of the age.' Sweeney left Belmont in 1862 for the mission at Bath, where in 1876 he produced his edition of *Sancta Sophia* which was promoted and given a high profile by his former colleague at St Michael's, Cuthbert Hedley, who in 1873 had been consecrated as auxiliary bishop to the Benedictine bishop of Newport, Joseph Brown. In a review of Sweeney's edition of *Sancta Sophia*, Hedley presented Baker

---

19. Augustine Clark, 'The Return to the Monasteries,' *Monks of England. The Benedictines in England from Augustine to the Present Day*, edited by D. Rees (London: 1997), pp.216–7.
20. Ampleforth Abbey Archives, MS 241 no. 105.

as the apostle of the contemplative life, for which Hedley observed:

> There must be solitude, a silence, which, if not perpetual, are at least such as are usually prescribed in a well-ordered monastic house... For a contemplative life then, both social recreation and apostolic work must be reduced to their lowest degree.[21]

Hedley must surely have known that such conditions would rarely be found in the male houses and missions of the English Benedictines, and that his views were likely to scandalise many of his former confreres, but he raised his head above the parapet to express the hope that his fellow monks would get a taste at least of contemplation in places such as Belmont. Such a life, he argued, was not just for nuns, it also 'ought to be' theirs:

> Father Baker, then, in *Sancta Sophia*, is writing for solitary, silent interior souls, such as are to be found in the cloisters of the enclosed orders of religious women, and such as ought to be most religious men, at least through the facilities afforded them by the considerable space they spend within their noviciates and houses of study.[22]

Hedley frankly admitted that Baker's teachings were not for every monk to imbibe. There could never be, he emphasised, full adherence to Baker within the English Benedictine Congregation, because for Hedley the Congregation followed *regula mixta*. He later opposed the later break up of the two Benedictine provinces and was uneasy with a doctrinaire quasi-medieval conventual monasticism which he saw developing among reformers who adopted Bakerism as their ensign.

Sweeney's edition of *Sancta Sophia* in 1876 did provoke a revival of interest in Bakerism, beginning at Belmont,

---

21. N. Sweeney, *The Life and Spirit of Father Augustine* Baker (London: 1861); C. Hedley, 'Art. III.–F. Baker's *Sancta Sophia*' in *Dublin Review* 27 (October 1876), p. 351.
22. Hedley, '*Sancta Sophia*', p. 353.

where, in the late 1870s, the novice master, Father Cuthbert Doyle (1862–1932), a monk of Douai, introduced *Sancta Sophia* to a new generation of novices, one of whom was Cuthbert Butler, the future Abbot of Downside and President of the English Benedictine Congregation. Butler later wrote:

> *Sancta Sophia* gave me a definite theory of the spiritual and monastic lives, and a high ideal to aim at... From it I got a firm grip of the great and fundamental principle that the Benedictine Order is contemplative and that we as English Benedictines ought to be contemplatives.[23]

One of the first novices at Belmont was Jerome Vaughan (1841–1896), the brother of both Father Bede Vaughan, the later Archbishop of Sydney, and Cardinal Herbert Vaughan. He has been described as being 'a highly strung romantic with delicate health but iron will.' He was ordained at Belmont in 1867, where he soon became Professor of Scripture and Junior Master. Vaughan went on to edit *The Spiritual Conflict and Conquest* by Lorenzo Scupoli, in which he made several allusions to the writings of Augustine Baker and in which he seems to be attempting to harness Baker's teachings to a distinctive monastic and English Benedictine spirituality which had little place for the missionary and parochial work traditional in the English Benedictine Congregation.

In the following decade a 'Constitutional crisis' erupted within the English Benedictine Congregation, when battle lines were drawn between those who favoured reform, and who wished to place the missions under the monasteries instead of the President of the Congregation and to make the monasteries autonomous communities with abbatial rank. They were opposed by those who were determined to preserve the missionary system. In the pamphlet war that broke out, it was not Baker's spiritual teaching, but his view of the English Mission that was used as ammuni-

---

23. Downside Abbey Archives, 3019, MS A, pp. 6–7.

tion by the reforming party. In 1881, for example, Laurence Shepherd quoted thirty three pages from Baker's 'Treatise on the English Mission' in a memorandum to Prior Boniface Krug, Claustral Prior of Monte Cassino, who had been appointed by the Holy See to conduct a visitation of the English Benedictine Congregation. In his memorandum, Shepherd used Baker to support his view that it was highly dangerous for monks to abandon their monasteries for the mission.[24] Similarly, in 1887, Dom Cuthbert Butler cited Baker in asserting that 'the English Benedictines are not essentially a missionary body: that however notable a feature the mission may be in the present condition of the body it is an *accident* and not an *essential* note or constituent'.[25]

The saga of the English Benedictine 'constitutional crisis' of the 1880s and 1890s and its outcome, lies beyond the scope of this paper, but it does provide some evidence that, at least for English Benedictine monks, it was not so much Father Baker, the mystical writer, but Father Baker, the polemicist, who influenced the Congregation at this crucial stage in its history. It would be left to the monks and nuns of the twentieth century to re-discover and rehabilitate Father Baker, the mystical writer.

---

24. M. Truran, 'Dom James Laurence Shepherd's Vision of the EBC' in *English Benedictine History Symposium Papers* (privately published: 1985), p. 4.
25. C. Butler, *Notes on the Origin and Early Development of the Restored English Benedictine Congregation, 1600–1661, from contemporary documents* (Downside: 1887), preface and pp. 46–49.

Index

The Abridgement of Perfection, 100–01
Adam, C., 157n.
Aire, English Poor Clares of, 131, 142
Allanson, A., 114n.
Allison, A. F., 23n., 135–36, 138n.
Alphonsus of Madrid, 125, 138
Alvarez, B., 129
Alvarez de Paz, J., 72, 119
Ampleforth, Priory and Abbey of St Laurence, 122n., 141, 194, 197, 199
Athanasius of Alexandria, 52
Angela of Foligno, 125
Anstey, B., 198n.
Apostolatus Benedictinorum in Anglia, 19ff., 179
Aquinas, St Thomas, 158, 161, 165n.
Aristotle, 58n., 158
Arius SJ, F., 142
Augustine of Hippo, St, 161–62, 165
Aveling, H., 187n.

Bagshaw, S., 33

Bainvel, J., 137n.
Baker, Augustine,
Abridgement, 125
Admittance, 124
All Virtues, 122n., 129
Alphabet (*Spiritual Alphabet*), 117n., 119n., 120, 123n., 124n., 125, 127, 140n.
Anchor of the Spirit, 90n., 121, 131, 170, 173n., 175
Apologie, 90, 106–08, 123n., 131
Autobiography, (*Concerning his own life*), 20, 130
Blosius: Spiritual Institution, 131
Bonilla–Quest of the Soul, 131
Book A, 114, 131
Book B, 114, 116n., 131
Book C, 114, 120, 131
Book E, 112n., 114, 116–17, 120, 131
Collections I–III, 118, 119, 124n., 131, 143n.
Confessiones Amantis (*More B*), 128

Conversio Morum, 44n.,45n., 46n., 47n., 78, 79, 80, 130, 138
Devotions (Gascoigne B), 120n., 130
Dicta sive Sententiae Sanctorum Patrum, 112n., 131
Directions for Contemplation. Book B, 112
Directions for Contemplation. Book D, 39, 46n., 82, 83, 112, 114–120, 131
Directions for Contemplation. Book F, 48n., 112, 115, 117–119, 121, 131
Directions for Contemplation. Book G, 112, 115, 116n., 120, 124, 131, 139, 140n.
Directions for Contemplation. Book H, 71, 92n., 112, 115, 117, 118n., 120n., 121, 123, 125
Directions for Idiot's Devotion (Idiot's Devotion B) 125n., 126
Discretion, 44n., 47n., 100, 122–24
Doubts and Calls, 34, 72, 73, 81, 117–19, 121, 127, 131, 143n.
Enquiry about the Author of the Treatises of the Abridgement and Ladder of Perfection, 100, 101, 122–24, 131
Examples, 126
Exposition of the Rule, 33, 36–7, 39n., 126n., 196. 196n.
Fall and Restitution of Man, 130
Five Treatises, 38n., 40, 41n., 120n., 123, 131

Flagellum Euchomachorum, 130
Harphius: Twelve Mortifications, 131
Idiot's Devotion, 118, 120n., 125–26
Library, 124, 131
Life (More A), 128, 129
Life and Death of Dame Gertrude More, 116n., 119n., 126n., 127, n, 129n.
Life and Death of Dame Margaret Gascoigne (Gascoigne A), 28n., 41n., 92, 120n., 130
Love of Enemies, 122n., 129
Mirror of Patience and Resignation, 112n., 122n., 129
Order of Teaching, 119n., 124, 131, 140
Reflection, 112n., 129
Relation of Fr Balthasar Alvarez, 129
Remains, 113, 128n.
Remedies against Temptations, 121, 131
Rythms, 130
Scandals, 123
Secretum sive Mysticum, 46n., 62–63, 65, 93–95, 98n., 99, 104n., 111–113, 124, 125, 126n., 131
Secure Stay in all Temptations, 38, 68–71, 73, 75–77, 112, 123, 124, 127, 131
Sickness with collections from the Book called Death, 113, 115, 117, 120, 121, 126, 127, 128n., 131

Index

Spiritual Alphabet for the Use of Beginners 68, 75, 117, 123, 124, 131
Spiritual Emblems, 122n. 129
Spiritual Exercises of....Dame Gertrude More, 128n.
Spiritual Treatise...called A.B.C., 72, 75n., 126n.
Substance of the Rule, 35, 36n., 38, 39n., 40
Summarie of Perfection, 90n., 121n., 130, 143n.
Tauler Part I, 131
Tauler Part 4, 131
Translations from Thomas à Kempis, 120n., 131
Treatise of the English Mission, 21
Treatise of the English Mission (Mission A), 29n.,112n., 230, 202
Treatise of the English Mission (Mission B), 130
Treatise on Confession, 38, 41n., 120, 121, 131, 141, 143n.
Twelve Mortifications of Harphius, 118n., 143n.
Vindication, 127
Vox Clamantis in Deserto Animae, 34–35, 114n., 126, 127, 129
Words of Brother Ricerius of Marchia, 129n.
Balthasar, H. U. von, 58n.
Barbanson, C., 14, 94, 105, 109, 115, 116, 119
Barbeau, T., 192n.
Barber, B., 197
Barber, L., 197n.
Barker, N., 139n.

Barlow, R., 4, 31, 32, 34n., 115–16, 118n., 130, 184, 188–89
Barnes, J., 23–25, 27
Barrett, M., 86n.
Bateman, J., 138
Bath, Benedictine mission in, 199
Batt, A., 141–42
Baudrillart, A., 134n.
Baxter, R., 66
Beech, A., 20–22
Bell, L., 96n.
Bellarmine, St Robert, 136
Bellenger, A., 99n.
Bellinzaga, C., 100, 122
Belmont, St Michael's Priory, 190–94, 199, 200–01
Benedict, Rule of St, 127
Bernard of Clairvaux, St, 8, 187n.
Birrell, T., 186–187n.
Birt, N., 189n.
Bishop, E., 28n.
Blois, G. de, 134n.
Blosius, L. (Blois, Francois, Louis de), 105, 118, 119, 125, 133ff.
Bodleian Library, Oxford, 4n.
Bonaventure, St, 103, 161, 162
Bonilla, J. de, 118, 143
Boylan, E., 2
Brathwaite, R., 136
Brent, C., 32
Broadway, 196
Brown, J., 199
Brudenell, J., 139
Brudenell, T., 139
Brussels, English Benedictine nuns of, 122
Buckley, M., 138
Buckley, S., 20–23

Bunyan, J., 74
Burnet, G., 6n.
Bury, A., 198
Butler, C., 194–95
Butler, C., 195n., 201–02
Butler, J., 169n.

Calvin, J., 65, 74
Cambrai, Abbey of Our Lady of Comfort, 4n., 24, 25, 31ff., 45, 85, 86, 90–93, 96n., 97, 117, 128, 138, 140, 186, 196
Camden, W., 28
Canfield, B., 16, 94, 105, 109, 112n., 116, 117, 119, 125, 143
Cary, A. C., 96n.
Cassian, St John, 126, 187n.
Catherine of Siena, St, 136
Charles V, Emperor, 136
Chase, S., 63n.
Chaucer, G., 102, 103, 104n.
Chaussy, Y., 24n.
Chelles, Abbey of, 23
Chevallier, P., 63n.
Chinnici, J. P., 195n.
Cicero, 168n.
Clancy, T. H., 143n.
Clark, A., 199n.
Clark, J., 29n., 31, 32n., 33n., 34n., 36n, 37n., 38n., 39n., 41n., 44n., 46n., 47n., 48n., 63, 65, 68n., 71n., 72n., 73n., 79n., 82n., 86n., 90n., 92n., 94n., 100–122nn., 124n., 125n., 126n., 128n., 129n., 130n., 138n., 139, 140n., 141n., 143n., 170n., 180, 197n.

Cloud of Unknowing, 8, 10, 12, 63, 67, 87, 88, 91–95, 99, 102, 105, 109, 111, 125, 127
Cluny, Order of, 23
Cockshoot, A., 197–99
Colledge, J, 87, n, 91n.., 98n.
Collingwood, E., 142
Collins, H., 91n.
Colwich, St Mary's Abbey, xi, 97n., 122n., 139, 196, 199
Combes, A., 55n., 63n.
Compton, M. X., 194n.
Condren, C., 153n.
Connolly, R. H., 20n., 21n., 22n., 23n., 25n., 27n., 28n., 29, 42n., 113n., 114n., 126n., 128n., 130n., 186n., 189, n, 191n., 197n.
Constable, B., 85, 112
Constable, H., 21–22
Coombes, W. H., 194n.
Coppens, C., 139n.
Costerus, F.,142
Cottingham, J., 153n., 157n., 159n., 174n., 178n.
Cotton, Sir R., 24–25, 28, 86, 97n.
Coxe, H. O., 25n.
Cramer, A., 122n., 124n., 194n., 197n.
Crampton, G. R., 96n.
Cressy, S., ii, 9, 17n., 32, 34n., 66n., 85, 91n., 112n., 113n., 137n., 140n., 141n., 180–92, 185, 189, 196, 197, 198n.

Darlington, Poor Clares of, 142n.
Desiderius, 118
Dieulouard, Priory of St Laurence, 161, 197

Index

Dijkgraaf, H., 139n.
Dionysius the Areopagite, 63n., 172, 174
Dondayne, H., 52n.
Douai Abbey, vii, xi, 187n.
Douai, Bibliothèque Municipale, 180n.
Douai, St Edmund's Priory, 196, 201
Douai, St Gregory's Priory, 33, 128, 129, 142, 189, 195
Downside Abbey, 92n. 197n., 201n.
Downside, St Gregory's Priory, 197, 199
Doyle, A. I., 89n.
Dullard, B., 196
Doyle, C., 201
Dubourg, P., 63n.
Dumeige, G., 63n.
Durham University, Library, 142n.
Durkin, M., 167n.
Dutton, E., 93n., 96n., 97n., 98n., 101n., 161n.

Eckhart, Meister (Eccardus), 117, 143, 189n.
Edwards, E., 31
Elizabeth of Bohemia, 177
Elizabeth of Schonau, 137
Ellis, T. P., 19–20
English Benedictine Congregation, x
Epistle of Privy Counselling, 88
Eriugena, J. Scotus, 52

Falkland, Lady E. C., 139
Farmer, D., 28
Feckenham, J., 27–28
Fisher, J. OSB, 194n.

Flèche, La, Jesuit College, 160
Flete, W., 92n., 121
Florentius a Monte, 138
Floreus Radewijns, 138
Francis de Sales, St, 136, 194
Francisco de Osuna, 57
Froius, 134

Gagliardi, A., 122
Galileo Galilei, 155
Gallus, T., 53–54, 63n.
Garnet, H., 135, 138n.
Gascoigne, C., 3, 33, 36, 126, 127
Gascoigne, F., 32n., 128
Gascoigne, M., 92, 97, 130
Gascoigne, P., 115
Gassendi, P., 175n.
Gaukroger, S., 153n.
Gerson, J., 54–57, 63n., 119
Gertrude the Great, St, 137, 140, 191
Gobinet, C., 194
Gorman, S., 97n.
Gregory the Great, Pope St, 187n.
Grosseteste, R., 52, 54
Guéranger, P., 191–92
Guigo II, 15n.

Hall, Bishop J., 6n.
Harphius (Henri de Herp), 116, 119, 137n., 143, 186, 189n.
Harrington, L. M., 63n.
Haskins, C. H., 52n.
Hayes, D., 192n.
Hedley, C., 194n., 199–200
Heil, G., 63n.
Herbert, G., 92n.
Hierotheus of Koblenz, 58, 60

Hildegard of Bingen, St, 137
Hilduin, 52
Hilton, W., 34, 86–88, 92, 109, 113, 126, 127
Hodgson, P., 8n., 67n.
Hogg, J., vii–viii, x, 85, 124n., 142n.
Holbeck, Jesuit Library, 139
Holland, H., 27n., 28
Holtzmann, W., 25, 26
Holy Wisdom (see also *Sancta Sophia*), ix, 66ff., 76, 78, 79, 81–83
Hopkins, A., 122
Hugh of Balma, 55
Hugh of St Victor, 52, 53, 57
Hughes, B., 20n.
Hull, F., 32, 34, 99, 106, 114, 127, 188
Hunter, I., 153n.
Husserl, E., 156n.
Hutchinson, D., 36n., 196

Ignatius of Loyola, St, 100, 160, 181
Imitation of Christ, 119, 134, 135, 187n.
Inge, W. R., 87n.
Ivanka, E. von, 63n.

Jackson, T., 6n.
Javelet, R., 63n.
Jeanes, H., 6n.
Jebb, P., 6n.
Jenkins, J., 97n.
Joannes a Jesu Maria (Juan de Jesus Maria), 116, 118, 119
John of the Cross, St, 9, 57, 62, 63, 144, 189n.
John Paul II, Pope Bl, 155, 158
Jones, L., 27, 32, 34n., 115
Jones, R., 31n.

Julian of Norwich, x, 85, 88, 90–93, 96–99, 109, 181, 183

Kempis, Thomas à, 119
Kenny, A., 157n.
Kenyon, A., 196
Knowles, D., 2, 17, 18, 25, 26, 28, 52n.
Krug, B., 202
Kuhn, S. M., 95n.

Lamennais, F. R. de, 134, 140
Lambspring, Abbey of SS. Adrian & Denis, 186, 196
Lanspergius, J. J., 137, 140n.
Lawes, R., 92n.
Leedham–Green, E., 139n.
Lefèvre d'Étaples, J., 137
Liessies, Abbey of, 133–34, 138
Lille, Archives du Nord, 31n., 35n., 37n., 38n., 39n., 40n., 41n., 42n., 138n.
Lingard, J., 195n.
Loarte, G., 135
Lorymer, A., 197n.
Louth, A., 58n., 63n.
Louvain, 136
Lovat, Lady, 134n.
Love, H., 141n.
Luis de Granada, 136
Lunn, D., 2, 21, 22,n., 179, 189n.
Luther, M., 74

Macdonald, T. C., 196
Madigan, L., 194n.
Maguire, B. P., 55n.
Main, J., 1, 2n.
Malebranche, N., 174
Marsten, J., 101n., 102
Matter, E. A., 62n.

Index

Mayhew (Maihew), E., 20, 23, 32n.
McCann, J., 4n., 17n., 20, n, 21n.., 25n., 27n., 28n., 29n., 32n., 42n., 85, 112n., 113, 114, 117n., 118n., 119–21, 123, 124, 126–31, 186n., 189n., 191n., 197
McAvoy, L. H., 96n.
McEvoy, J., 54n.
McGinn, B., 53n., 59n., 60n., 61n., 62n., 89n., 90n.
McKenty, N., 2n.
Mechthild of Magdeburg, 90n., 137
Meyer, A., De, 134n.
Millward, P., 28n.
Minnis, A., 103n., 104
More, G., 116, 119, 126–28, 180n., 188
Morris, C., 52n.
Murdoch, D., 157n.

Newsham, C., 135

Okie, L., 110n.
Oulton Abbey, 32n.
Owen, H. W., 96n.
Oxford, Jesus College, 24–27

Palmer, R. R., 190n.
Paris
 Abbey of Saint-Denis, 52
 Abbey of Saint-Victor, 52f.
 Abbey of Our Lady of Good Hope, 96n., 142, 186
 Bibliothèque Mazarine, 142n.
 Bibliothèque Nationale, 96n.
 St Edmund's Priory, 139, 141

Parma, Abbey of St John the Evangelist, 198
Pascal, B., 165–66
Paul, St, 167n., 176n.
Péguy, C., 154n.
Percy, M., 100, 122
Perin, Dr, 143n.
Perne, A., 139
Philip II, King of Spain, 136
Plato, 162
Platus (Hieronymus Plautus, Jerome Piatti), 122, 162, 187n.
Polding, J. B., 194n.
Pollard, A. W., 136n.
Porete, M., 90n.
Power, Edmund (D. J.), 160n., 176n.
Preston, T., 20–22
Price, W., 196
Prichard, L., 20, 25, 27, 36n., 85, 112, 118, 120n., 128
Pseudo–Dionysius, 52, 53, 55–9, 61, 62, 88, 99, 174
Pseudo–Suso, 117
Pseudo–Tauler, 117
Puente, Luis de la, 129

Quentin, D., 139n.
Quignones, Francisco de, 138

Ramridge, J., 139
Rau, H. Defos du, 192n.
Redgrave, G. R., 136n.
Reidy, J., 95n.
Reyner, C., 27, 180
Reypens, L., 189n.
Rhodes, J., 119n., 141n., 143n.
Richard of St Victor, 53, 57, 63n., 88
Richerius of Marchia, 128
Ritter, A. M., 63n.

Rocques, R., 62n.
Rodriguez, A., 193–94, 193n.
Rogers, D. M, 23n., 135–36, 138n., 142n., 143n.
Rolle, R., 86–88, 92, 121
Rorem, P., 53n., 60n.
Rowell, B., 122n., 196n.
Ruysbroeck, J., 119, 137, 138, 141
Ryle, G., 176n.

Sadler, V., 20
Salvin, P., 4n., 17n., 113n., 137n., 138, 140n., 141n., 196
Sancta Sophia (see also *Holy Wisdom*), 91, 112, 159, 160n., 162, 163–66, 171–72, 181–83, 187, 190, 191, 197–201
Sander, N., 28
Sarracenus (Peter Thomas Saracenus), 52, 54
Sarrazin, J., 63n.
Scott, G., 153n., 194n., 195
Scupoli, L., 193, 194, 201
Shakespeare, W., 101–02
Shaw, D. J., 139n.
Shepherd, L., 191, 198, 199, 202
Shoreham, William of, 96n.
Sitwell, G., 2n.
Smith, M. P., 32n.
Solesmes, Abbey of, 191
Solignac, A., 63n.
Spearritt, P., 186–87
Stanbrook Abbey, 196, 197–99
Stapleton, T., 27
Stillingfleet, E., 181–90
Stoothoff, R., 157n.
Suchla, B., 63n.
Summit, J., 86n.
Surius, L., 117, 137
Suso, H., 117, 137

Svartvik, J., 176n.
Sweeney, N., 1n., 66n., 182n., 190n., 191, 198n., 199, 200
Syon Abbey, Lisbon, 142

Tannery, P., 157n.
Tauler, J., 105, 117, 118n., 136–38, 189n.
Teresa of Avila, St, x, 57, 62, 105
Thomas a Jesu, 75
Torquemada, Juan de, 22
Tresham, T., 139n.
Truran, M., 141n., 186–87, 197n., 202n.
Turner, D., 62n., 174, n
Turner, J., 194n.
Tyler, P., 178n.

Ullathorne, B., 194, 196, 197
Underhill, E., 87–92, 167n.
Upholland College, Baker Anthology, 96, 98, 141, 142n.
Ushaw College, Durham, 142n.

Van Cauwenbergh, Et., 134n.
Van Engen, J., 137n.
Van Hyning, V., 86n., 91n., 92, 94n., 161n.
Vaughan, B., 201
Vaughan, H., 201
Vaughan, J., 201
Vitae Patrum, 126

Walgrave, F., 23
Walgrave, W., 4n.
Walker, C., 93n.
Walmesley, C., 187
Walsh, E., 87, n, 91n.., 98n.
Walsh, J., 10n.

Watkin, E. I., 2
Watson, N., 87, 88, 90–92, 97n., 110
Wekking, B., 85, 116n., 119n.,
Wharton, H., 180–81
Whitford, R., 142n.
Who were the nuns? (database project), 96n.
Wickes, G., 22n.
Wilberforce, B. A., 135n., 138n., 144n.
Williams, B., 155n.
Winghe, Antonius de, 135, 150
Winken de Worde, 92n.
Wiseman, N., 135
Witham, C., 142
Witham, M., 142
Witham, T., 142
Wittgenstein, L., 51n.
Wolfe, H., 86n., 139n.
Woodward, L. J., 189n.

www.ingramcontent.com/pod-product-compliance
Lightning Source LLC
Chambersburg PA
CBHW032251150426
43195CB00008BA/409